Network Technology Foundations:
Self-Study Guide

Chief Executive Officer

Narasimhan (Nat) P. Kannan

Senior Vice President and General Manager

Lindsay Miller

Vice President, Publishing

Todd Hopkins

Senior Content Developer

Kenneth A. Kozakis

Content Developer

Irina Heer

Managing Editor

Susan M. Lane

Senior Editor

David C. Oberman

Editor

Sarah Skodak

Project Manager/Senior Publisher

Tina Strong

Customer Service   ComputerPREP, Inc.
A division of
VCampus Corporation
410 N. 44th Street, Suite 600
Phoenix, AZ 85008
(602) 275-7700

Network Technology Foundations
Self-Study Guide

Developers

Ken Kozakis and Irina Amstutz

Contributors

James Stanger, Ph.D., and Patrick T. Lane

Editor

Sarah Skodak

Project Manager/Publisher

Tina Strong

Trademarks

Prosoft is a trademark of Prosoft Learning, a VCampus Company. All product names and services identified throughout this book are trademarks or registered trademarks of their respective companies. They are used throughout this book in editorial fashion only. No such use, or the use of any trade name, is intended to convey endorsement or other affiliation with the book. Copyrights of any screen captures in this book are the property of the software's manufacturer.

Disclaimer

Prosoft Learning, a VCampus Company, makes a genuine attempt to ensure the accuracy and quality of the content described herein; however, Prosoft makes no warranty, express or implied, with respect to the quality, reliability, accuracy, or freedom from error of this document or the products it describes. Prosoft makes no representation or warranty with respect to the contents hereof and specifically disclaims any implied warranties of fitness for any particular purpose. Prosoft disclaims all liability for any direct, indirect, incidental or consequential, special or exemplary damages resulting from the use of the information in this document or from the use of any products described in this document. Mention of any product or organization does not constitute an endorsement by Prosoft of that product or corporation. Data used in examples and labs is intended to be fictional even if actual data is used or accessed. Any resemblance to, or use of real persons or organizations should be treated as entirely coincidental. Prosoft makes every effort to ensure the accuracy of URLs referenced in all its material, but cannot guarantee that all URLs will be available throughout the life of a course. When this course/CD-ROM was published, all URLs were checked for accuracy and completeness. However, due to the ever-changing nature of the Internet, some URLs may no longer be available or may have been redirected.

Copyright Information

Table of Contents

List of Labs

List of Activities

List of Optional Labs

List of Quizzes

List of Figures

List of Tables

Course Description

Network Technology Foundations teaches essential networking technologies and skills, including TCP/IP, stable network creation, wireless networking and network troubleshooting. You will learn to use various network components and protocols that enable users to share data quickly and easily. You will explore the different types of transmission media, and will learn how network architecture and topologies provide for efficient and secure communication. In addition, you will learn about the OSI reference model and its relationship to packet creation, and you will compare and contrast the OSI model with the Internet architecture model.

You will study the functions and features of internetworking server types, and will achieve competency in performing basic hardware and operating system maintenance procedures. In addition, you will learn about the importance of RFCs and where to locate the most recent RFC documents. You will also learn about the importance of routing, and will explore IP addressing, IP address classes and subnet masks. This course will also teach you essential network security concepts, including authentication, encryption and firewalls. Finally, you will explore career opportunities in the IT industry, and will discuss effective ways of communicating technical information.

All CIW Foundations courses offer Case Studies about real-world skills applications, and updated topics such as project management and the relationship between technology and business operations. The CIW Foundations courses prepare you to take the CIW Foundations certification exam.

Guided, step-by-step labs provide opportunities to practice new skills. You can challenge yourself and review your skills after each lesson in the Lesson Summary and Lesson Review sections. Additional skill reinforcement is provided in Activities, Optional Labs and Lesson Quizzes that are included in the coursebook and on the companion CD-ROM.

The companion CD-ROM contains the lab files used in the course. To practice the skills presented in the coursebook or to perform any labs that were not completed, refer to the Course Setup Guide And System Requirements section for information about system requirements and using the lab files.

Series

Network Technology Foundations is the third course in the CIW Foundations series. CIW Foundations consists of the following courses:

* Internet Business Foundations

* Site Development Foundations

* *Network Technology Foundations*

Prerequisites

No prior experience using the Internet, developing Web pages or configuring networks is necessary. However, you should be familiar with an operating system such as Microsoft Windows XP before starting this course. The CIW Foundations courseware does not provide entry-level computer literacy. Rather, it builds upon computer literacy training and certifications such as Microsoft Office Specialist (*www.microsoft.com*) and IC³ (*www.certiport.net*).

Certification

The CIW Foundations series of courses prepares you to take the high-stakes CIW Foundations certification exam. Those who pass the CIW Foundations exam earn the highly respected CIW Associate certification, which is recognized throughout the industry as validating essential Internet skills for the workplace. The CIW Associate certification proves that an individual has evolved from being an Internet consumer to an Internet producer, capable of producing real-world Internet applications. A CIW Associate certificant can use common Internet-ready applications, can create properly formed HTML/XHTML documents, knows CGI and database essentials, and can troubleshoot networks. For information about taking the Foundations exam, visit *www.CIW-certified.com*.

Self-Study Courseware

This coursebook was developed for self-directed training. Along with comprehensive instructional text and objectives checklists, this coursebook provides easy-to-follow hands-on labs and a glossary of course-specific terms. It provides Internet addresses needed to complete some labs, although due to the constantly changing nature of the Internet, some addresses may no longer be valid. The coursebook also includes margin notes that provide additional tips and commentary to supplement course narrative, and that direct you to material relating directly to specified CIW Foundations exam objectives. Each course lesson includes practice, study and assessment materials such as preview and review questions, Case Studies, Application Projects, pen-and-paper-based Activities, Optional Labs and Quizzes.

The coursebook includes a companion CD-ROM that provides files needed to complete labs, and supplemental movie clips that review concepts in a multimedia format. The companion CD-ROM also includes an appendix listing the CIW Foundations certification exam objectives and locations of corresponding material in the coursebook. The companion CD-ROM provides all answers to Activities, Optional Labs and Lesson Quizzes. Lesson Quizzes are provided as study and self-assessment resources only; success on these materials in no way guarantees a passing score on the CIW Foundations certification exam. The movies provide supplementary instruction in a multimedia format, and enhance the coursebook narrative and labs. However, movie content does not comprehensively address CIW Foundations exam objectives and is not intended to replace coursebook content.

After you have finished the course, you will find this coursebook to be a valuable resource for reviewing labs at home or in the workplace and applying the skills you have learned.

Additional online resources

In addition to the material found in the coursebooks, you can visit CIW Online at *www.vcampus.com/cciivv/CIW-Online/index.html* to help you prepare for the CIW Foundations certification exam. CIW Online provides a variety of online tools you can use to supplement the Official CIW Courseware, including:

- **Course review questions** — More than 1,300 new course review questions. The multiple-choice questions cover numerous topics throughout the Foundations course material, not just those topics addressed by the CIW exam objectives. The questions are completely integrated with material from the book and can be used to assess your understanding of the course material.

- **Interactive exercises** — Activities that consist of fill-in-the-blank, true-or-false, categorizing, matching and crossword puzzle exercises. The self-testing exercises provide immediate scoring and feedback after completion, allowing you to focus on topics that require additional study. The exercises are based on Foundations content and prepare you to excel in tests and quizzes that feature multiple-choice questions.

- **Online flashcards** — Approximately 400 glossary flashcards that test your vocabulary of important Foundations terms. The interactive flashcards show a vocabulary term on one side and the definition on the other. You may move through the flashcards as necessary for extra review.

Course Objectives

After completing this course, you will be able to:

- Identify network components and major network operating systems.

- Describe the packet creation process and explain the Open Systems Interconnection (OSI) reference model.

- Compare and contrast the functions of network protocols, and describe network transmission media and types.

- Identify network architectures and topologies, and describe the Internet architecture model and Internet protocols.

- Explain the routing process, IP addressing, IP address classes, default subnet masks and the use of private IP addresses.

- Use diagnostic tools for troubleshooting TCP/IP networks.

- Identify and describe the functions and features of various internetworking server types.

- Identify maintenance issues for common system components.

- Describe the characteristics of file system types and use file system management tools.

- Identify and suggest corrective measures for operating system boot problems and application failures, and identify methods to remotely manage workstations.

- Identify essential network security concepts.

- Explore career opportunities in the IT industry and discuss effective ways of communicating technical information to non-technical audiences.

Course Setup Guide and System Requirements

In order to implement this course, you will need to set up your computer based on the hardware, software and connectivity requirements listed in the following sections. However, you may want to use additional software to further explore network interaction or related technologies.

Hardware requirements

The following table summarizes the hardware requirements for all courses in the CIW program.

Hardware Specifications	Minimum Requirements
Processor	Intel Pentium III processor (or equivalent) with a processor speed greater than or equal to 800 MHz
L2 cache	256 KB
Hard disk	20 GB
RAM	128 MB
CD-ROM	32X
Network interface card (NIC)	10BaseT or 100BaseTX (10 or 100 Mbps)
Sound card/speakers	Required for movie clips
Video adapter	4 MB
Monitor	Super VGA (800 x 600) resolution video graphics card and 17-inch monitor with 256 colors

* Must meet universal CIW hardware requirements.

Software requirements

If you are taking all three CIW Foundations self-study courses sequentially, there is no need to reformat your computers for each course. The recommended software configurations for computers used to complete the labs in this book are as follows.

Internet Business Foundations

To be installed before starting the course:

- Microsoft Windows XP Professional Service Pack 2 (typical installation)

- Microsoft Internet Explorer 7.0 with Outlook Express (typical installation)

You can also use Microsoft Windows XP Home Edition to complete this course. Some lab steps may vary slightly.

To be installed during course labs:

- Firefox 2.0 (binary provided in the C:\CIW\Internet\LabFiles\Lesson02 folder)

- Adobe Reader 8.0 (binary provided in the C:\CIW\Internet\LabFiles\Lesson03 folder)

- Aethera (binary provided in the C:\CIW\Internet\LabFiles\Lesson05 folder)

- Thunderbird 2.0 (binary provided in the C:\CIW\Internet\LabFiles\Lesson05 folder)

- TightVNC, Bzip2 and Bunzip2 (binaries provided in the C:\CIW\Internet\LabFiles\Lesson06 folder)

- Ad-Aware SE Personal (binary provided in the C:\CIW\Internet\LabFiles\Lesson07 folder)

- GanttProject (binary provided in the C:\CIW\Internet\LabFiles\Lesson08 folder)

Site Development Foundations

To be installed before starting the course:

- Microsoft Windows XP Professional Service Pack 2 (typical installation)

- Microsoft Internet Explorer 7.0

You can also use Microsoft Windows XP Home Edition to complete this course. Some lab steps may vary slightly.

To be installed during course labs:

- Lynx (binary provided in the C:\CIW\Site_Dev\LabFiles\Lesson01 folder)

- Mozilla SeaMonkey 1.1.2 (binary provided in the C:\CIW\Site_Dev\LabFiles\Lesson10 folder)

- Apache2Triad 1.1.9 (C:\CIW\Site_Dev\LabFiles\Lesson11\apache2triad)

Network Technology Foundations

To be installed before starting the course:

- Microsoft Windows XP Professional Service Pack 2 (typical installation)

- Microsoft Internet Explorer 7.0 with Outlook Express (typical installation)

You can also use Microsoft Windows XP Home Edition to complete this course. Some lab steps may vary slightly.

To be installed during course labs:

- Java 2 Runtime Environment (binary provided in the C:\CIW\Network\LabFiles\Lesson01 folder)

- Phex 3.0.2.100 (binary provided in the C:\CIW\Network\LabFiles\Lesson01 folder)

- FineCrypt 9.1 (binary provided in the C:\CIW\Network\LabFiles\Lesson05 folder)

The CIW *Network Technology Foundations* course teaches you to use diagnostic tools such as ping and traceroute. If you have installed a firewall on your computer, it may not allow ICMP packets to access the Internet. As a result, you may not be able to use ping and traceroute.

Installing and configuring Microsoft Windows XP Professional

The three CIW v5 Foundations self-study courses can be completed without reinstalling the operating system for each course. Install Windows XP Professional with the default settings. The only requirement is that your system must be able to access the Internet in order for you to perform the hands-on labs in all CIWv5 Foundations self-study courses.

Note: If you have already installed Windows XP Professional and have Internet access, you can skip this section. You can also use Microsoft Windows XP Home Edition to complete this course; some lab steps may vary slightly.

The instructions for installing Windows XP Professional are as follows:

1. Start the Windows XP Professional setup by inserting the installation CD-ROM into the CD drive and rebooting the system. You may have to enter CMOS to ensure that the drive searches and boots from a CD.

2. Accept the licensing agreement by pressing F8.

3. Install Microsoft Windows XP Professional with the following parameters.

When This Information Is Required	Use
Phase 1	
Partition Location	Default (C:)
Partition Size	Entire hard disk drive
Partition File System	NTFS
Location	Default (C:\windows)
Phase 2	
Regional Settings	Customize for your location
Name	Your name
Organization	Your organization, if applicable
CD Key	The CD key for your copy of Windows XP Professional
Licensing Modes	Per server
Concurrent Connections	The number of computers in your system (at least one)

When This Information Is Required	Use
Computer Name	Your name
Administrator Password	**password** (all lowercase letters)
Date and Time Settings	Customize for your location
Network Settings	Custom settings
Networking Components	Select **Internet Protocol (TCP/IP)** and click **Properties**. Select the **Use The Following IP Address** radio button, and manually enter the IP address information specific to your system. You can use DHCP if you prefer; however, prepare the system for networking. Install TCP/IP using valid IP addresses. *Note: No DNS configurations are entered during Windows setup. DNS will be configured during the labs.*
Workgroup or Computer Domain	Select **No, This Computer Is Not On A Network, Or Is On A Network Without A Domain**. In the Workgroup Or Computer Domain field, enter **Classroom**.
Verification	Verify that the system is working and that it can communicate with other systems on the Internet.

Connectivity requirements

Internet connectivity is required for this course. You will experience optimal performance with a dedicated Internet connection (e.g., a cable/DSL modem or a T1 line). However, you can complete the course using slower connections (e.g., 56-Kbps modem).

CIW v5 Foundations Self-Study Kit Companion CD-ROM

Each coursebook includes a companion CD-ROM. The files on the CD-ROM are referenced and used throughout the course. The CD-ROM also includes supplemental movies.

When you insert the CIW v5 Foundations Self-Study Kit Companion CD-ROM, you will see a list of folders for the courses and movies. Select the course folder and the appropriate executable file. This executable file will create a directory of all supplemental materials for the course. You can choose to download the directory to the default location, which is C:\CIW\[*Course_Title*].

Optionally, you can select another location. After you choose the location and unzip the file, a directory will be created on your hard drive. All supplemental files for the course will be downloaded to this directory. You can then create a shortcut to this directory on your Desktop. As you perform the course labs, you can use this shortcut to access your lab files quickly.

CIWv5 Foundations movies

The CIW v5 Foundations courses offer movie files from LearnKey that discuss selected technology topics. The movies are available on the CIW v5 Foundations Self-Study Kit Companion CD-ROM.

To view the CIW v5 Foundations movies:

- You need a Windows Internet Explorer 5.5 (or later) browser.

- You need Windows Media Player 9 and all necessary codecs.

- You can use Windows Update to obtain the latest versions of Internet Explorer and Media Player.

Note that you will install Windows Media Player software on your system during an Internet Business Foundations course lab.

Consider the following points about the CIWv5 Foundations Movies:

- The movies provide supplementary instruction in a multimedia format, and enhance the coursebook narrative and labs. However, movie content does not comprehensively address CIW Foundations exam objectives and is not intended to replace coursebook content.

- CIW Foundations coursebooks include Movie Time alert boxes that signal appropriate points at which to view the supplemental movies.

- Do not distribute unlicensed copies of this copyrighted material.

Conventions and Graphics

The following conventions are used in this coursebook.

Terms	Technology terms defined in the margins are indicated in **bold type** the first time they appear in the text. However, not every word in bold type is a term requiring definition.
Lab Text	Text that you enter during a lab appears in ***italic bold type***. Names of components that you access or change in a lab appear in **bold type**.
Notations	*Notations, comments, and code and utility keywords appearing in narrative are indicated in italic type.*
Program Code or Commands	Program code or operating system commands appear in the Lucida Sans Typewriter font (in examples) or in *italic* type (in narrative).

The following graphics are used in this coursebook.

 Tech Notes point out exceptions or special circumstances that you may find when working with a particular procedure. Tech Notes that occur within a lab are displayed without the graphic.

 Tech Tips offer special-interest information about the current subject.

 Warnings alert you about cautions to observe or actions to avoid.

 This graphic signals the start of a lab or other hands-on activity.

 The Movie Time graphic signals appropriate points in the course at which to view movie clips. All movie clips are © 2007 LearnKey, Inc.

 Each lesson summary includes an *Application Project*. This project is designed to provoke interest and apply the skills taught in the lesson to your daily activities.

 Each lesson concludes with a summary of the skills and objectives taught in that lesson. You can use the *Skills Review* checklist to evaluate what you have learned.

 This graphic indicates a line of code that is completed on the following line.

Lesson 1: Introduction to Networking

Objectives

By the end of this lesson, you will be able to:

🖋 Identify and describe the functions of servers, workstations and hosts.

🖋 Identify major network operating systems and their respective clients.

🖋 Discuss packets and describe packet creation, and explain the Open Systems Interconnection (OSI) reference model.

🖋 Compare, contrast and discuss the functions of network protocols, including TCP/IP.

🖋 Describe the basics of local area networks (LANs) and wide area networks (WANs).

🖋 Identify and describe the function of network access points (NAPs).

🖋 Describe transmission media and types, including cabling, asynchronous and synchronous, simplex, half duplex, full duplex, baseband and broadband.

🖋 Identify network architectures, and describe basic network topologies and carrier systems (for example, T and E carriers).

Pre-Assessment Questions

1. Which network topology provides multiple communication paths so that an alternative path may be used if a connection fails?

   a. Ring
   b. Bus
   c. Star
   d. Mesh

2. Which category of twisted-pair cable includes four twisted pairs, is typically used for 100BaseT Ethernet, and supports transmission rates of up to 100 Mbps?

   a. Category 2
   b. Category 3
   c. Category 4
   d. Category 5

3. A packet consists of what three elements?

_____

Version 1.2

infrared
A spectrum of light used for communication between various network-enabled devices.

network interface card (NIC)
A circuit board within a computer's central processing unit that serves as the interface enabling the computer to connect to a network.

Open Systems Interconnection (OSI) reference model
A layered network architecture model of communication developed by the International Organization for Standardization (ISO). Defines seven layers of network functions.

NOTE:
Watch the Warriors of the Net video, located at *www.warriorsofthe. net,* at least once during the first two lessons of this course. The video explains how the Internet works. It is available in various resolutions and languages.

OBJECTIVE:
3.1.1: Convergence networks

Internet Service Provider
An organization that maintains a gateway to the Internet and rents access to customers on a per-use or subscription basis.

Overview of Networks and Protocols

A network can be defined as two or more connected computers that share data by way of a transport medium. This configuration can include a small business network in one room, two Personal Digital Assistants (PDAs) that communicate by means of **infrared**, or a worldwide network connecting millions of users, such as the Internet. In fact, networking on the Internet has been given its own name: internetworking.

Networks have become extremely popular because they allow users to share data quickly. In the past, users had to place files on a floppy disk or print them, and deliver them to the destination in person or by mail. Networks allow information to be distributed easily and quickly through a system of protocols, cables and other hardware.

To communicate efficiently, networks require a standard, or protocol. Network protocols are established rules that enable data to flow from one **network interface card (NIC)** to another. Network protocols correspond (roughly, in some cases) to the **Open Systems Interconnection (OSI) reference model**.

Local area networks (LANs) and wide area networks (WANs) are the basis of networking and internetworking. The two systems can work together to allow companies to transmit data internally and externally.

In this lesson, you will learn about networking basics, network protocols, and LANs and WANs.

Telephony Networking

Before examining specific types of computer networks, we will turn our attention to one of the oldest existing networks — the public switched telephone network (PSTN). The PSTN has connected millions of users for decades, and remains a cornerstone in internetworking today.

Traditional telephone network

Since the inception of the telephone, voice has been carried over circuit-switched connections of the PSTN. Originally, all phone service was analog. Today, however, the network is entirely digital except for the portion that extends from the central office of the local telephone company to the user.

Typically, to exchange data over the public telephone network using a dial-up connection, a modem is necessary. A modem (modulator/demodulator) is a device that translates, or modulates, a digital signal coming from your computer into an analog signal that can be carried over the phone line. A modem attached to the receiving computer demodulates the analog signal back into a digital one.

Today, the PSTN is a hybrid network. About 80 percent of today's telephone users begin a telephone conversation in their homes using analog technology. The signal is then converted into a digital signal at the central office, and this digital signal is sent across a major portion of the telephone network. As necessary, signals are converted back into analog at the central office, to which the destination telephone is linked.

The PSTN is still an integral part of the Internet infrastructure because it furnishes most of the long-distance connections. Most **Internet Service Providers (ISPs)** pay long-distance providers for access to telephone lines.

IP telephony and Voice over IP (VoIP)

Internet Protocol (IP) telephony is a technology that uses packet-switched connections to exchange voice, fax and other forms of data that were previously carried on circuit-switched connections. (You will learn about packets later in this lesson.) Using the Internet, the packets of data are sent over shared lines. IP telephony enables users to avoid the tolls charged on telephone company lines because most ISPs absorb this cost.

Voice over IP (VoIP)
A technology that transmits voice in digital form as packets of data using Internet Protocol.

Voice over IP (VoIP) is voice information delivered in digital form as packets of data using Internet Protocol instead of the traditional circuit-switched lines of the PSTN. VoIP is free for users if they already have Internet access, allowing them to avoid the tolls charged for using ordinary phone lines. VoIP is forcing telephone companies to offer consumers better deals in order to keep their business.

Most local and long distance providers, cable TV companies and ISPs now offer (or soon will offer) IP telephony services.

Networking Evolution

Originally, networks were operated on a centralized, or mainframe, model, which usually limited networks to large, well-funded institutions, such as universities and Fortune 500 companies. By the late 1980s, however, many business networks adopted the client/server model, which used a more modular approach and allowed small- to medium-sized businesses to create powerful networking solutions. The advent of the Internet led to another shift to Web-based, increasingly decentralized and more affordable networking.

Mainframe

Mainframe (or centralized) computing provided the first practical network solution. This centralized approach used central servers, or mainframes, and remote terminals. Usually, these terminals were diskless, or "dumb" stations that could only request information. Most information processing occurred on the "back end" (the server), not on the "front end" (the client).

Retrieving information from mainframes

Obtaining information from a mainframe traditionally involves a great deal of processing by the mainframe. A terminal sends an information request to the mainframe, which in turn processes the query and obtains the desired information from a database or other source. After this processing is finished, the mainframe structures the information and returns it to the terminal. You will see how the client/server model differs somewhat from this model. Figure 1-1 shows a mainframe model.

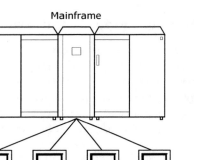

Figure 1-1: Mainframe model

Mainframe liabilities

The mainframe-computing model has two main liabilities. The first is that the mainframe must handle all the processing work. The second is that the request and response packets sent between the terminal and the mainframe occupy a relatively large amount of the network's bandwidth. In large, heavily used networks, these two liabilities create unacceptable network congestion.

The future of mainframes

Owing to the overwhelming investment in mainframes over the decades by universities, businesses and other institutions, the mainframe model is still quite prevalent, and will not disappear soon. However, with the advent of the Web and more sophisticated computing technologies, Web-based interfaces and other bridging technologies will replace, or at least greatly modify, the traditional "dumb terminal" and mainframe environment. Furthermore, fewer institutions are investing in the traditional mainframe model, opting instead for client/server and Web-based solutions. Often, mainframes remain in use, but users will not interact with them directly. In many cases, you will be using client/server technologies on the **front end** to gain access to information, but will in fact be accessing mainframes that perform some of the work on the **back end**.

Client/Server Model

The client/server model, also called distributed computing, attempts to reduce network slowdown by dividing processing tasks between the **client** (the front end) and the **server** (the back end). The back-end computer is generally more powerful than the front end, and is responsible for storing and presenting information. A client/server example is illustrated in Figure 1-2.

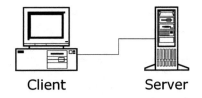

Figure 1-2: Client/server model

front end
A client that acts as an interface to a collection of servers (for example, mainframes or PC-based servers). A Web browser is a typical front-end client.

back end
A series of systems that fulfill requests made by a client. Back-end systems can include mainframes and servers containing information databases.

client
An individual computer connected to a network. Also, a system or application that requests a service from another computer (the server), and is used to access files or documents (such as a Web browser or user agent).

server
A computer in a network that manages the network resources and provides, or serves, information to clients.

Client/server model databases and SQL

bottleneck
A point in network communication at which information is processed more slowly. Also, any element (a hard drive, I/O card or network interface card) that slows network connectivity rates.

The client/server model contains two types of databases: single database servers and distributed databases. A distributed database involves information storage across several computers, while still allowing searches and transactions to occur as if the information were stored centrally. The primary advantage of this approach is that it divides the task among several powerful computers and network connections. Such distribution tends to decrease the number of network **bottlenecks**.

Databases store information in an organized, tabular format. To enable transactions between these databases and users, the client/server model must translate human-readable language into machine-readable code. Thus far, the most efficient way to accomplish this task is by using the Structured Query Language, or SQL (pronounced "sequel").

NOTE:
This example refers to a specific server-based application example.

SQL allows users to phrase queries on the front end that can be understood by the back end. Requesting data from a server in SQL involves the following process:

1. The user requests **data**.

data
Information being stored, usually in a database.

2. The client computer translates the request into SQL.

3. The client sends the request to the server.

4. The server processes the request, which might involve communicating with a remote database or server.

NOTE:
TPC/IP and ODBC provide a framework for interoperability, but do not guarantee that the systems will be able to work together. Appropriate applications and, possibly, custom client software are also required.

5. The server delivers the response to the client.

6. The client delivers the response to the computer screen.

The key difference between this retrieval model and the one used by mainframes is that the client processes much of this request.

Client/server advantages

In addition to shared task processing, client/server benefits include a modular approach to computing. Because the client/server model allows you to add new system components, you are not limited to one solution. At one time, network administrators had to choose between one system and another. However, with the advent of open standards such as Transmission Control Protocol/Internet Protocol (TCP/IP) and Open Database Connectivity (ODBC), heterogeneous systems can work together more efficiently. For example, UNIX and Windows servers that use TCP/IP can work together, allowing businesses to scale solutions according to customer demand. The client/server model is scalable because it gives you the ability to adjust to new demands. The client/server model also allows users more control over their own files.

NOTE:
Multitier computing models are typically referred to in the context of an enterprise application model rather than a networking model. Microsoft's COM+ and .NET framework are examples.

Two-tier and three-tier computing

legacy model
A model that, because of its age, may not support modern technologies without manipulation or upgrades.

Traditional client/server relationships are similar to two-tier computing in that both computers are responsible for part of the processing task. In two-tier computing, one computer is responsible only for formatting the information on the screen. The other computer is responsible for both the process logic and the data storage. Client/server relationships distribute the task more evenly between the two computers. Client/server and two-tier computing are often considered **legacy models**.

business logic
The coding (usually in SQL) necessary to create relationships in the data stored in a database.

presentation responsibilities
The forms in which the data and business logic are presented on your screen. Presentation responsibilities include XHTML and HTML forms, and application-specific interfaces such as Web browsers.

Developers and networking professionals have cooperated further to create more efficient models: three-tier and n-tier. These models separate **business logic**, **presentation responsibilities**, and data into at least three separate levels, called tiers.

In a common three-tier model, a Web server contains the business logic, a Web browser is responsible for presentation, and a database server contains the data. An n-tier model uses multiple systems to divide responsibilities further. It is a more sophisticated version of three-tier computing in which many different individual systems help process information. Whenever you perform a transaction on a site such as eBay or Amazon.com, you are using either the three-tier or the n-tier model.

Advantages of three-tier computing

Separating these responsibilities into at least three different tiers provides the following benefits:

- **Flexibility** — It is possible to upgrade or change components in one tier without necessarily having to change components in the other two.

- **Increased speed** — Because responsibilities are divided among at least three tiers, each tier can concentrate only on certain data to speed information processing. This division of responsibilities can reduce network latency.

Sometimes, three-tier/n-tier networking is referred to as Web-based networking because clients often use a Web browser to access network services.

OBJECTIVE:
3.1.8: Network Operations Centers (NOCs)

Network Operations Center (NOC)

A Network Operations Center (NOC) is a specific location, usually a dedicated room, from which a network is managed, monitored and maintained. The term originally was used in relation to telecommunications networks, but is now used widely in relation to data networks. As data and telephony networks continue to converge, distinctions among equipment types will probably disappear as they relate to NOCs.

The NOC is the central point for network maintenance and troubleshooting. It contains workstations that are configured to display all activities and functions of the networks being monitored. For example, workstations are configured with packet sniffers and monitoring software that allow NOC administrators to quickly identify anomalous traffic (for example, worms, viruses, traffic spikes and downed networks). These workstations also contain management software, including firewall and router configuration software, and ways to control workstations remotely.

Application Service Provider (ASP)
A company that provides applications and services (over the Internet) to individual or enterprise subscribers that would otherwise need to provide those applications and services on their own servers.

NOCs also generally include multiple, redundant network connections and redundant power supplies to help ensure communication and power. Most NOCs for larger companies also have dedicated telephones from a separate provider and cell phones to ensure that they can communicate with the company and all ISPs and **Application Service Providers (ASPs)** in an emergency, or if the company's standard telephone provider experiences problems.

Networking Categories

All networks consist of the same three basic elements, as follows:

- **Protocols** — communication rules on which all network elements must agree. You will learn about networking protocols later in this lesson.

- **Transmission media** — media that enable all networking elements to interconnect. You will learn about transmission media later in this lesson.

- **Network services** — resources (such as printers) that are shared with all network users. You will learn about network services later in this course.

Aside from these similarities, two basic types of networks exist: peer-to-peer and server-based. A third network architecture — enterprise network — combines peer-to-peer and server-based types.

Peer-to-peer network types

Peer-to-peer networks are subdivided into the following two types:

- **Microsoft peer-to-peer** — a legacy model in which Microsoft-based systems communicate with one another without using a centralized system to control authentication and access.

- **P2P** — a modern model that supports many thousands of simultaneous users who can download and upload files on a worldwide network.

Microsoft peer-to-peer network

Microsoft peer-to-peer networks tend to be less expensive and easier to work with than server-based networks. However, they are less secure, support fewer users (no more than 10) and experience more problems with file system management. Figure 1-3 illustrates a Microsoft peer-to-peer network.

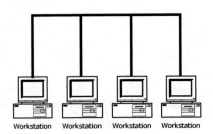

Workstation   Workstation   Workstation   Workstation

Figure 1-3: Peer-to-peer network model

Various Microsoft operating systems support peer-to-peer networking, including Windows 95, Windows 98, Windows Millennium Edition (Me) and Windows XP.

P2P network

A modern P2P network is created when a workstation uses add-on software to participate in large, decentralized networks that are usually located on the Internet. First popularized by the now-defunct free version of the Napster network, P2P networks include:

- Gnutella (*www.gnutella.com*).

- KaZaA (*www.kazaa.com*).

WARNING! *Do not download files (for example, MP3s or unauthorized software) from these networks. Doing so may be illegal, and can result in punitive action against you. Discussion of P2P networks should never be misconstrued as support for them, or as an encouragement to use them.*

NOTE:
Never download files (for example, MP3s or pirated software) from other users on P2P networks.

These networks are often used to illicitly share copyrighted information (for example, audio files and software). However, these networks can be used for legitimate purposes. Following are the two types of P2P networks:

- **Centralized** — This type of network requires logging on to a central server, which maintains a database of all attached peer clients. Because logging on to a central server is required, this type of network is not a true peer-to-peer network. Napster is an example of this type of network. The fact that a group of central servers was used to maintain the database of remote clients allowed the service to be shut down easily.

- **Decentralized** — This type of network consists of groups of clients/servers that communicate with one another to create a network that has no single central database. The Gnutella network is an example.

Server-based network

node
Any entity on a network that can be managed, such as a system, repeater, router, gateway or firewall. A computer or other addressable device attached to a network; a host.

A server-based network is a configuration of **nodes**, some of which are dedicated to providing resources to other **hosts** on the network. Dedicated nodes that make their resources available are called servers. These resources can include printers, applications and documents.

Server-based networks offer user security because a central database can track the resources that users can access. However, dedicated servers can be expensive. They may also require a full-time network administrator.

host
A computer that other computers can use to gain information; in network architecture, a host is a client or workstation.

Figure 1-4 illustrates a server-based network.

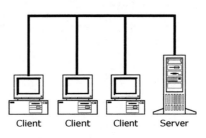

Figure 1-4: Server-based network model

Examples of server nodes include:

- Print servers.
- File servers.
- Mail servers.
- Web servers.
- Database servers.

Client nodes can access these resources over the network. Examples of client/server networks include:

- Novell NetWare.
- UNIX/Linux.

- Microsoft LAN Manager.

- Microsoft Windows NT/2000/2003 Server.

Authentication

Network resources require users to authenticate before accessing resources. Server-based networks enable **authentication** in the following two ways:

- **Centralized** — In this mode, users access a single server or set of servers and present authentication information (for example, a user name and a password, or biometric information).

- **Decentralized** — In this mode, users access each individual server and present authentication information.

Centralized authentication has become increasingly popular because it simplifies the administration of users and user credentials.

Network Topologies

Topologies are basic configurations that information systems personnel use to wire networks. They are the basic design of any network. Topologies used to connect computer networks include bus, star, ring and hybrid.

Bus topology

Bus topology networks require that all computers, or nodes, connect to the same cable. When a computer sends data, that data is broadcast to all nodes on the network. The term *bus* connotes an actual bus, which must stop at each bus stop along its route. Only the destination computer reads the sent message; the other computers ignore it. Figure 1-5 illustrates a bus topology.

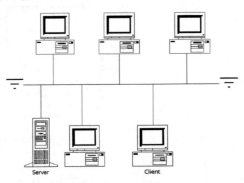

Server   Client

Figure 1-5: Bus topology with terminators

Small offices often use bus networks. If the network grows, a star network is usually the replacement topology. Bus networks require terminators at each end to ensure that network traffic does not echo back through the network. Following are the advantages and disadvantages of bus topologies:

- **Advantages** — Bus networks are relatively simple, inexpensive, easy to operate and reliable. They also use cable efficiently.

- **Disadvantages** — Isolating problems is difficult; if a cable breaks, the entire network can be affected. The network is likely to slow during peak traffic periods.

Star topology

Star topology networks connect network nodes through a central device, usually a hub or a switch (you will learn about hubs and switches later in this course). Because each computer's network connection terminates in the hub, this arrangement greatly reduces the risk of an entire network failure. For instance, if a cable breaks or a node fails, only that cable segment or node will be affected. The rest of the network will continue to function. Figure 1-6 illustrates a star topology.

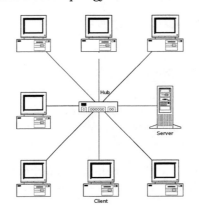

Figure 1-6: Star topology

Network administrators can troubleshoot networks far more easily in a star topology because the failure is usually isolated. Following are the advantages and disadvantages of star topologies:

- **Advantages** — The network is usually not affected if one computer fails. Network expansion and reconfiguration are relatively simple. Network management and monitoring can be centralized.

- **Disadvantages** — If the hub (or centralized connection point) malfunctions, the entire network can fail.

Ring topology

Ring topologies do not have a central connection point. Instead, a cable connects one node to another, until a "ring" is formed. When a node sends a message, the message is processed by each computer in the ring. If a computer is not the destination node, it will pass the message to the next node, until the message arrives at its destination. If the message is not accepted by any node on the network, it will travel around the entire ring and return to the sender. Figure 1-7 illustrates a ring topology.

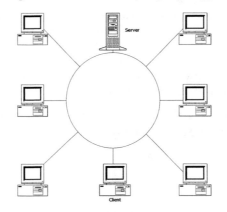

Figure 1-7: Ring topology

Ring networks often connect through a central device called a Multistation Access Unit (MAU), which you will learn more about later in this course. Isolating problems is difficult on a ring topology network. If one node fails, the entire network can fail. Following are further advantages and disadvantages of ring topologies:

- **Advantages** — All computers have equal access to data. During peak use periods, the performance is equal for all users. Ring networks perform well with heavy network traffic.

- **Disadvantages** — Network expansion or reconfiguration will affect network operation.

Hybrid network

Larger networks combine the bus, star and ring topologies. This combination allows expansion even in enterprise networks. Two common examples are star ring and star bus. In a star ring network, two or more star topologies are connected using a Multistation Access Unit as a centralized hub.

backbone
The highest level in the computer network hierarchy, to which smaller networks typically connect.

In a star bus network, two or more star topologies are connected using a bus trunk. The bus trunk serves as the network's **backbone.** Figure 1-8 illustrates a star bus network.

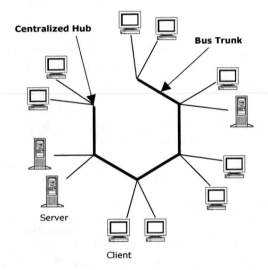

Figure 1-8: Star bus network

media
Any material that allows data to flow through it or be stored on it; includes hard and floppy disks, wire, cable, and fiber optics.

Note that each star network contains two nodes that are connected to a centralized hub, and that the hubs are connected by linear bus trunks. This topology is excellent for larger companies because the backbone can implement **media** that support high data transmissions. Following are further advantages and disadvantages of star bus topologies:

- **Advantages** — Network expansion is relatively simple. The network is usually not affected if one computer fails.

- **Disadvantages** — If the hub malfunctions, computers on that hub will be unable to communicate. Connections between the malfunctioning hub and other hubs will fail.

Mesh topology

NOTE:
The Internet is probably the most recognizable implementation of a mesh topology.

Mesh topologies connect devices with multiple paths so that redundancies exist. Messages sent on a mesh network can take any of several possible paths from a source to a destination. Mesh networks differ from other topologies in that the component nodes can all connect to each other via multiple hops (that is, by going through intermediate nodes along the way).

There are two types of mesh topologies: full mesh and partial mesh. In a partial mesh topology, some nodes are organized in a full mesh, but other nodes are connected to only one or two other nodes in the network. Partial mesh is less expensive to implement and is usually found in peripheral networks connected to a full mesh backbone. Figure 1-9 illustrates a partial mesh topology based on the star bus hybrid topology.

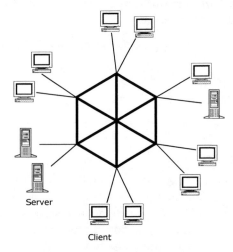

Server

Client

Figure 1-9: Mesh topology

Notice that in the partial mesh network shown in the preceding figure, each node can communicate with any other node even though the source and destination nodes are not directly connected to each other.

In a full mesh topology, all devices are cross-connected so the best path can be chosen at any given moment. A full mesh is very expensive but is the most reliable because it provides the greatest amount of redundancy. If one node fails, network traffic can be redirected to any of the other nodes. Full mesh is generally reserved for backbone networks supported by public carriers such as the phone company.

The advantages and disadvantages of mesh topologies are as follows:

- **Advantages** — Mesh topologies are the most fault-resistant network type. If one connection is terminated, another can be chosen to deliver the data to the destination.

- **Disadvantages** — Additional hardware can make private mesh topologies expensive.

Many P2P networks use a mesh topology. This approach is not necessarily expensive because it relies on the Internet, which has already been created. However, private mesh topologies are more expensive to build.

Network Operating System

network operating system (NOS)
An operating system that manages network resources.

A **network operating system (NOS)** manages resources on a network, and offers services to one or more clients. A NOS can manage multiple users on a network; provide access to file and print servers; provide services such as Web, File Transfer Protocol (FTP) and e-mail; and implement network security. NOSs such as Novell NetWare, Microsoft Windows 2000 and UNIX are very popular.

A NOS enables clients to access remote drives (those not on the user's computer) as if the drives were on the client's own computer. NOSs also allow servers to process requests from a client and decide whether that client can use a particular resource.

NOTE:
Systems in a peer-to-peer network are commonly referred to as peer servers or member servers, depending on the operating system that they are running.

Similar to a client/server relationship, part of the NOS must run from the client, and part of it must run from the server. In a peer-to-peer network, each client can serve as both the client and the server.

This section will discuss three of the most popular network operating systems, as follows:

- Microsoft Windows

- UNIX/Linux

- Novell NetWare

Interoperability

interoperability
The ability of one computer system to communicate with another; often refers to different operating systems working together.

All three major NOSs (Microsoft Windows NT/2000, UNIX and Novell NetWare) can operate with one another. This feature, called **interoperability**, makes it easier for corporations with different clients and servers to create a network, even though the clients and servers all use different operating systems. Figure 1-10 illustrates how the three major NOSs can interoperate with their clients and servers.

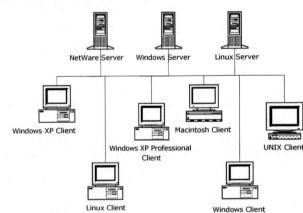

Figure 1-10: NOS interoperability

In most cases, software must be installed on the server and client for interoperability. The following sections explain the fundamentals of the three major NOSs.

Microsoft Windows Servers

NOTE:
Novell's directory
services servers
existed before
Microsoft Active
Directory.

Microsoft Windows New Technology (NT) is a family of network operating systems that began in 1993. It is widely implemented and gaining in popularity. The server versions are as follows:

- Windows NT 3.1 (1993)

- Windows NT 3.5 (1994)

- Windows NT 3.51 (1995)

- Windows NT 4.0 (1996)

- Windows 2000 (2000)

- Windows Server 2003 (2003)

NOTE:
Windows 9x,
Windows NT and
Windows 2000 can
all be easily
deployed on the
same network.

The Windows NT family first consisted of Windows NT Server and Windows NT Workstation. With the release of Windows 2000, Windows NT 4.0 Server was updated to Windows 2000 Server. Windows NT Server Enterprise Edition has become Windows 2000 Advanced Server. Windows NT Workstation was replaced by Windows 2000 Professional and Windows XP Professional. Windows 2000 Server and Windows Server 2003 include the software necessary for Microsoft's .NET program. This new technology provides a ready-made networking platform that allows companies to transfer information by means of various types of servers (for example, Web, database and e-mail).

NOTE:
**Optional Lab 1-2:
Reviewing network
operating systems**
provides a brief
additional
introduction to
Windows
networking.

Windows Servers support all Windows clients, such as Windows 3.1, Windows 95/98, Windows Millennium Edition (Me), Windows 2000 Professional, Windows XP Professional and Windows XP Home Edition.

Windows 2000, Windows 2003 and Windows XP use TCP/IP as the default network protocol, and have a user interface similar to Windows 95/98/Me.

NOTE:
Remember that the
labs in this course
use Windows XP
Professional.

The labs in this course use Windows XP to teach networking skills and concepts. For in-depth experience with network operating systems, such as modern Windows servers and Linux, you should enroll in the Master CIW Administrator track.

UNIX

kernel
The essential part of an operating system; provides basic services; always resides in memory.

UNIX was developed by AT&T's Bell Telephone Laboratory (now part of Lucent). In 1969, Ken Thompson, Dennis Ritchie and others worked on a team for AT&T in developing a mainframe computer system called MULTICS. This team created an alternative operating system that could work well on relatively small computers. This alternative was named UNIX, as a pun on MULTICS. Since the 1970s, many versions of UNIX have evolved from the original **kernel**. However, there is no single version of UNIX. Instead, several different versions, known as "flavors," of UNIX have been developed over the years. Each flavor is based on the following basic platform strategies:

- **System V** — a version of UNIX developed by AT&T.

- **Berkeley Systems Distribution (BSD)** — the version of UNIX developed by students at the University of California, Berkeley.

- **Open Software Foundation (OSF)** — an attempt to unify various vendor operating systems.

Some of the more popular flavors of UNIX today are as follows:

- **Linux** (which contains elements of both System V and BSD) — This flavor was developed by Linus Torvalds, the GNU organization (*www.gnu.org*) and the open source community. Various flavors of Linux exist, including Slackware (*www.slackware.com*), Red Hat (*www.redhat.com*), Mandriva (formerly Mandrake; *www.mandriva.com/en*) and SuSE (*www.novell.com/linux/*).

- **Sun Solaris** (based on System V) — Traditionally the premier version of UNIX, Sun Solaris (*www.sun.com*) runs primarily on non-Intel systems.

- **BSD** — This flavor includes FreeBSD (*www.freebsd.net*), which was the first BSD-based operating system that was free and available on various platforms. Apple's OSX, available on all newer Macintosh systems, is based on FreeBSD, NetBSD and OpenBSD. NetBSD (*www.netbsd.org*) was a redesign of FreeBSD that provided additional stability and ease of use as a server. OpenBSD (*www.openbsd.net*) was a thorough redesign of FreeBSD with a better-than-average security record.

UNIX systems have been tried and tested for years, and are widely considered the workhorses of the Internet. The majority of Web, e-mail, FTP and database servers still run one form of UNIX or another. When properly configured, UNIX systems have a reputation for stability and efficient use of resources. However, they often require a knowledgeable administrator and more administration time; an improperly configured UNIX server can be difficult to administer and can cause security problems.

As with any operating system, UNIX systems consist of at least one kernel, a file system and a **shell**. UNIX systems are often associated with a shell because, often, you must enter commands from a command line rather than a graphical user interface (GUI).

Because there are more than 600 UNIX commands, GUIs were developed to simplify UNIX operations. The most popular GUI is the **X Window** system, which consists of the following:

- **Server** — provides access to the computer; provides the actual interface.

- **Font server** — provides fonts for use in GUI windows and menus.

- **Client** — attaches to the server.

- **Window manager** — provides borders and menus.

The X Window server, font server and client often reside on the same computer, though they need not necessarily do so.

UNIX uses TCP/IP as its native core networking protocol. Additional protocols can be installed if necessary.

Linux

As you have already learned, Linux was developed by Linus Torvalds, the GNU organization, and the open source community. The Linux kernel is copyrighted to Linus B. Torvalds under the terms of the General Public License (GPL), which states that the source code must be freely distributed and that anyone is allowed to make copies for their own use, or to sell or give to other people (with a few restrictions). If any changes are made to the kernel, then these changes must be made freely available.

Linux can operate as a client or as a server and supports all of the most common Internet protocols, including TCP/IP, SMTP, POP, NNTP, Telnet, HTTP, FTP, IRC, DNS and more. Linux is an excellent choice for LANs, regardless of the combination of clients —

NOTE:
Visit any Linux vendor. Then visit a popular open-source software site: *www.freshmeat.net* or *www.sourceforge.net*

These sites offer Windows, Linux-based and UNIX-based software. GNU's name is an acronym for "GNU's Not UNIX." However, GNU has been developing UNIX-like software for some time, and has effectively become associated with the UNIX name.

---

shell
A command-based interface that allows a user to issue commands.

X Window
A windowing system used with UNIX and all popular operating systems.

NOTE:
Linux can be thought of as an open source, work-alike "clone" of UNIX.

including Macintosh, DOS, Windows, Windows NT, Windows 95, Novell, OS/2 — which can all use their own native communication protocols. Linux also includes a free X Window Graphical User Interface (GUI), allowing most X-based programs to run under Linux without any modification. Windows programs can run inside X Window with the help of an emulator called WINE.

Various flavors of Linux exist, and they are distributed by several commercial and non-commercial organizations that enhance the basic functions of the operating system. SuSE Linux, for example, is a distribution of Linux that has features of the core Linux kernel plus enhancements, which are specific to that distribution.

Novell

Although widely known for its proprietary network operating system called NetWare, Novell recently acquired SuSE Linux and now offers Open Enterprise Server, which combines NetWare and SuSE LINUX Enterprise Server. You can use NetWare, SuSE LINUX or a combination of both technologies.

Novell NetWare

Novell was incorporated in 1983, and helped popularize the LAN market. Novell NetWare is the most widely installed family of network operating systems. It uses stand-alone servers that provide LAN services such as file storage, network printing and directory services. See *www.novell.com* for more information about NetWare.

NOTE:
Systems after NetWare 5 continue to provide support for IPX/SPX, but IPX/SPX is not a default installation option.

Before NetWare version 5, NetWare was a proprietary NOS that communicated using the Internetwork Packet Exchange (IPX) protocol, the Sequenced Packet Exchange (SPX) protocol and the NetWare Core Protocol (NCP). These protocols were necessary for all network computers to communicate. Although Novell operating systems can function in several capacities (for example, as Web, file and database servers), Novell specializes in directory services. A directory services server allows a company to organize its resources securely and logically. Directory services servers store information about a company's resources in a centralized database. Using a secure logon protocol allows a user to access the database quickly and learn the location of the needed resource.

NetWare 5 supports TCP/IP as its networking protocol and Java as its application language. Because TCP/IP is the language of the Internet, and Java is a programming language that operates across various platforms (e.g., on Windows, UNIX, etc.), NetWare 5 is more flexible than previous versions.

The Need for Protocols

NOTE:
The network protocol is the "language" that a computer speaks to communicate with other computers. Two computers must have at least one protocol in common to be able to communicate, but a common protocol alone does not guarantee communication.

Earlier, you learned that network protocols are established rules that enable data to flow from one NIC to another. Unless you understand the specific rules applied to network communications, you will not be able to administer a network efficiently. You need protocols so that systems developed by various vendors can communicate with one another.

Various protocols are mapped to specific layers of the OSI reference model (often called the OSI/RM). Without the OSI/RM standard, and without standardized protocols, network communication would be haphazard at best.

OSI Reference Model

OBJECTIVE:
3.1.4: OSI reference model

The OSI/RM was defined by the International Organization for Standardization (ISO) in 1983 (see *www.iso.org*). The OSI/RM has three practical functions, as follows:

- It gives developers necessary, universal concepts so they can develop and perfect protocols that can work with operating systems and network products developed by other vendors.

- It explains the framework used to connect heterogeneous systems. In other words, it allows clients and servers to communicate even if they are using different applications and operating systems; all they need is a common protocol, such as TCP/IP or IPX/SPX.

- It describes the process of packet creation. You will learn more about packet creation shortly.

NOTE:
The OSI/RM is a framework and does not provide specific implementation instructions.

The OSI/RM allows systems from various vendors to communicate with one another; significant deviance from the OSI/RM will result in communication failures.

Networks are built using the OSI/RM, just as a building is constructed from a blueprint. For instance, Microsoft Windows and UNIX refer to the OSI/RM when creating their networking software. The OSI/RM provides a common framework that allows these network operating systems to interoperate.

The OSI/RM is an example of a protocol-layering model because protocols are mapped to various layers in the model. For example, whenever protocols such as IP and IPX are discussed, they are usually linked to the network layer (Layer 3) of the OSI/RM. Several other networking models exist. While few manufacturers follow the OSI/RM guidelines exactly, most models closely parallel the OSI standard.

The OSI/RM consists of seven layers, described in Table 1-1. We will review each layer carefully because they help explain how information is sent over a network.

Table 1-1: OSI/RM layers

NOTE:
You must understand the OSI/RM and what occurs at each layer in the model.

Consider the following associations with layers of the OSI/RM:

Transport — TCP or UDP packet, encased in an IP packet

Network — IP packet

Data link — frame

Physical — bit

Layer	Layer Number	Description
Application	7	The interface to the user in a networking environment. Networking applications such as file transfer and e-mail function here. The first layer is used when a packet is being created in a system.
Presentation	6	Provides useful transformations on data to support a standardized application interface and general communications services. For example, it converts text from American Standard Code for Information Interchange (ASCII) format into Extended Binary Coded Decimal Interchange Code (EBCDIC). Encryption occurs at this layer, and codecs operate here as well.
Session	5	Responsible for describing how protocols build up and tear down connections (or sessions). Also adds traffic flow and synchronization information.
Transport	4	Provides reliable, transparent transport between end points (the source and destination hosts). Also supports end-to-end error recovery and flow control. This layer is responsible for the accuracy of data transmission.

Table 1-1: OSI/RM layers (cont'd)

Layer	Layer Number	Description
Network	**3**	Responsible for logical addressing. Organizes data into packets. Provides reliable addressing services among hosts and networks. Ensures that packets are forwarded and routed to their destinations.
Data link	**2**	Defines how data is formatted for transmission and how access to the network is controlled. Frames are created and transmitted with the necessary synchronization, error control and flow control. In short, the data link layer prepares the information so it can be placed on the transmission medium, such as a copper wire. In the IEEE 802 series of LAN standards, the data link layer is divided into two sublayers: the Logical Link Control (LLC) layer and the Media Access Control (MAC) layer.
LLC sublayer		The Logical Link Control (LLC) sublayer is responsible for separating network layer protocols from the underlying network technology. It provides Service Access Points (SAPs) between the MAC sublayer and the network layer protocols. A SAP identifies which network layer protocol (such as IP or IPX) generated and is to receive the frame. The LLC is also responsible for error and flow control.
MAC sublayer		The Media Access Control (MAC) sublayer defines the network adapter interface options and the access method used on the network. The MAC sublayer is responsible for placing data on the transmission medium.
Physical	**1**	Associated with transmission of unstructured bit streams (electrical impulses, light or radio signals) over a physical link (such as copper wire or fiber-optic cable). Responsible for the mechanical, electrical and procedural characteristics that establish, maintain and deactivate the physical link. This layer controls how data is transmitted and received across the media.

The OSI/RM provides the concepts and nomenclature you need to be able to discuss packet creation and networking protocols.

OSI/RM layers and communication

NOTE:
Layers cannot be skipped. Communication flows from layer to layer. For the application layers on two systems to communicate, the data must pass through all layers on both systems.

Like any other networking model, the OSI/RM describes how systems communicate with one another. For Host A to "talk" to Host B, Host A must encapsulate its data and send it over the network to Host B. Host B must then de-encapsulate the data. That is, an application on Host A may pass a request down through the layers of the OSI/RM to the physical media, and an application on Host B will pull that request up from the physical media through the layers of the OSI/RM in order to process the request.

For example, if a client sends a request to a server, the request might begin with a mouse click by a user on a Web page hyperlink. The mouse click occurs at the client's application layer. The request travels down the OSI/RM until it reaches the data link layer, where it is placed onto a copper wire, or whatever transmission medium is used (the physical layer).

The client's request travels across the wire until it reaches the server. The server's data link layer pulls the request off the wire (physical layer) and sends it up the server's OSI/RM, as illustrated in Figure 1-11. When the request arrives at the server's application layer, the request is processed. The server then returns a response to the client, using the same method.

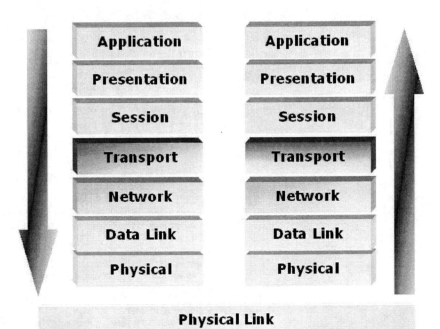

Figure 1-11: OSI model layers

In the preceding figure, the left column contains the seven OSI/RM layers that exist on the client. The right column contains the same seven layers that exist on the server. The upper four layers are used whenever a message passes to or from a host. The lower three layers are used whenever a message passes through a host. If the message is addressed to the particular host, the message is passed to the upper layers. If the message is addressed to another host, it is not passed to the upper layers, but is forwarded to another host.

If the client sends a request to the server, the request might begin with a mouse click by the user on a Web page hyperlink. The mouse click occurs at the client's application layer. The request travels down the OSI/RM until it reaches the data link layer, where it is placed onto a copper wire, or whatever transmission medium is used (the physical layer).

The client's request travels across the wire until it reaches the server. The server's data link layer pulls the request off the wire (physical layer) and sends it up the server's OSI/RM. When the request arrives at the server's application layer, the request is processed. The server then returns a response to the client, using the same method.

Data Encapsulation

The process of passing information through the layers of the OSI/RM is called encapsulation or packetization. A Protocol Data Unit (PDU) is a packet of information that is created by a computer and passed from one layer of the OSI/RM to another. A PDU contains information specific to each layer. Each layer adds a header to the data being passed through it to prepare it for transfer. At the end of the encapsulation process, a frame is formed.

Packet creation: Adding headers

NOTE:
Header information
is protocol-specific.

Data encapsulation
can be compared
to nesting
matryoshka dolls.

The packet creation process begins with Layer 7 (the application layer) of the OSI/RM, and continues through Layer 1 (the physical layer). For example, when you send an e-mail message or transfer a file from one computer to another, this message or file undergoes a transformation from a discrete (i.e., complete) file into smaller pieces of information (packets). Beginning with the application layer of the OSI/RM, the file continues to be divided until the initial discrete message becomes smaller, more manageable pieces of information sent at the physical layer.

NOTE:
Figure 1-12 shows
specific headers
being added to the
application data
during the
packetization
process. The letters
"AH" stand for
"application
header," "NH" stands
for "network
header," and so
forth. Notice that
there is no physical
header.

As shown in Figure 1-12, each layer adds its own information (the header) to the packet. This information enables each layer to communicate with the others, and also allows the receiving computer to process the message. Keep in mind that each layer considers whatever has been passed down to it from an upper layer to be "data." It treats the entire higher-layer message as a data payload. It does not concern itself with what was added by the upper layers.

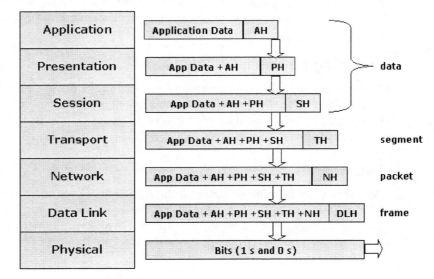

Figure 1-12: Headers added at each OSI/RM layer

Data, segments, packets and frames

The terms data, segment, packet and frame are the protocol data unit names assigned to information at specific points in the encapsulation process. That is, they refer to information at the application (and presentation and session), transport, network and data link layers, respectively. An item of information is considered data as it is generated and passed down through the upper three layers of the OSI, which are often collectively known as the application layer.

Data: The application, presentation and session layers

Data is passed down to the transport layer, where it is encapsulated to include source and destination port numbers that identify the applications (such as FTP or e-mail) between which the data should be passed. At this point, the data is considered a segment.

Segment: The transport layer

A segment is passed down to the network layer, where it is encapsulated and given source and destination IP addresses. At this point, the segment becomes a packet.

Packet: The network layer

A packet is passed down to the data link layer, where it is encapsulated and given source and destination MAC addresses, and an error-checking mechanism called a cyclical redundancy check (CRC). At this point, the packet becomes a frame.

Frame: The data link layer

Frames are passed down to the physical layer, where they are sent across the medium as a bit stream.

Cyclical redundancy check (CRC)

A cyclical redundancy check (CRC) is a mathematical calculation that allows the receiving computer to verify whether a packet is valid. When a sending host transmits a packet, it calculates a CRC by summing all the ones in the payload and storing this sum as a hexadecimal number, which is then stored in the trailer. When the receiving host reads the packet, it runs its own CRC, then compares it with the CRC stored in the trailer. If the two match, the packet is not damaged, and the receiving host processes the packet. If the CRCs do not match, the receiving host discards the entire packet. The CRC occurs at OSI Layer 2 (the data link layer).

Removing headers

When a receiving host processes a packet, it reverses the packet-creation process and de-encapsulates or removes each header, beginning with Layer 1 and ending with Layer 7. All that is left at the end of this process is the original, unaltered data, which the host can then process.

Peers

Network communication is based on the principle of peer layers. In a single system, each OSI layer has one or two adjacent layers (the layer above it and the layer below it) with which it interacts. For example, the data link layer receives packets from the network layer. The data link layer encapsulates the packets into frames and then passes them to the physical layer.

On the receiving end of a communication is another system. Within that receiving system, any given layer communicates only with that same layer on the sending system. That is, when the network layer on the sending system adds information (such as a destination IP address), that information will be of use only to the network layer (its peer) on the receiving system.

Packets

Although a unit of information technically becomes a packet when it passes through Layer 3 of the OSI/RM, the term packet is loosely used to describe any fixed piece of information sent across a network.. Whenever you send information across any network, you begin the packet creation process. A packet consists of the following three elements:

- A header (OSI/RM layer information).

- The actual data (for example, the client request or server response).

- A trailer (often contains techniques ensuring that errors do not occur during transmission).

Many networking professionals use the terms "packet," "datagram" and "frame" interchangeably. Although this usage is accurate most of the time, "packet" is a generic term for any piece of information passed through a network. A datagram is a packet at the network layer of the OSI/RM. A frame is a packet at the data link layer (used to traverse an Ethernet network). Even though the concepts are slightly different, these terms are used synonymously.

NOTE:
You need only be familiar with how packets are created. You need not memorize the content.

As shown in Figure 1-13, the header contains several different pieces of information, such as addressing information and an alert signal to the incoming computer.

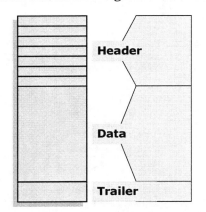

Figure 1-13: Packet structure

The packet also contains the original data (also called a payload) sent by the application, such as a page request sent by a Web browser. The trailer contains information signifying that the end of the packet has been reached, and also usually contains information that validates the packet. For example, it could contain cyclical redundancy check (CRC) information.

OSI/RM Protocol Examples

NOTE:
NWLink is listed as both a transport-layer protocol and a network protocol because it combines the functionality of both IPX and SPX in a single protocol.

Various protocols, as well as network components, are mapped to particular layers of the OSI/RM. Many protocol suites (also called protocol stacks) overlap the borders of the seven-layer model because they operate at multiple layers (for example, several application-layer protocols overlap into the presentation and session layers). Most protocols map to the application, transport and network layers.

The application layer allows applications to speak to one another across networks. The transport layer provides reliable data delivery, and the network layer provides addresses used on a network and rules for particular networks. Protocols do not map to the physical layer; the physical layer affects hardware.

The networking protocols listed in Table 1-2 are examples of common protocols that operate within the OSI/RM layers. The protocols listed in the first row of the table are those found in the upper layers of the OSI/RM, which are the application, presentation and session layers. No specific section is available for the presentation and session layers because these layers include the upper-layer protocols.

Table 1-2: OSI/RM protocol examples

Layer(s)	Corresponding Protocol	Protocol Description
Application (upper layer) **Presentation** **Session**	Simple Mail Transfer Protocol (SMTP)	Used to send e-mail messages
	Post Office Protocol 3 (POP3)	Used to allow clients to log on to a remote server and obtain e-mail messages
	Internet Message Access Protocol (IMAP)	Used to allow clients to access and manage e-mail messages without first downloading them
	Hypertext Transfer Protocol (HTTP)	Used to interconnect Web pages
	Server Message Block (SMB)	Allows files to be shared on a Microsoft network
	NetWare Core Protocol (NCP)	Allows files and printers to be shared on a NetWare network
	Network file system (NFS)	Allows files and printers to be shared on a UNIX network
Transport	Transmission Control Protocol (TCP)	Part of the TCP/IP protocol suite; provides reliable delivery and manages sessions
	Sequenced Package Exchange (SPX)	Part of the IPX/SPX protocol suite; similar to TCP in that it manages communication sessions
	NWLink	Microsoft's implementation of IPX/SPX; operates at both the transport and the network layers
	NetBEUI	Allows different applications on different computers using NetBIOS to communicate with one another; a nonroutable protocol that operates at both the transport and the network layers
Network	Internet Protocol (IP)	Part of the TCP/IP protocol suite; responsible for addressing hosts and routing packets in any network running TCP/IP
	Internetwork Package Exchange (IPX)	Provides addressing services for the Novell IPX/SPX suite
	NWLink	Microsoft's implementation of IPX/SPX; operates at both the transport and the network layers
	NetBEUI	Allows different applications on different computers using NetBIOS to communicate with one another; a nonroutable protocol that operates at both the transport and the network layers
Data link	Ethernet	A LAN protocol that was created by Xerox, Digital Equipment Corp. and Intel; the most popular LAN technology
	Token Ring	A LAN protocol that was created by IBM to provide more reliability than Ethernet; not as commonly implemented

NOTE:
The fact that a protocol is listed as a network protocol does not imply that it operates at the network layer of the OSI/RM. Ethernet is a lower-level protocol. NetBEUI does not include any network-layer information.

You will learn more about the TCP/IP protocol suite throughout this course.

Major Networking Protocols

NOTE:
TCP/IP is the current *de facto* standard for local and wide area PC networks. All others mentioned in this list are not as commonly used.

Several networking protocols and architectures exist, all based on the OSI/RM. Earlier, you were introduced to TCP/IP and IPX/SPX; however, many additional protocols are used for networking. This section will explain several important networking protocol properties. Following are some important networking protocols:

- TCP/IP

- IPX/SPX

- NetBEUI

- AppleTalk

Connection-oriented (stateful) and connectionless (stateless)

NOTE:
Connection-oriented protocols operate with a broadcast and acknowledgment. The receiving system acknowledges the packets it receives. Acknowledgments are not used with connectionless protocols. The packets are broadcast without expecting a reply.

Some network protocols require that a host establish a connection, or session, before they transfer information. Because of this requirement, session-oriented (or connection-oriented) protocols are often called stateful protocols. A state is the name given to a session. Connection-oriented protocols are considered more reliable because they first gain a system's attention, prepare it to receive information, and then send the information in a process commonly known as "handshaking." However, connection-oriented protocols require more system overhead, and are not always appropriate for certain networking tasks. An example of a connection-oriented protocol is TCP.

Other network protocols do not require a previously established session; they rely on a "best-effort" technology that sends the information, hoping that it will reach the other system. This type of protocol is called connectionless, or stateless. An example of a stateless protocol is IP, which provides addresses for the TCP/IP suite. Many connectionless protocols send information by means of short messages called datagrams.

You might assume that a connection-oriented protocol is more important or reliable, but this is not necessarily true. Each protocol type has its own place in a network.

Routable and nonroutable protocols

Some protocols can travel through LANs and WANs and beyond because they can pass through a router. Routable protocols include TCP/IP and IPX/SPX.

NOTE:
NetBEUI is typically seen in networks supporting legacy network operating systems only. DLC has become less common as more printers directly support TCP/IP.

Nonroutable protocols use predefined, or static, routes that cannot be changed. Some protocols are nonroutable because they do not use the functions of the OSI/RM network layer. Nonroutable protocols include NetBEUI, NetBIOS, Local Area Transport (LAT) and the Data Link Control (DLC) protocol. You will learn more about routing later in the course.

To use a nonroutable protocol effectively, you can add a bridge (bridges are discussed later in this lesson) to your network or encapsulate the nonroutable protocol within a routable protocol, such as TCP/IP. Encapsulation is also called tunneling.

TCP/IP

OBJECTIVE:
3.1.5: TCP/IP

On January 1, 1983, the major networks that make up the Internet adopted the TCP/IP suite as the Internet's official protocol. One reason for the Internet's rapid growth and powerful communication ability is its adoption of this suite, which was originally developed in Berkeley, California.

The TCP/IP suite is the current *de facto* standard for both local and wide area networking. Most operating systems include TCP/IP support as a default selection for installing and configuring network support, including current Windows family operating systems, Novell NetWare and all flavors of UNIX. Windows 2000 and Windows XP, for example, install only TCP/IP on a default Windows installation. In addition to being used as a communication protocol on private networks, TCP/IP is required for Internet access.

TCP/IP is used as the primary or sole communication protocol on nearly all new computer network installations. In addition, most existing networks either have converted or are converting to TCP/IP. TCP/IP is a routable protocol that can be used in nearly any LAN or WAN configuration.

NOTE:
TCP/IP version 4 is commonly referred to as IPv4. Windows XP provides limited support for IPv6, primarily for application development purposes and testing.

Currently, the Internet fully supports TCP/IP version 4. However, TCP/IP version 6 (known as IPv6) is expected to gain full support in the coming decade. TCP/IP is not tied to any one vendor, and therefore allows heterogeneous networks to communicate efficiently.

A collection of protocols

TCP/IP is a collection of protocols that includes Transmission Control Protocol, Internet Protocol, User Datagram Protocol (UDP) and many others that will be discussed later in this course. Each of these protocols has a specific function. This lesson will discuss only TCP, UDP and IP.

TCP

NOTE:
TCP provides sequencing, acknowledgment, socket identifiers and data integrity checks.

TCP ensures reliable communication and uses ports to deliver packets. It is a connection-oriented protocol. TCP also fragments and reassembles messages, using a sequencing function to ensure that packets are reassembled in the correct order. In TCP, a connection must be built using a handshake process before information is sent or received. All e-mail protocols (for example, SMTP, POP3 and IMAP) are TCP-based.

UDP

UDP is a connectionless protocol: It allows information to be sent without using a handshake process. It is often used to transfer relatively small amounts of information.

IP

NOTE:
IPv4 uses 32-bit addresses. IPv6 uses 128-bit addresses.

IP is a connectionless protocol responsible for providing addresses of each computer and performing routing. TCP/IP version 4 uses 32-bit addresses. The address scheme falls into five classes, only three of which are available for standard network addressing. The original plan was to assign class A addresses to large networks, class B addresses to medium-sized networks, and class C addresses to smaller networks. Class D addresses are used for multicasting, and class E addresses are experimental. You will learn more about these classes later in this course. IP also includes Internet Control Message Protocol (ICMP), which is used for troubleshooting connectivity between systems, as well as sending error and control messages between routers and switches. Thirty-two-bit IPv4 addresses are divided into halves: the network portion and the host portion. The subnet mask helps determine which bits form the network and host portions.

IPX/SPX

Novell, Inc., developed this once-dominant LAN and WAN protocol. Like TCP/IP, IPX/SPX is a protocol suite rather than a single protocol. UNIX systems support IPX/SPX. Microsoft also supports IPX/SPX, although the corporation has renamed it NetWare Link (or NWLink). Microsoft uses an emulation protocol rather than IPX/SPX because IPX/SPX is a proprietary Novell protocol.

 NetWare networks newer than NetWare version 4 use TCP/IP rather than IPX/SPX as their default networking protocol. Earlier versions used the default of IPX/SPX, and some early versions supported IPX/SPX only.

You will typically need to install NWLink support only when configuring Windows family systems for use on a legacy NetWare network or when the user needs to communicate with systems running IPX/SPX as the only protocol. A limited number of legacy applications use SPX communications. NWLink is required when supporting these applications.

IPX

IPX is a connectionless protocol that resides at the network layer of the OSI/RM. The function of IPX in IPX/SPX is similar to that of IP in TCP/IP. IPX is responsible for network addressing and forwarding packets to their destination, a task known as routing.

SPX

SPX is a connection-oriented transport-layer protocol that uses services provided by IPX. The function of SPX in IPX/SPX is similar to that of TCP in TCP/IP. SPX provides reliability to IPX: It ensures that packets arrive intact at their destination. Because this protocol resides at the transport layer, it ensures reliable data delivery and manages sessions.

IPX/SPX frame types

frame
Data passed between a system that contains addressing and link control information. Like all network protocols, IPX/SPX encapsulates its communications into frames.

Older versions of IPX/SPX use different **frame** types from those of newer versions; these differences can cause conflicts. IPX/SPX frame types include:

- Ethernet 802.2.

- Ethernet 802.3.

- Ethernet II.

- Token Ring.

- Token Ring SNAP.

Ethernet networks use frames to communicate; if two systems use different frame types, they will not be able to communicate. The frame type is a property setting for IPX/SPX bound to a NIC. In Microsoft systems, this protocol is called NWLink/IPX/SPX/NetBIOS Compatible Transparent Protocol.

NOTE:
For more information about internal and external network numbers, go to http://support. microsoft.com/kb/ 150546, or search the Microsoft Web site for the phrase "internal network number."

In most Windows XP installations, the frame type property is set to Auto Detect by default. If you find that you are unable to communicate with an older IPX/SPX system, such as a Novell3 system, you may need to adjust the frame type setting on the newer system to match the frame type specified on the old system.

A system running IPX/SPX can have two different types of network numbers: internal and external. A network number helps an IPX/SPX-enabled system to determine how to route packets. An external network number must be unique for each network segment (that is, each portion of the network separated by a router or bridge). An internal network number is used for routing inside a particular segment and is a unique identifier for the computer. You will learn more about routing later in the course.

Like TCP/IP, IPX/SPX and NWLink support NetBIOS, which is a naming system that enables systems to communicate with one another without using the Domain Name System (DNS). Internal LANs have traditionally used NetBIOS, but newer systems use DNS by default. You will learn about DNS later in this course. You may need to enable NetBIOS support if you are running NetBIOS applications on the network. You will learn more about NetBIOS shortly.

IPX/SPX internal network number

Media Access Control (MAC) address
The hardware address of a device connected to a network.

In IPX/SPX, each host uses its **Media Access Control (MAC) address** to help it identify a NetWare host within a particular virtual IPX/SPX network. If the internal network number is not set, you will probably still be able to communicate with another IPX-enabled system on your local network. Before NetWare 5.x, routing was built into the NetWare kernel, requiring an internal network number during installation of a NetWare server. However, setting the internal network number makes communication more efficient if you are routing IPX/SPX because the internal network number allows the system to identify itself to remote subnets. You must use an internal network number in the following situations:

- You are using your system to route IPX/SPX on a network.

Service Advertising Protocol (SAP)
A protocol designed to provide file and print services for Novell NetWare networks.

- You are using your system to run applications that use NetWare's **Service Advertising Protocol (SAP)**, and you are running IPX/SXP. These applications often include databases, such as those provided by SAP (*www.sap.com*) and Microsoft (*www.microsoft.com*).

IPX/SPX advantages and disadvantages

You have already learned that IPX/SPX is not a vendor-neutral protocol. It was developed by Novell and is used mostly with Novell NetWare networks. TCP/IP has eclipsed IPX/SPX as the standard enterprise protocol because of its open nature. However, IPX/SPX is still common and has typically performed better than TCP/IP.

Virtual Private Network (VPN)
A secure network between two sites using Internet technology as the transport; an extended LAN that enables a company to conduct secure, real-time communication.

Although IPX/SPX is not supported on the Internet, thousands of IPX/SPX WANs use private networks or **Virtual Private Networks (VPNs)** to communicate over long distances.

Novell has adopted TCP/IP as its default protocol in Novell NetWare 5, although the company still supports IPX/SPX.

NetBEUI

NOTE:
NetBEUI is typically found on legacy networks only.

NetBEUI (pronounced "Net-boo-ee") is an acronym for Network Basic Input/Output System (NetBIOS) Extended User Interface. It was first developed by IBM, but Microsoft has since implemented it as a solution for its peer-to-peer networks. NetBEUI is a nonroutable protocol, which limits its usefulness in many networks.

NetBIOS

NOTE:
Technically, NetBIOS is not a protocol but an application programming interface (API) that can be implemented over different protocols. NetBIOS names are not required for Windows 2000 and Windows XP systems.

NetBIOS was originally designed for use with NetBEUI (hence the name NetBIOS Extended User Interface). Because NetBEUI is declining in popularity, NetBIOS is mainly used as a programming interface for applications. It resides at the session layer (Layer 5) of the OSI/RM. NetBIOS can operate over NetBEUI, as well as over routable protocols such as TCP/IP and IPX/SPX. Microsoft Windows computers use NetBIOS names to identify one another and communicate on a network.

AppleTalk

AppleTalk, a routable protocol, is used only in Apple networks, and is thus proprietary. AppleTalk Phase II allows this protocol to work with other protocols. Rather than using the term domain or network, AppleTalk divides groups of computers into zones.

Choosing and Combining Protocols

Despite its prevalence, TCP/IP is not the only protocol you need to learn and use. You should know about other protocols, as well. For example, small peer-to-peer networks do not require TCP/IP or IPX/SPX. A simple protocol such as NetBEUI would be the most appropriate for these networks, mainly because it is fast, and is easy to configure and maintain. However, a large LAN or a WAN would require a more capable protocol such as TCP/IP.

Combining protocols

NOTE:
Multiple protocols should be used on a network only when necessary. The preferred network configuration is to use a single protocol, if possible.

Networks commonly use two routable protocols, such as TCP/IP and IPX/SPX, although this combination could cause problems with system overhead in large sites experiencing heavy traffic. Such a combination provides system redundancy and can speed connectivity.

Sometimes routable and nonroutable protocols should be combined, even in a routed network. A nonroutable protocol such as NetBEUI can be quite useful in a LAN or WAN because it can deliver traffic to local computers without the overhead associated with TCP/IP. If a user sends a message to an employee in the same LAN, NetBEUI will handle the entire transaction. However, if someone sends a message to a recipient on another LAN (activity that involves a router), the system will automatically use a routable protocol such as TCP/IP.

 Using multiple protocols can increase the time required to maintain and troubleshoot a network. In addition, the more protocols you use, the more system overhead you create.

Binding protocols

Whenever you use a protocol such as TCP/IP, you must attach, or bind, it to your NIC. To create a network, you must first obtain and install a NIC, use a compatible NIC driver, and choose a protocol.

In UNIX systems, you perform this attachment by reconfiguring the kernel because the UNIX kernel incorporates all drivers and protocols. Whenever you want to change a driver or protocol, you must incorporate it directly into the kernel.

In Windows XP, however, you bind a protocol to the NIC using the Local Area Connection Properties dialog box, shown in Figure 1-14.

NOTE:
This figure shows TCP/IP as an installed protocol. The fact that a protocol has been installed does not necessarily imply that it is bound to a network interface card.

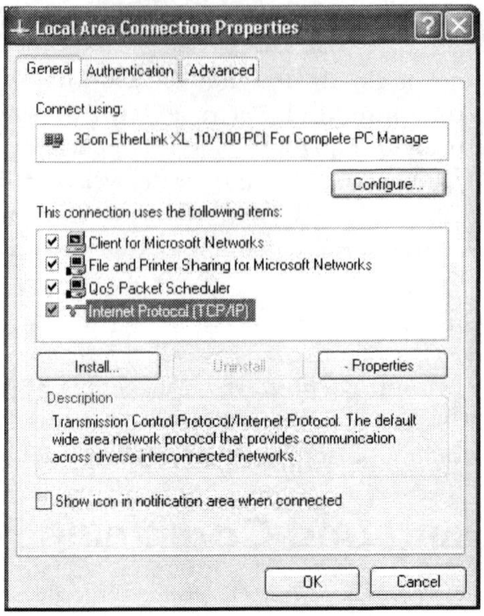

Figure 1-14: Windows XP Local Area Connection Properties dialog box

Protocols and binding order

If you are using multiple protocols, the binding order determines the first protocol that the system will use to send information. If the first protocol is unavailable, the system will use the second protocol to deliver the packets.

Incoming packets are compared with bound protocols in binding order until a matching protocol is found. The protocol that is used for most of the computer's traffic should be bound as the first protocol.

Many operating systems, including Linux, Windows NT, Windows 2000, Windows XP and Windows Server 2003, allow you to choose the binding order of network protocols. Older operating systems, such as Windows 95/98/Me, do not allow you to choose binding order. These systems automatically order protocols.

Local Area Network (LAN)

OBJECTIVE:
3.1.6: LANs and WANs

local area network (LAN)
A group of computers connected within a confined geographic area.

A **LAN** is a group of computers connected within a confined geographic area. Figure 1-15 illustrates a LAN.

hub
A device used to connect systems so that they can communicate with one another; a repeater or a bridge.

switch
A device used to connect either individual systems or multiple networks.

Layer 1 switch
A device that connects individual systems; a Layer 3 switch connects networks.

wide area network (WAN)
A group of computers connected over an expansive geographic area so their users can share files and services.

router
A device that routes packets between networks based on network-layer address; determines the best path across a network. Also used to connect separate LANs to form a WAN.

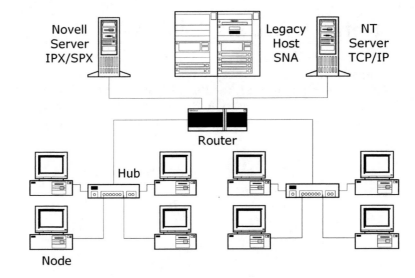

Figure 1-15: LAN example

LANs allow users to share files and services, and are commonly used for intraoffice communication. They can extend over several hundred feet, and generally represent one locale, such as a corporate office in Phoenix, Arizona, for example. You would use a **hub** or a **Layer 1 switch** to connect computers so that they create a LAN. Modern LANs are structured around distributed computing, and often consist of workstations and servers.

Wide Area Network (WAN)

A **WAN** is a group of computers connected over an expansive geographic area, such as a state or country, allowing users to share files and services. Figure 1-16 illustrates a WAN. A WAN often connects two LANs using the communications lines of a public carrier, such as the PSTN. The connection is called a WAN link. You will learn about various types of WAN links later in this course.

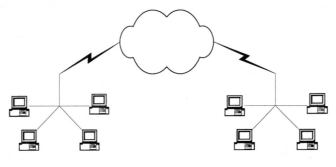

Figure 1-16: WAN example

The primary difference between a LAN and a WAN is the fact that a WAN involves two separate networks. Either a **router** or a switch is required to create these two networks. In many ways, the Internet is an extremely large, complex WAN. You will learn more about network components such as routers and switches later.

Network Access Point (NAP)

OBJECTIVE:
3.1.7: Internet
infrastructure

You have already learned that the Internet is a series of interconnected networks. A network access point (NAP) is a junction between one high-speed network and another. As shown in Figure 1-17, the three key NAPs in the United States are in New York, Chicago and San Francisco. All these NAPs are run by telephone companies. These three exchange points, plus Washington, D.C., are the four original NAPs in the United States.

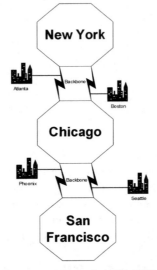

Figure 1-17: Three key U.S. NAPs

OBJECTIVE:
3.1.7: Internet
infrastructure

NAP connections are usually made by either a router or a switch. These high-speed networks are called Internet backbones because they provide essential connectivity for the rest of the Internet. Backbones can cover long or short distances, and smaller networks typically connect to them.

The backbone network connected by a NAP is known as a very high-speed Backbone Network Service (vBNS). Most of the NAPs in use today run in excess of 1 gigabit per second (Gbps), and are designed to reduce congestion from increasing Internet use.

Throughout most of the Internet's history, regional and governmental agencies were responsible for providing the physical connections. Beginning in 1995, commercial ISPs began to fund the Internet. This group of ISPs is called the National Research and Education Network (NREN). It uses NAPs for connectivity.

Segment

segment
Part of a larger
structure; common
term used in
networking.

A **segment** is any piece or part of a larger structure. On the Internet, a segment can be the part of the backbone that connects San Francisco to Chicago, as shown in the previous figure. On a smaller scale, a segment can be the connection between your company's network and its NAP. The term segment also describes subnetworks in a LAN (see the *Bridges* and *Routers* sections later in this lesson).

Common Network Components

Computer networks usually require a great deal of equipment to function properly. LANs and WANs typically include network interface cards, repeaters, hubs, bridges, routers, brouters and switches. These devices affect the way traffic is controlled and moved throughout a network. Before investigating the individual devices, you should be familiar with the following terms that are associated with network traffic:

- **Collision domain** — a logical area in a computer network where a group of Ethernet devices compete for access to the media. In traditional Ethernet networking, only one device can transmit at any one time. When two devices transmit at the same time, the simultaneously transmitted frames collide and are destroyed. The more collisions there are, the less efficient the network is.

- **Broadcast** — a transmission from one node that is intended for transmission to all other nodes on the network. Whenever a device needs to send out information but does not know which device to address it to, it sends out a broadcast. Broadcasts are vital to the function of a network, but they generate a large amount of traffic and must be handled wisely to keep a network running efficiently.

- **Broadcast domain** — a logical network segment in which any connected device can transmit to any other device in the domain without having to go through a routing device. Broadcast traffic is limited to the confines of a broadcast domain.

Equipment configuration for a typical network is shown in Figure 1-18.

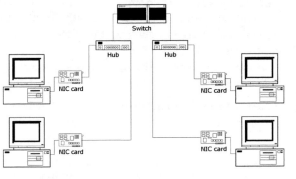

Figure 1-18: Networking components

Network interface card (NIC)

OBJECTIVE:
3.2.2: Hardware/ software connection devices

adapter
A device that provides connectivity between at least two systems.

NOTE:
Many PCs include NIC hardware built into the system hardware rather than implemented as a separate adapter card.

Each node in a network contains a NIC, often called a network **adapter** card. The NIC is the interface between the computer and the network (that is, it is the physical connection between the computer and the network cabling), as shown in Figure 1-19.

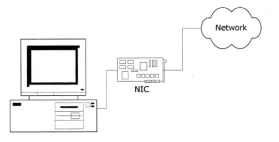

Figure 1-19: Network interface card (NIC)

Networks transmit data serially, or one bit at a time. The network adapter converts the data from the computer into a format appropriate for transmission over the network. A

NIC generally resides in the motherboard expansion slot and communicates with the computer through a NIC device driver. Networking cable connects the NIC to the network. NICs vary for Ethernet and token-ring networks, which you will learn about in a later lesson. NICs operate at the data link layer of the OSI/RM.

A NIC requires a device driver, which is specialized software that must be installed on the system to enable the NIC to function properly.

transceiver
A device that transmits and receives digital or analog signals.

Most NICs contain a **transceiver**, a network device that transmits and receives analog or digital signals. The term is short for transmitter-receiver.

In LANs, the transceiver places data onto the network wire, and detects and receives data traveling across the wire. Some network types require an external transceiver. Most NICs have more than one transceiver. Each transceiver is attached to a different connector available on the back of the card.

A NIC can be attached to a computer by any of the following:

- **Peripheral component interconnect (PCI) card** — a standard method for attaching any internally attached system card.

- **Universal Serial Bus (USB) device** — a method for attaching external interfaces, including NICs. Two USB standards exist, 1.0/1.1 and 2.0. USB 1.0 cards support data rates of up to 12 megabits per second (Mbps). USB 2.0 cards support data rates of up to 480 Mbps.

- **IEEE 1394 (FireWire) device** — similar to USB, though the original USB 1394 standard supports speeds of up to 400 Mbps. Commonly found on Macintosh systems, but increasingly found on IBM-compatible systems. IEEE 1294 cards have connectors for both internal and external devices. The Institute of Electrical and Electronics Engineers (IEEE) is an organization that creates standards for computers and communications. You will learn more about IEEE standards later in this lesson.

- **Industry Standard Architecture (ISA) card** — considered a legacy standard for connecting internal cards. Largely superseded by PCI cards, though still in use.

Most new NICs are PCI Ethernet cards with an RJ-45 port to connect to unshielded twisted-pair cable. Older NICs included an RJ-45 port and a BNC port, which was used to connect the PC to legacy Thinnet (10Base2) coaxial cable.

Every NIC has a physical, or MAC, address that identifies an individual machine on a network. While the NIC's interface itself is defined at the physical layer (Layer 1) of the OSI model, the physical address of the adapter, as well as its drivers, are located at the MAC sublayer of the data link layer (Layer 2).

Repeater

NOTE:
Repeaters will amplify any electronic "noise" on the line along with the data signal.

A repeater is a low-level device that amplifies the electronic signal traveling on a cable segment. It ensures that electronic signals do not degrade. Therefore, a repeater can connect computers that are farther apart than the defined network standards, as shown in Figure 1-20.

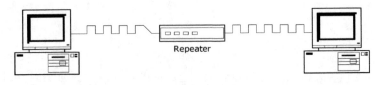

Figure 1-20: Repeater

Repeaters operate at the physical layer (Layer 1) of the OSI/RM. They transmit binary code, which consists of ones and zeros. A cable segment that approaches its maximum length causes the data signal to weaken and eventually break down. A repeater can strengthen this signal by retransmitting it.

Hub

A hub connects computers in a star-configured network so they can exchange information. It has several ports, each connected to a single node. By interconnecting the nodes, a hub serves as the concentration point for a network. Most hubs are called active hubs because they regenerate electronic signals (the same as a repeater). Figure 1-21 illustrates a hub.

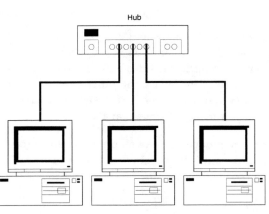

Figure 1-21: Hub connecting workstations

Hubs operate at the physical layer (Layer 1) of the OSI/RM. They can be connected to other hubs, or "daisy-chained," to provide more ports for a larger network. You can also connect hubs to switches or routers to increase the number of network nodes.

In technical terms, a hub connects multiple devices into the same collision domain and allows frame collision. Hubs do not divide a network into discrete segments the way switches do; a hub takes a signal coming from any node and passes it on to all the other nodes on the network.

This traditional Ethernet topology is often called shared Ethernet, because all hosts must share the bandwidth, only one can transmit at a time, and each host is responsible for collision detection and retransmission. A shared Ethernet network provides for only half-duplex transmission (data can be transmitted in only one direction at a time). Hubs have been replaced widely by switches in modern networks.

Bridge

Bridges are devices that filter frames to determine whether a specific frame belongs on a local segment or another LAN segment. Because bridges operate at Layer 2 of the OSI/RM, they use hardware addresses to determine which segment will receive the frame.

Bridges can reduce network traffic by dividing one network into two segments, thereby creating two separate (smaller) collision domains. They can also connect network segments with the same or different data link protocols, enabling those segments to communicate. For example, a bridge can connect an Ethernet network to a token-ring network, or two token-ring networks. Figure 1-22 illustrates two network segments connected by a bridge.

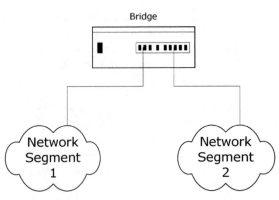

Figure 1-22: Bridge connecting network segments

NOTE:
Remember that bridges are typically invisible to upper-layer protocols. When you use a routable protocol, all segments connected by a bridge will be part of the same subnetwork.

Bridges recognize hardware (MAC) addresses between networks. Suppose one computer sends information to another in an Ethernet network. The bridge determines whether the destination computer resides on the same network segment by verifying the MAC address. If the destination computer resides outside that segment, the bridge passes the message to another segment. Through this screening process, network traffic is reduced and more bandwidth is made available.

Bridges are independent of all upper-layer protocols. This independence enables bridges to forward frames from many different upper-layer protocols. Bridges have also been largely replaced by switches in modern Ethernet networks because switches are faster.

Router

OBJECTIVE:
3.2.2: Hardware/software connection devices

Routers are conceptually similar to bridges, except that they operate at the network layer (Layer 3) of the OSI/RM. Instead of using MAC addresses, routers forward and control network protocols, such as IP and IPX. They forward, or route, data from one network to another, instead of only to network segments. Thus, they are efficient tools for creating discrete network segments, which can help reduce network traffic.

NOTE:
The term "gateway" is used to refer to routers in a TCP/IP network environment. This usage can lead to confusion if the context in which "gateway" is being used is not known.

Routers direct data packets between networks. They identify the destination computer's network address, and then determine the most efficient route for transmitting data to it. As a result, routers do not forward broadcast traffic (unless they are specifically configured to do so). Routers limit broadcast domains at the network layer (Layer 3).

Figure 1-23 illustrates a router connecting two networks.

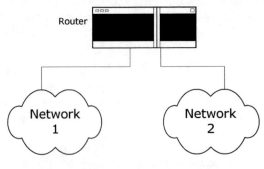

Figure 1-23: Router connecting networks

Suppose a computer on Network 2 sends data to another computer on Network 2. In this case, the router will not pass the data to Network 1. This filtering process conserves network bandwidth. You can measure a router's capability by its packets per second (PPS) rate.

Routers are protocol-dependent: They rely on the address system defined by the protocol used (IPX, IP and so forth). Different types of routers work with different protocols. For example, IP routers operate with the inherent IP 32-bit address structure. To use the IPX addressing protocol, a router that supports IPX is required. Routing will be discussed in more detail later in this lesson.

Routing table

Routers often need to communicate with one another in order to keep their information current. Routers store network information in files called routing tables. Whenever a router needs to update another router's routing table, routing protocols are used. As you will see later in the course, interior and exterior routing protocols are used, depending on the location of the router.

Switch

OBJECTIVE:
3.2.2: Hardware/ software connection devices

On a network, a switch directs the flow of information directly from one node to another. There are several different types of switches, as you will learn shortly. A Layer 2 switch, also called a LAN switch, provides a separate connection for each node in a company's internal network.

A switch segments a collision domain into as many segments as there are connections between nodes. That is, the collision domain is reduced so that only the two nodes in any given connection coexist within each collision domain. Essentially, a LAN switch creates a series of instant networks that contain only the two devices communicating with each other at that particular moment.

NOTE:
You should know that, by definition, switches operate at the data link layer (Layer 2) of the OSI/RM.

Switches provide full-duplex communication. A switch cross-connects all hosts connected to it and can give each sender/receiver pair the line's entire bandwidth, instead of sharing the bandwidth with all other network nodes. A switch can handle multiple simultaneous communications between the computers attached to it, whereas a hub can handle only one communication at a time. Switches forward broadcast traffic.

By definition, a switch operates at the data link layer (Layer 2) of the OSI/RM; however, there are several types of switches that operate at various OSI layers.

Types of switches

Layer 2 switch
A device that forwards traffic based on MAC addresses.

Switches can operate at several layers of the OSI/RM. A Layer 1 switch, called a switching hub, has replaced the much slower and less efficient traditional hub. A **Layer 2 switch**, also called a LAN switch, forwards traffic based on MAC addresses and is much faster than a bridge.

Layer 3 switch
A device that connects networks.

A **Layer 3 switch** forwards traffic based on Layer 3 information, and is called a routing switch if it supports network protocols, such as IP and IPX. These switches are much faster than routers because they can act on Layer 2 information as well as Layer 3 information, and are replacing routers in many installations in the core network.

Layer 4 switches make forwarding decisions based on Layer 4 information (such as the specific TCP/UDP port that an application uses), as well as on Layer 2 and 3 information.

Packet switching

A LAN switch establishes a connection between two network segments just long enough to send the current packet. This process is called packet switching. An incoming frame contains an IP packet as the payload with a header that includes the MAC address information for the source and destination. The MAC address in the frame's header is read and compared to a list of addresses maintained in the switch's lookup table. Switches can use store-and-forward or cut-through methods for forwarding traffic:

- **Store-and-forward** — The switch saves the entire packet in its buffer and checks it for CRC errors before forwarding it. Packets that contain errors are discarded.

- **Cut-through** — The switch reads the MAC address as soon as the frame begins to enter the switch. After reading the destination MAC address, the switch immediately begins forwarding the frame. This method provides no error detection or correction.

Many switches combine the two methods for forwarding traffic.

Benefits of using switches

Switches offer the following benefits for networks:

port
A logical opening in an operating system or protocol stack that allows the transfer of information. Not the same as a TCP or UDP port.

- **Simple installation** — For many bridges and hubs, installing a switch requires you to unplug connections from existing devices and plug the connections into the switch **ports**.

- **Higher speeds** — Switches have high-speed backplanes (the connections within the switch itself) that allow full bandwidth between any two users or segments. This feature eliminates the switch as a potential network bottleneck.

- **Bandwidth control** — Using a switch, it is possible to control the bandwidth available to a client or server.

virtual local area network (VLAN)
Logical subgroup within a LAN created with software instead of hardware.

- **Creation of logical computer groupings** — You can create a group of systems called a **virtual LAN (VLAN)**. A VLAN allows you to organize systems according to their logical function on the network, as opposed to their physical location. For example, a VLAN can allow systems residing in New York, Bangalore and London to all belong to the same group, in spite of their obviously different physical locations. Network hubs allow you to group systems only by their physical location.

- **More default security** — Using a VLAN, you can isolate individual systems. Also, it is slightly more difficult to "sniff" (examine data traveling over a network) network connections in a switch-based network than in a standard hub-based network, because each connection made in a switch is dedicated; in a hub-based network, any one system can see all connections made on the network.

Figure 1-24 illustrates a routing switch that connects two networks.

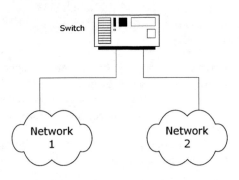

Figure 1-24: Switch connecting networks

Increased LAN traffic

Following are three options for handling increased LAN traffic.

- **Use a bridge** — This traditional method reduces the number of users on a network by separating it into two network segments.

- **Use a LAN switch (a Layer 2 switch)** — LAN switches are available for Ethernet, fast Ethernet, Token Ring and Fiber Distributed Data Interface (FDDI). You will learn about these network standards later in the course.

- **Increase the network bandwidth** — One way to increase bandwidth is to move to a higher-speed standard such as FDDI. This approach requires you to change adapters, rewire the building and possibly change system software. Upgrading to FDDI is expensive. Upgrading from Ethernet to fast Ethernet is more economical.

Gateway

Gateways, also called protocol converters, can operate at any layer of the OSI/RM. The job of a gateway is much more complex than that of a router or switch. Typically, a gateway must convert one protocol stack into another and can be used to connect networks with dissimilar protocols or architectures. For example, a gateway may connect an AppleTalk network to nodes on a DECnet network, or a TCP/IP network to an IPX/SPX network, as shown in Figure 1-25.

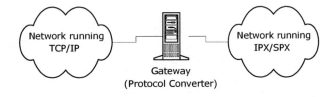

Figure 1-25: Gateway

You will learn about another gateway type, the default gateway, later in this course.

Channel Service Unit/Data Service Unit (CSU/DSU)

A Channel Service Unit/Data Service Unit (CSU/DSU) terminates physical connections. This device is required when using dedicated circuits, such as T1 lines. The digital data stream is translated by the CSU/DSU into bipolar signals, which are suitable for line transmission.

For example, a dedicated T1 line enters a building through a Registered Jack-45 (RJ-45) connector, which resembles a large phone jack (phone jacks use RJ-11 connectors). The CSU/DSU then transmits the signal to the network, as illustrated in Figure 1-26.

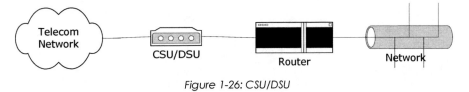

Figure 1-26: CSU/DSU

The CSU/DSU also performs some error-reporting and loopback functions. CSU/DSUs operate at the physical layer (Layer 1) of the OSI/RM.

OBJECTIVE:
3.2.2: Hardware/
software
connection devices

Modem

A modem is a device that enables a computer to communicate with other computers over telephone lines by translating digital data into audio/analog signals (on the sending computer) and then back into digital form (on the receiving computer). This type of modem is called a traditional or analog modem.

The term "modem" is widely used, but does not always denote an analog-to-digital translation. For instance, cable, DSL and Integrated Services Digital Network (ISDN) modems are used on all digital networks — no translation to analog is required. The term "modem" has been used to describe any device that adapts a computer to a phone line or cable television network, whether it is digital or analog.

NOTE:
Most modems can auto-detect connectivity settings, so detailed configuration is usually not required.

A single modem can be shared on a network for all users. The computer that is physically attached to the modem must be configured properly. When setting up a modem for WAN access (or any other connectivity purpose), you must define several items to ensure successful modem function. These items include:

- Serial port interrupt request (IRQ).

- Input/output (I/O) address.

- Maximum port speed.

Serial port IRQ

An IRQ line is used by components such as modems, network cards and keyboards to request attention from the processor of the system. Serial modems can use IRQ Lines 3 or 4, which are both used for serial ports.

I/O address

The I/O address transfers information between the CPU and a specific device. The base I/O port settings for a modem are 3F0 to 3FF for COM1, and 2F0 to 2FF for COM2. You will learn more about COM ports later in the course.

Maximum port speed

Modems are available in different capacities for sending and receiving data. When configuring your modem, you must set the maximum port speed for the modem to ensure that it functions properly. This setting will provide the most reliable connection for the modem, and the optimal transmission rate for your session.

Figure 1-27 illustrates two modems (any type) used for WAN connectivity between two company sites.

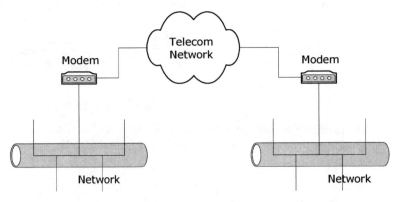

Figure 1-27: Modems used for WAN connectivity

Modem AT commands

ATtention (AT) commands are instructions that activate features on modems. These commands were developed by Hayes Microcomputer Products in 1978 and have become standard modem commands, officially called the Hayes Standard AT Command Set. The AT command is a prefix that initiates each modem command, and informs the modem that commands are being sent.

With the advent of user-friendly Internet software, the AT commands are usually run automatically when a computer accesses the Internet with a modem. The commands are responsible for dialing, answering, transmitting and receiving. Before user-friendly Internet software, modems had to be sent commands through a command-line interface, such as the MS-DOS prompt, the Windows NT/2000/XP command prompt or a UNIX/Linux terminal. Today, you can use these commands from a command-line interface for troubleshooting purposes. Table 1-3 lists the basic commands that modems require.

NOTE:
Memorizing AT commands is not required. However, you should know the purpose of AT commands.

Table 1-3: Basic AT commands for modems

AT Command	Description
ATA	Answer command. The modem waits to answer a call, then answers the incoming call and communicates with another modem.
ATD	Dial command. The modem dials a telephone number to begin communication with another modem.
ATH	Hang-up command. The modem disconnects the session and hangs up the telephone line.
ATX	Extended result codes command. The modem indicates connection result codes when a connection is established. If a connection is not established, the modem sends a code indicating otherwise, such as no carrier, ringing, dial tone and busy signal detection.
ATZ	Reset command. The modem disconnects the session and hangs up the telephone line, and then restores settings (stored settings or factory defaults).

Movie Time!

Watch the following CIW v5 Foundations Movie to learn even more about this topic.

Signals and Modems (approx. playing time: 04:45)

All movie clips are © 2007 LearnKey, Inc.

Patch panel

patch panel
A group of sockets that manually switches data between inbound and outbound transmissions.

A **patch panel** is a group of sockets (usually consisting of pin locations and ports) mounted on a rack. It is a central point where cables from different rooms or departments can be connected to one another (forming a LAN, for example). It can then be used to connect a network to the Internet or another WAN.

Patch panels are usually placed in a central point, such as a closet or a company's server room. They may have numerous ports and pin locations, depending on the company's size.

One side of the patch panel contains rows of pin locations. A punch tool is used to "punch down" the wires to make a connection. These connections often originate from wall jacks throughout a building. For example, in an accounting department in a large cubicle-filled room, each accountant's computer may be connected to a hub. The hub is then connected to a wall jack, which is connected to the patch panel.

The other side of the patch panel contains a row of female ports, which are used to connect to other network devices, such as routers and switches. For example, the patch panel may be connected to a router, which is then connected to the Internet, as shown in Figure 1-28.

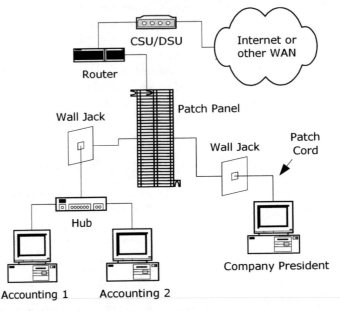

Figure 1-28: Patch panel

Patch cords are used in ports to cross-connect networked computers that are wired to the patch panel. Patch cords also connect network devices to a wall jack.

Firewall

A firewall is a secure computer system placed between a trusted network and an untrusted one, such as the Internet. A firewall acts as a barrier against potential malicious activity, while still allowing a "door" for people to communicate between a secured network and the open, unsecured network. A network firewall is most commonly placed between a corporate LAN and the Internet. By connecting to the Internet through firewalls, no computer on the corporate LAN is actually connected to the Internet, and any requests for information must pass through the firewall.

Transmission Media

To transmit data, a medium must exist, usually in the form of cables or wireless methods. The following section explains the most common cable types: twisted pair, coaxial and fiber optic. It concludes with a discussion of wireless media.

Twisted-pair cable

Twisted-pair cable is perhaps the most widely used cabling system in Ethernet networks. Two copper wires are intertwined to form the twisted-pair cable. Depending on the category, several insulated wire strands can reside in the cable. Cable categories will be discussed later in this lesson.

A twisted-pair segment cannot exceed 100 meters. Twisted-pair cable is used for many types of network standards. For example, 10BaseT Ethernet networks use twisted-pair cable; the name "10BaseT" denotes a network running at 10 Mbps, using baseband transmission and twisted-pair cable.

Twisted-pair cable is available in two basic types: shielded twisted-pair (STP) and unshielded twisted-pair (UTP).

- **STP** — Shielded twisted-pair copper wire is protected from external electromagnetic interference by a metal sheath wrapped around the wires; STP is harder to install and maintain than UTP.

- **UTP** — Unshielded twisted-pair cable is the most common type of twisted-pair wiring; it is less expensive than STP, but less secure and prone to electromagnetic interference. This course focuses on UTP.

STP and UTP are available with two varieties of wire: stranded and solid.

- **Stranded** — the most common type; flexible and easy to handle around corners and objects.

attenuation
The weakening of a transmission signal as it travels farther from its source.

- **Solid** — can span longer distances without as much **attenuation** as stranded wire, but is less flexible; will break if bent multiple times.

Six twisted-pair standards are specified by the Telecommunications Industry Association/Electronic Industries Alliance (TIA/EIA) 568 Commercial Building Wiring standard. An additional level, Category 7, is commercially available, but is not standardized. Table 1-4 outlines these categories.

OBJECTIVE:
3.2.1: Networking cable types

Tech Tip

As you study Table 1-4, consider the designations Mbps and megahertz (MHz) for Ethernet cabling. The phrase "bits per second" refers to the speed at which information can be transferred across a wire. Standard Ethernet, for example, operates at 10 Mbps (10 million bits per second). Fast Ethernet can transmit (or push) bits across a wire at 100 Mbps (100 million bits per second). Alternatively, the term "Hertz" describes the number of times a signal cycles in one second. The MHz value of a wire should be considered because Ethernet transmissions do more than simply push bits across a wire. They also transmit a particular signal. Standard Ethernet requires a cable that supports at least 10 MHz (signals that cycle 10 million times in one second). Fast Ethernet requires a cable that can support signals of 100 MHz (signals that cycle 100 million times in one second).

Table 1-4: TIA/EIA 568 twisted-pair cable categories

Cable Grade	General Use	Bandwidth	Specific Network(s)
Category 1	Some voice and limited data transfer	1 Mbps	Intercom and doorbell wiring; previously used in the telephony industry
Category 2	Data	4 Mbps. Can sustain rates up to 2 MHz.	Early token-ring networks and ISDN
Category 3	Data	10 Mbps. Can sustain rates up to 16 MHz.	Standard telephone networks after 1983
Category 4	Data	20 Mbps. Can sustain rates up to 20 MHz.	Rarely used; 16-Mbps token ring, ISDN lines
Category 5	Data	100 Mbps. Can sustain rates up to 100 MHz.	A popular implementation; 10BaseT and 100BaseTX networks, as well as some FDDI and ATM networks

Table 1-4: TIA/EIA 568 twisted-pair cable categories (cont'd)

Cable Grade	General Use	Bandwidth	Specific Network(s)
Category 5e	Data	1,000 Mbps. Can sustain rates up to 100 MHz.	Gigabit Ethernet and other high-speed networks
Category 6	Data	10 Gbps. Can sustain rates up to 250 MHz.	Supports networks of up to 10 Gbps. If you want to upgrade a Category 5 network and still use wires, consider using this category of cable.
Category 6E	Data	10 Gbps. Can sustain rates up to 550 MHz.	10-Gbps (and faster, more powerful) networks
Category 7	Data	10 Gbps. Can sustain rates up to at least 600 MHz.	Proposed standard

Category 1 is not considered an acceptable medium for network data transmissions, but does support low-speed serial communication such as connections to dial-up lines. Category selections are made according to network data transmission requirements.

Registered Jack-45 (RJ-45) connector

NOTE:
Typically only four wires are connected and used.

Registered Jack-45 (RJ-45) connectors are commonly used on certain types of Ethernet and token-ring networks, which you will learn about later in this lesson. The connector holds up to eight wires, and is used with twisted-pair wire. To attach an RJ-45 connector to a cable, the connector must be crimped using a tool called a crimper.

To crimp an RJ-45 connector, place the connector on the cable with the wires correctly positioned (the wire position depends on the network standard used, which will be discussed in this lesson). Place the connector in the crimper with the cable, and squeeze the crimper handles firmly.

The crimper pushes two plugs from the RJ-45 connector into the cable. One plug pushes into the cable jacket to attach the connector and cable. The other plug pushes eight pins through the cable jacket and into the respective wires. Figure 1-29 illustrates an RJ-45 connector.

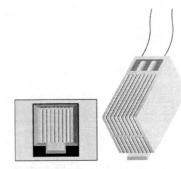

Figure 1-29: RJ-45 connector and jack

An RJ-45 connector is slightly larger than the RJ-11 standard telephone connector, which holds four wires. (An RJ-11 six-wire version also exists.) An RJ-48 connector is similar to an RJ-45 in that it has the same number of connectors. However, the RJ-48 is used when connecting T1 lines, and has a slightly different wiring pattern. An RJ-21 connector is a 50-pin connector on one end that expands to 12 RJ-45 connectors on the other.

OBJECTIVE:
3.2.1: Networking
cable types

NOTE:
For more about
crossover cables,
see the Data
Communications
Cabling FAQ at
www.faqs.org/faqs/
LANs/cabling-faq.

coax
High-capacity two-
wire (signal and
ground) cable; inner
wire is the primary
conductor, and the
metal sheath serves
as the ground.

plenum
Space between
building floors;
usually contains air
and heating ducts,
as well as
communication
and electrical wires.

NOTE:
Thicknet coax was,
at one time, a
common choice for
backbone cable
applications, but
has fallen out of
favor, primarily due
to its limited
bandwidth. Thinnet
is also considered a
legacy network
topology.

NOTE:
Most newer Ethernet
cards do not
include a BNC
connector. They
provide an RJ-45
connector only.

Crossover cable

A crossover cable for Ethernet networks is a specialized cable that allows you to connect two computers directly without using a hub. The crossover cable reverses, or crosses over, the respective PIN contacts. Crossover cables can be used in various situations, including the following:

- You want to connect two workstations together to transfer information quickly between them, and you do not have a hub or switch available.

- You need to connect a router to certain cable modems. If connecting a standard Ethernet cable to the cable modem does not work, try a crossover cable.

Coaxial cable

Coaxial cable, known as **coax** (pronounced "co-axe"), is a high-capacity cable used for video and communication networks. Coaxial cable has remained in common networking use because cable companies are often a preferred choice for high-speed Internet access.

Coaxial cable contains a signal wire at the center, which is either stranded or solid, surrounded by a metallic shield that serves as a ground. The shield is either braided or solid and is wrapped in plastic. If a cable travels through a **plenum**, it is coated in a fire-safe material such as Teflon.

Several types of coaxial cable exist for different purposes. For instance, coaxial cable is designed for baseband, broadband and television networks.

Common coax types are listed in Table 1-5.

Table 1-5: Common coax cable types

Cable Type	Use	Impedance
RG-6	Cable television, video, some cable modems; often for short distances (e.g., 6 feet)	75 Ohms
RG-8	Thick Ethernet (10Base5); maximum segment length of 500 meters	50 Ohms
RG-11	Broadband LANs	75 Ohms
RG-58	Thin Ethernet (10Base2); maximum segment length of 185 meters	50 Ohms
RG-59	Television	75 Ohms
RG-62	ARCnet	93 Ohms

You will notice an impedance value listed for each of the cable types. Impedance is a measure of a cable's resistance to a changing signal.

BNC connector

The British Naval Connector, or Bayonet Neil-Concelman (BNC) connector, is commonly used to connect coaxial cable to NICs, hubs and other network devices. The BNC connector is crimped to the cable using a bayonet mount. The bayonet mount technique connects the two wires (signal and ground) in the coaxial cable to the connector. The connector is then inserted into another connector and turned, which causes the bayonet mechanism to pinch several pins into the BNC's locking groove. A BNC connector is illustrated in Figure 1-30.

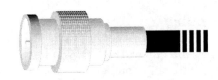

Figure 1-30: BNC connector

Fiber-optic cable

Fiber-optic cable can accommodate data transmissions much faster than coaxial or twisted-pair cable. Fiber-optic lines can transmit data in the gigabits-per-second range. Because they send data as pulses of light over threads of glass, the transmissions can travel for miles without a signal degradation. No electrical signals are carried over the fiber-optic line, so the lines are free of electromagnetic interference and are extremely difficult to tap.

Fiber-optic cables consist of two small glass strands: One strand sends and one receives. These strands are called the core, and they are sometimes made of plastic. Each core is surrounded by glass cladding. Each core and cladding element is wrapped with a plastic reinforced with Kevlar fibers.

Laser transmitters send the modulated light pulses and optical receivers receive them. Following are the two major types of fiber-optic cable:

- **Single-mode** — uses a specific light wavelength. The cable's core diameter is 8 to 10 microns. It permits signal transmission at extremely high bandwidth and allows very long transmission distances (up to 70 km, or 43 miles). Single-mode fiber is often used for intercity telephone trunks and video applications.

- **Multimode** — uses a large number of frequencies (or modes). The cable's core is larger than that of single-mode fiber, usually 50 microns to 100 microns, and it allows for the use of inexpensive light sources. It is used for short to medium distances (less than 200 m, or 656 feet). Multimode fiber is the type usually specified for LANs and WANs.

Fiber-optic cable is expensive, and installation can be tedious and costly. Attaching connectors to fibers used to involve a tedious process of cutting and polishing the ends of the glass strands and mounting them into the connectors. Modern tools and newer connectors cut and polish in one step.

Wireless Network Technologies

Wireless network connections have become extremely popular, both in enterprises and in homes. Wireless networking is usually implemented in a hybrid environment, in which wireless components communicate with a network that uses cables. For example, a laptop computer may use its wireless capabilities to connect with a corporate LAN that uses standard wiring.

The only difference between a wireless LAN and a cabled LAN is the medium itself: Wireless systems use wireless signals instead of a network cable. A standard system that uses a wireless NIC is called an end point. Following is a discussion of various media used to enable wireless networks.

Wireless networking media

spread spectrum
Technologies that consist of various methods for radio transmission in which frequencies or signal patterns are continuously changed.

Wireless communications use **spread spectrum** technologies. In spread spectrum technologies, a signal is generated by a system (for example, a computer with a wireless NIC), and then sent (in other words, spread) over a large number of frequencies to another system. That system then reassembles the data. Wireless networks can use the following types of spread spectrum transmissions:

- **Orthogonal Frequency Division Multiplexing (OFDM)** — OFDM splits a radio signal into smaller subsignals that are transmitted simultaneously on different frequencies. IEEE 802.11a and 802.11g networks can use OFDM. The 802.11a DSSS networks can operate at 54 Mbps at 5.4 GHz.

wideband
A large set of frequencies capable of carrying data at higher rates (for example, 1.544 Mbps). Usually carries digital signals. Includes DSL and cable Internet access.

- **Direct Sequence Spread Spectrum (DSSS)** — Rather than hopping from one frequency to another, a signal is spread over the entire band at once through the use of a spreading function. For this reason, DSSS is considered a **wideband** networking method. DSSS is used by 802.11b and 802.11g networks. The 802.11b (Wi-Fi) networks communicate as fast as 11 Mbps at 2.4 GHz, and 802.11b NICs have been available in stores for years. The 802.11g NICs and networks are becoming increasingly common, and can operate at rates between 20 and 54 Mbps at 2.4 GHz. The 802.11g wireless networks are backward-compatible with 802.11b networks.

narrowband
A specific set of frequencies established for wireless communication (usually for voice). Communicates at lower rates than broadband.

- **Frequency Hopping Spread Spectrum (FHSS)** — Originally developed during World War II, FHSS is a **narrowband** transmission technology that involves changing the frequency of a transmission at regular intervals. Signals move from frequency to frequency, and each frequency change is called a hop. Both the client and the server must coordinate the hops between frequencies. That is, they retune at regular intervals during the transmission. FHSS is ideal for networks in which interference is a problem. However, FHSS networks are slower than DSSS networks, achieving speeds between 2 Mbps and 3 Mbps. Even though FHSS networks use hop sequences, they do not make connections any more secure than those found in DSSS networks. It is possible for 802.11 networks to use FHSS, but FHSS has not been as widely adopted.

The 802.11b networks have the same frequency as standard 2.4-GHz cordless phones, Bluetooth networks, and even equipment such as microwaves. As a result, wireless networks can interfere with transmissions or be interfered with by other equipment.

Wireless networking modes

OBJECTIVE:
3.9.1: Ad-hoc and infrastructure mode

The following two types of wireless modes exist for 802.11a, 802.11b and 802.11g networks:

- **Ad-hoc** — in which systems use only their NICs to connect with one another. Ad-hoc mode is useful when two or more systems need to communicate with one another for only a short time. This mode is also known as peer-to-peer mode.

- **Infrastructure** — in which systems connect via a centralized access point, called a wireless access point (WAP). Infrastructure mode is a preferred method because a WAP allows some centralized access control and network protection. Also, a WAP can be used to connect a wireless network to a wired network. When the WAP is plugged into a standard hub, wireless and wired systems can communicate with one another if they are on the same IP network.

Software provided with the NIC allows the system administrator to choose between infrastructure and ad-hoc mode.

Figure 1-31 illustrates the two types of wireless networks.

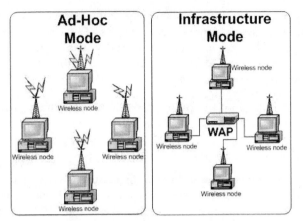

Figure 1-31: Ad-hoc vs. infrastructure mode

OBJECTIVE:
3.9.2: Wireless
access points
(WAPs)

Wireless access point (WAP)

As you just learned, a WAP is a device that acts much like a standard hub or switch in that it allows wireless systems to communicate with one another, as long as they are on the same network. It is possible to attach a WAP to a standard Ethernet hub or switch, and thus extend your network without having to lay down wires, which can be inconvenient. It is also possible for a WAP to include a router, which enables multiple wireless and wired networks to communicate with one another.

Wireless cell

A wireless cell is a collection of wireless clients around a specific WAP. The farther a client is from a WAP, the less that client is inclined to belong to a particular cell because the WAP beacon becomes too weak, and interference results.

 Resources often call a wireless cell a "sphere of influence" that is generated by a specific WAP.

If multiple cells exist in close proximity, a client may reside in several wireless cells at one time. Because of the nature of wireless networks, a mobile client (for example, a laptop computer) can be moved from one wireless cell to another. As a result, people can move from one wireless cell to another to gain (sometimes illicit) access to a wireless network and its resources. Resources can include files, printers and other networks, such as the Internet.

Basic Service Set Identifier (BSSID)

A Basic Service Set Identifier (BSSID) is provided by a WAP, and has one function: to differentiate one wireless cell from another. The BSSID does not contain authentication information. In fact, it is most often the MAC address of the WAP.

OBJECTIVE:
3.9.5: Secure Set
Identifier (SSID)

Service Set Identifier (SSID)

A Service Set Identifier (SSID) is a unique name for each wireless cell (or network). A SSID (pronounced "Sid") is used to control access to a particular wireless cell. Usually, a SSID is a simple text string entered into a WAP, although a SSID can also be established by hosts participating in an ad-hoc wireless network. After a WAP has a SSID entered, this WAP immediately becomes differentiated from other wireless cells. SSID values are case-sensitive and can be up to 32 characters long. They can also be encrypted.

Tech
Note

A SSID is not the same as a BSSID.

Common default WAP SSIDs include the following:

- ANY (in lowercase and/or uppercase letters).

- The vendor name (for example, Linksys®, Belkin — also in uppercase and/or lowercase). Cisco Aironet® cards use the word "tsunami."

Some cards default to a blank SSID. To begin to secure your system, change default SSID settings.

Figure 1-32 shows the configuration interface for a common WAP.

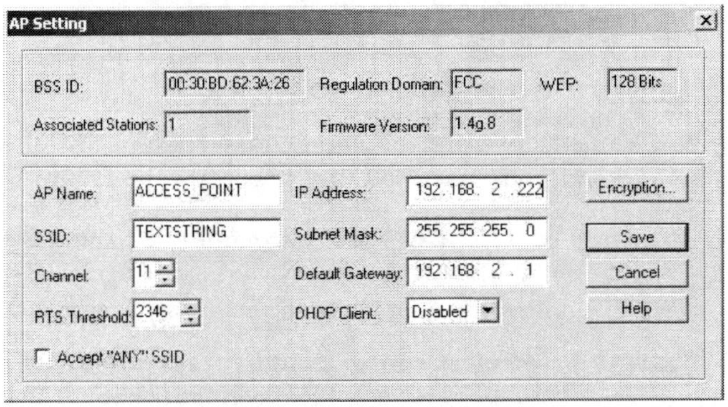

Figure 1-32: Configuration interface for common WAP

Notice that values exist for the BSSID as well as the SSID. It is also possible to configure a WAP so that it has its own IP address information. The default channel is often 11.

WAP beacon management frame

Whenever a WAP is ready to accept connections, it sends a special Ethernet frame called a beacon management frame. This beacon informs clients about the WAP's availability. Clients that are not specifically configured to use a particular WAP use this beacon to determine their participation in a wireless network. If a client knows where to go, it does not rely on a WAP's beacon. The beacon contains the SSID.

WAP security features

OBJECTIVE:
3.9.7: Wireless network security issues

A WAP provides centralized control and security features, and acts as a hub. Such measures are important because many hackers take advantage of wireless networks by placing their wireless systems in open mode, in which their systems search for all access points. Hackers then drive through a neighborhood or business district, trying to discover unsecured wireless networks. This practice is called "war driving." Both WAPs and wireless routers provide the following features to help stop war driving:

OBJECTIVE:
3.9.4: Wired Equivalent Privacy (WEP)

- **Wired Equivalent Privacy (WEP)** — WEP encryption can be in 64-bit, 128-bit and 256-bit keys. Generally, WEP is considered a weak form of encryption because the 64-bit and 128-bit symmetric keys used to encrypt the network transmissions have been cracked. Any system that does not encrypt transmissions cannot use the WAP. Because each system uses a key to encrypt transmissions, this form of encryption is called shared-key encryption. When configuring an end point to use WEP, you must provide a shared key. Similar to using a SSID, you must configure the WAP device to use the shared key, and then configure each end point to use this shared key. Many security experts consider WEP encryption trivial because the symmetric-key algorithm used — called RC4 — has been cracked. Nevertheless, using WEP is always recommended because it makes hacking into the network much more difficult.

OBJECTIVE:
3.9.6: MAC address filtering

- **MAC address filtering** — This feature enables the device to allow only certain MAC addresses to access the network. In MAC address filtering, a WAP is configured so that it allows only certain system MAC addresses to communicate with the rest of the network. MAC address filtering can be performed using either of two policies: Exclude all by default, then allow only listed clients; or include all by default, then exclude listed clients. MAC address filtering is also problematic from a security standpoint because hackers are able to forge MAC addresses. Forged (or spoofed) MAC addresses can then be used to fool an access point's filtering features.

NOTE:
You will learn more about spoofing in a later lesson.

Both WEP and MAC address filtering are useful tools that help systems administrators keep illicit users from attaching their systems to the network. Illicit systems that attach to the network are often called rogue systems.

Wireless management software

A WAP can accept programming to enable WEP, MAC filtering and other features. A standard end point uses software to control the following:

NOTE:
After a WAP is fully configured, wired and wireless systems can manage it. It is best not to depend on wireless systems to manage the WAP because one simple misconfiguration in the WAP software can cause the wireless systems to be disconnected from the network. Thus, they will be denied access to the WAP.

- **The end point's NIC** — Software must be loaded onto the end point's system to enable it to configure its own NIC in order to use a specific wireless channel, use WEP, monitor the connection strength and use other features.

- **A WAP or wireless router's configuration** — Software must be loaded onto an end point so that this end point can configure the WAP device. Generally, this type of software is capable of conducting a scan to locate the device. After the software finds the device, you can enter a password and begin configuring the device.

Following is a summary of what you can configure and/or manage on a WAP:

- Set the administrative password.

- Configure WEP and MAC address filtering.

- Set the WAP device's IP address, which can allow it to be managed by both wired and wireless systems.

- Upgrade the device's firmware (in other words, its operating system).

- Configure the device to become a Dynamic Host Configuration Protocol (DHCP) client.

The WAP or wireless router will have a default IP address. To change this address so that you can configure it, you must first configure a wireless system to access this IP address. You can then reconfigure the device to use the IP addresses for your network.

OBJECTIVE:
3.9.8: Wireless LAN practicality

Suitability of a wireless LAN

You must consider several factors when evaluating the practicality of a wireless LAN in your organization. Using wireless may be less expensive than installing new cable, especially in an old building. However, if your network is spread across a wide geographic region, you must consider how many access points you will need. You should also consider the following issues when considering incorporating a wireless LAN:

- **Security** — Wireless security presents certain challenges. Will WEP and/or MAC address filtering be sufficient? How will you control or limit the exchange of sensitive data over your wireless LAN? Will you need to update your existing network policies and procedures? Will you need to train employees in the secure use of wireless technology?

- **Learning curve** — Your Information Technology (IT) staff may require time to learn how to implement and maintain wireless technologies. IT employees may be accustomed to working with office hardware only. Wireless devices are mobile, and can be in use anywhere. Other employees, too, may need time to learn how to use wireless technologies effectively.

- **Network management** — The addition of wireless LANs often complicates the management of the existing wired network. For example, will you have enough ports in which to plug in access points? What new equipment or software might you need to secure the wireless network?

Attaching a WAP to a wired network

OBJECTIVE:
3.9.3: Wireless to wired LANs

In addition to providing centralized wireless client access, a WAP also has an RJ-45 plug that allows you to attach it to a standard, wired Ethernet network. After you attach a WAP to a hub or a switch, all wireless clients will be able to access all the services available to standard Ethernet clients (for example, Internet access, intranet access and company e-mail). Figure 1-33 illustrates how a WAP attached to a hub allows wireless clients access to the standard Ethernet network, which itself has access to the Internet.

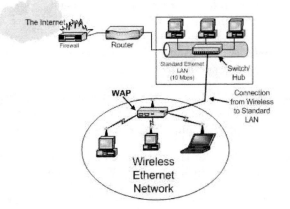

Figure 1-33: WAP attached to Ethernet hub or switch

Without the connection to the standard network, these wireless clients would be able to communicate only with one another and not with the rest of the network or the Internet.

Troubleshooting wireless connections

OBJECTIVE:
3.9.9:
Troubleshooting wireless connectivity

As you work with wireless connections, consider the following issues:

- **Power** — Make sure that the WAP has power; technicians periodically assume that a problem exists with a particular workstation or laptop, but find that the WAP was unplugged. If the WAP is attached to a standard Ethernet hub or switch, make sure that all equipment is plugged in and powered on.

- **Encryption** — Make sure that all clients are using the same level of encryption as the WAP.

- **SSID** — One minor change in a system's SSID may cause the wireless connection to fail.

- **MAC address filtering** — Check the WAP to see whether filtering settings are blocking your system from the network. You may need to add your system's MAC address, or you may need to remove your system's MAC address from the WAP's filtering list.

Configuring a wireless network

Following are the steps necessary for configuring a wireless network.

1. **Plug in the WAP** — An obvious step, but one that is sometimes inadvertently omitted.

2. **Configure the WAP's SSID, encryption level and shared key** — You must use the software that ships with your WAP. This software can be installed on any computer supported by the vendor. Microsoft-based programs are most often provided. Choose a SSID for your WAP; never use the default value. Use the highest encryption that all clients can use. When choosing a shared key, use one that is not easily guessed. Make sure that you record all information so that you can enter the correct values in each wireless NIC that connects to the WAP.

3. **Insert the wireless NIC into the computer** — Wireless NICs come in various forms, including PCI, USB and Personal Computer Memory Card International Association (PCMCIA). You may need to repeat this step on multiple computers.

4. **Choose a networking protocol and configure the protocol for each client** — A logical choice may be TCP/IP, but use a protocol that is appropriate. If you choose TCP/IP, make sure that each NIC is configured so that it participates on the same network; failure to ensure that each NIC is configured to participate on the same network may cause you to mistake a problem specific to TCP/IP for one specific to the wireless NIC or the WAP.

5. **Configure each computer's wireless NIC to use the WAP** — Insert the appropriate values (for example, SSID, encryption level and the shared key) using management software that ships with each NIC.

6. **Troubleshoot the connection** — Verify that the wireless NICs and WAP are functioning by making sure that the computers can communicate.

7. **Configure additional security features** — After you have verified basic connectivity, further secure the wireless network. Measures can include MAC address filtering, as well as encryption and authentication supplements.

8. **Plug the WAP into a wired network (optional)** — If you want to provide Internet access, attach the WAP to a wired network using the WAP's RJ-45 jack.

Next-generation (3G) wireless

Next-generation (3G) wireless networks are not IEEE 802.11 networks. Rather, they are networks dedicated to personal devices, including PDAs and cellular telephones. Next-generation wireless networks are called 3G networks because they represent the third iteration of personal wireless technology.

First-generation (1G) wireless networks included the crude mobile telephones used in the 1970s as well as analog cell phones used in the 1980s and early 1990s. Second-generation (2G) wireless networks included the introduction of digital phones as well as the use of Code-Division Multiple Access (CDMA), which is a set of protocols that allow multiplexing of signals onto one channel. This multiplexing allows both voice and data to be used on cellular networks. The original CDMA version 1 had a capacity of 14.4 Kbps, and only one channel. However, an extension allows the use of eight channels, and a top speed of 115 Kbps.

Cellular networks are often required to process an increasing amount of data traffic. Devices such as cell phones and PDAs are providing video and data ports and technologies. To accommodate these demands, 3G networks use additional access protocols for multiplexing, including the following:

- **CDMA 2000** — has data rates of 144 Kbps to 2 Mbps. Adopted by the International Telecommunication Union (ITU).

- **Wideband CDMA** — supports speeds between 384 Kbps and 2 Mbps. When this protocol is used in a WAN, the top speed is 384 Kbps. When it is used in a LAN, the top speed is 2 Mbps. Also adopted by the ITU.

All 2G and 3G networks are digital in nature, which makes the transfer of data more efficient because modulation and demodulation of data are not necessary.

NOTE:
Security has become an increasing concern with the advent of 3G networks.

Third-generation technology allows a cell phone or PDA user to have access to networks throughout North America, Europe and Japan, and to have access to voice and data at 2 Mbps. With the maturity of 3G networks, once-incompatible devices will be able to work together, and data should become even more available in various formats and places.

Transmission Types

After a network is in place, the data must be transmitted across the cable. This section will discuss several data transmission concepts, including asynchronous and synchronous transmission modes, data transmission flow, baseband and broadband. It will conclude with a brief discussion of the differences between logical and physical topologies.

Synchronous transmission

With synchronous transmission, the access device and network device share a clock and transmission rate. The transmissions are synchronized.

Data is exchanged in character streams called message-framed data. A start-and-stop sequence is associated with each transmission. The access and network devices need to be synchronized so that the entire message is received in the order in which it was transmitted. T1 lines use synchronous transmissions (you will learn about T-carrier services later in this lesson).

Asynchronous transmission

Asynchronous transmission is characterized by the absence of a clock in the transmission media. The access device is not synchronized with the network device. However, the transmission speeds must be the same. Therefore, data is transmitted as individual characters. Each character is synchronized by information contained in the start (header) and stop (trailer) bits. Dial-up modems use asynchronous transmissions.

Data transmission flow

NOTE:
Dial-up modems also use half-duplex communication.

The three methods of circuit operation are as follows:

- **Simplex** — Data travels in only one direction, similar to a public address (PA) system.
- **Half duplex** — Data travels in two directions, but in only one direction at a time, similar to a walkie-talkie. Ethernet uses half-duplex transmissions.

- **Full duplex** — Data travels in two directions simultaneously, similar to a phone conversation. Full-duplex Ethernet, an extension of Ethernet, supports full-duplex transmissions in a switched environment.

Baseband and broadband transmissions

bandwidth
The amount of information, sometimes called traffic, that can be carried on a network at one time. The total capacity of a line. Also, the rate of data transfer over a network connection; measured in bits per second.

In networking, **bandwidth** is the measure of transmission capacity for a given medium. This rate is quantified as the number of bits that can be transmitted per second. A transmission medium's bandwidth can be divided into channels; thus, each channel is a portion of the total capacity available to transmit data. The two methods used to allocate bandwidth to channels are baseband and broadband.

Baseband

Baseband uses the entire media bandwidth for a single channel. Although it is most commonly used for digital signaling, baseband can also conduct analog signals. Most LANs, such as Ethernet and token-ring networks, use digital baseband signaling.

Baseband uses a transmission technology called time division multiplexing (TDM). TDM sends multiple signals over one transmission path by interweaving the signals. For instance, three signals (X, Y and Z) can be sent as XXYYZZXXYYZZ. The recipient device separates this single stream into its original three signals. Statistical TDM (StatTDM) gives priority to more urgent signals.

Broadband

Broadband divides the media bandwidth into multiple channels, and each channel carries a separate signal. This method enables a single transmission medium to carry several conversations simultaneously and without interference.

Broadband uses a transmission technology called frequency division multiplexing (FDM). Like TDM, FDM also transmits multiple signals over a single transmission path. However, each signal in FDM transmits within a unique frequency range, or carrier. Broadband transmission is commonly used for cable television and wireless systems.

The term broadband is also commonly used to describe any high-speed data transmission that provides services at T1 rates (1.544 Mbps) and higher. However, the capabilities of broadband technology vary greatly depending on the situation, and actual transmission rates may fail to reach T1 rates or may far exceed them. Generally, however, broadband implies higher transmission speeds than those that have been widely available in the past.

Logical and physical topologies

Network topology describes a network's physical layout, or how cables, nodes and connection devices are linked together. Topologies are determined by the networking method used, the physical space available, the structured cabling available on the premises, and the networking requirements of the enterprise.

A LAN has both a physical and a logical topology. Logical topologies refer to the way electronic signals pass through the network from one device to the next without regard to the physical interconnection of the devices. Bus and ring are two types of logical topologies. Logical topologies are bound to the network protocols that direct how data moves across the network and are not necessarily the same as the network's physical topology. A logical bus network generates a signal to all devices on the network. A logical ring network generates a signal that travels in one direction along a determined path. This lesson will further discuss logical networks by introducing access methods.

Physical topologies refer to the way network devices are connected to each other by their cables. You studied physical topologies — including bus, star, ring and mesh topologies — in a previous section of this lesson. It is important to understand the difference between logical and physical topologies.

IEEE LAN Standards

Carrier Sense Multiple Access/Collision Detection (CSMA/CD)
The LAN access method used by Ethernet. Checks for network access availability with a signal.

As you learned earlier, the IEEE is an organization of professionals that create standards for computers and communications. The IEEE 802 series of standards specifies various LAN technologies. See the IEEE Web site at *www.ieee.org* for more information.

A distinguishing factor among LAN technologies is their access methods. Access methods refer to the way data is placed on the physical wire for transmission. The 802 series includes the **Carrier Sense Multiple Access/Collision Detection (CSMA/CD)**, token, and demand priority access methods. Each method will be discussed shortly.

NOTE:
You need a thorough understanding of network standards, cable types and appropriate cable use.

This section covers the following IEEE 802 network standards:

- IEEE 802.2

- Ethernet/IEEE 802.3

- IEEE 802.3u — fast Ethernet

- IEEE 802.3z and 802.3ab — gigabit Ethernet

- IEEE 802.3ae — 10-gigabit Ethernet

- IEEE 802.5 — Token Ring

- IEEE 802.12 — 100VG-AnyLAN

IEEE 802.2

All standards in the IEEE 802 series use the 802.2 standard. The standard is also used by the Fiber Distributed Data Interface (FDDI) network, which is not an IEEE standard. The 802.2 standard divides the OSI/RM data link layer into two sublayers: Logical Link Control (LLC) and Media Access Control (MAC).

The LLC sublayer provides connection-oriented and connectionless services at the data link layer, which manages transmissions and can provide flow control.

NOTE:
Regardless of the upper-level protocol used, packets addressed to a specific computer will include a MAC address.

The MAC sublayer provides:

- Access to the LAN media. The MAC is responsible for placing the data on the wire.

- The MAC address (also called a hardware address, physical address or Ethernet address).

Although Ethernet does not technically use the 802.2 standard, Ethernet is compatible with it and shares several important elements with the standard, such as the MAC sublayer.

MAC addresses

MAC addresses are unique addresses that are burned on a NIC. The terms MAC-48 and EUI-48 (Extended Unique Identifier) are also used for MAC addresses. Each address is burned by the manufacturer and used to identify a computer on a network.

MAC addresses are called physical addresses, as opposed to logical addresses. Logical addresses are found at the network layer (Layer 3), and include IP and IPX addresses. Logical addresses are used to send data over internetworks to a remote destination. Physical addresses are found at the data link layer (Layer 2), and are often part of the physical interface. Physical addresses are used only to send data between two devices on a single network link.

MAC addresses use 12 **hexadecimal** digits to form a 48-bit address (6 **bytes**). Each half of the address is used for a different purpose, as shown in Figure 1-34.

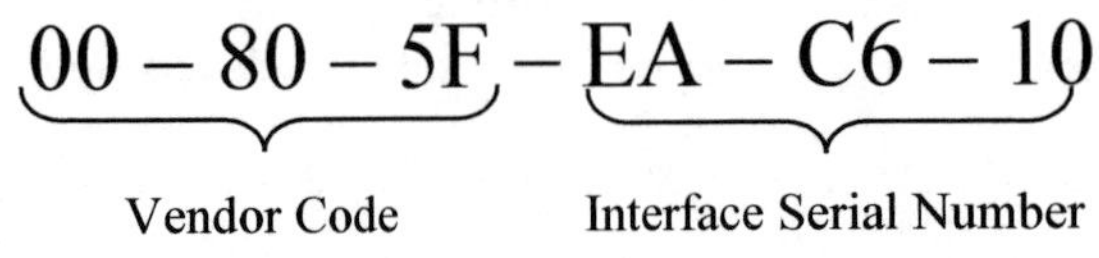

$$\underbrace{00-80-5F}_{\text{Vendor Code}} - \underbrace{EA-C6-10}_{\text{Interface Serial Number}}$$

Figure 1-34: MAC address components

The vendor code is identified in the first 24 bits (3 bytes). The vendor code in Figure 1-34 is for Compaq. Other vendor codes include Sun (08-00-20) and Cisco (00-00-0c). The vendor code is also known as the Organizationally Unique Identifier (OUI).

The interface serial number is identified in the last 24 bits. Determined by the vendor, the serial number is always unique to that vendor. In theory, no two MAC addresses are identical.

Even in a routed network environment — in which IP addresses determine where a packet will be sent — the MAC address is used to send the packet to its final destination once that packet has reached the local network segment on which the destination system resides.

In the following lab, you will view the MAC address on your system. Suppose you are troubleshooting a wireless system and you want to make sure that your system's MAC address is not being filtered out by the wireless network's security settings. You can view the MAC address to verify address components.

Lab 1-1: Viewing the MAC address on your system

In this lab, you will use the `ipconfig` command to view the MAC address on your system.

1. Select **Start | Run**, and enter **cmd** in the Open text box.

2. Press **ENTER**.

3. After a command prompt opens, enter the following command:

    `ipconfig /all`

    Note: In Linux, you would use the `ifconfig` *command, without any options or arguments.*

4. Press **ENTER**.

5. You will see a printout of all information relevant to your system's NIC.

6. Look for the following parameter:

   `Physical Address`

7. The Physical Address parameter records your system's MAC address. Write your system's MAC address in the space provided:

   _____

8. Underline the vendor code portion of the MAC address.

9. The `ipconfig` command should tell you about the NIC vendor. Sometimes, however, this information is not available. The `ipconfig` command may not reveal this information, or you might be using another operating system that is less informative. If you have Internet access, open a browser and go to a search engine such as Google or AltaVista.

10. Type the vendor code portion of the MAC address in the browser's search text box.

    Note: You might also want to use the words "vendor code" (in quotation marks) in your search.

11. **Write your NIC's vendor in the space provided:**

    _____

12. Close your command prompt.

*Tech Note: In Windows XP, you can also view the MAC address by clicking the **Support** tab of the **Local Area Connection Status** dialog box, then clicking the **Details** button.*

In this lab, you used the `ipconfig` command to view your system's MAC address.

Ethernet/IEEE 802.3

Ethernet is one of the most successful LAN technologies and is a predecessor to the IEEE 802.3 standard. Ethernet is a broadcast system for communication between systems. It uses the 10Base2, 10Base5 or 10BaseT wiring standards. It can also use fiber-optic cabling.

Even though Ethernet and IEEE 802.3 are supported together and used interchangeably, Ethernet does not totally comply with the 802.3 standard.

The differences between IEEE 802.3 and Ethernet do not hinder hardware manufacturers because IEEE 802.3 and Ethernet both support MAC addresses and the same physical layer. In addition, software that differentiates between the sublayers is available.

Ethernet/IEEE 802.3 access method

All networks that use Ethernet/IEEE 802.3 (including IEEE 802.3u, IEEE 802.3z and IEEE 802.3ab) use CSMA/CD. A station must make sure no other transmission is already in progress. If no other station is transmitting, the sender can begin immediately. Collisions occur when two or more stations sense the channel is idle and begin to transmit simultaneously. If a collision occurs, all transmission ceases while the colliding stations are notified. The colliding stations then wait a random amount of time before transmitting.

NOTE:
Many situations will
call for a router,
rather than a
bridge, to segment
and isolate traffic.

NOTE:
Most newer Ethernet
NICs are 10/100
cards, supporting
both 10-Mbps and
100-Mbps Ethernet
and automatically
configuring
themselves online
based on the traffic
detected on the
network.

Transmissions are broadcast to all stations. Only the destination system responds; all other systems discard the transmission. This process can create heavy traffic on a network. Therefore, it is important to divide larger Ethernet networks into segments (using a bridge, for example).

IEEE 802.3u — fast Ethernet

Fast Ethernet is a faster version of IEEE 802.3. It was originally developed by vendors such as 3Com, Cabletron, SynOptics, Digital, Grand Junction Networks and Intel. The IEEE 802.3 committee is responsible for fast Ethernet. The major objective of the fast Ethernet standard is to promote the use of Ethernet at 100 Mbps using the same access method, CSMA/CD.

Fast Ethernet supports the 100BaseTX and 100BaseT4 wiring standards, which require Category 5 UTP wiring to support 100 Mbps. It can also use 100BaseFX, which is fiber-optic cabling. Vendors support fast Ethernet cards that use data rates of both 10 Mbps and 100 Mbps.

Many network administrators are upgrading their 10BaseT networks to 100BaseTX or 100BaseT4. In many cases, this upgrade can be accomplished by replacing 10BaseT NICs with 100BaseTX or 100BaseT4 NICs, and upgrading hubs to support both 10BaseT and 100BaseTX or 100BaseT4. This process is usually less expensive than upgrading to a 100BaseFX, 16-Mbps token-ring, 100VG-AnyLAN or FDDI network.

Table 1-6 displays the key differences between Ethernet and fast Ethernet.

Table 1-6: Ethernet vs. fast Ethernet

Category	Ethernet	Fast Ethernet
Speed	10 Mbps	100 Mbps
IEEE standard	IEEE 802.3	IEEE 802.3u
Access method	CSMA/CD	CSMA/CD
Topology	Bus/star	Star
Cable support	Coax/twisted pair/fiber	Twisted pair/fiber
UTP link distance (maximum)	100 meters	100 meters

IEEE 802.3z and 802.3ab — gigabit Ethernet

Gigabit Ethernet, which offers a tenfold increase in data rates over the previous standard, is used primarily for network backbones. The gigabit Ethernet standard transfers data at 1,000 Mbps using the CSMA/CD access method over either twisted pair or fiber.

The two types of gigabit Ethernet are IEEE 802.3z and 802.3ab.

802.3z

The 802.3z standard is specified for the following two types of fiber-optic cable:

- **1000BaseLX** — uses a long wavelength laser. Will work over distances of up to 2 km over single-mode fiber (although many manufacturers guarantee distances of up to 10 km or 20 km). Over multimode fiber, the maximum cable length is 550 m.

- **1000BaseSX** — uses a near-infrared light wavelength over multimode fiber. Maximum cable length is 220 m. Popular for intrabuilding links in large corporations.

Cost must be considered when determining which fiber standard to implement.

802.3ab

The 802.3ab standard specifies gigabit Ethernet over UTP cable.

- **1000BaseT** — requires Category 5 cable at a minimum, according to the standard, but a minimum of Category 5e is strongly recommended. Category 6 cable can also be used. Maximum segment length is 100 meters.

Unlike slower versions of Ethernet, 1000BaseT wiring uses all four pairs of wires.

IEEE 802.3ae (supplement) — 10-gigabit Ethernet

10-gigabit Ethernet (10GbE) is the fastest of the Ethernet standards, offering data rates of 10 Gbps (10 times faster than gigabit Ethernet). The standard provides for transmission over the following types of fiber-optic cable:

- **10GBaseSR** — used for short distances (26 m to 82 m) over multimode fiber. Also supports 300 m over new multimode fiber.

- **10GBaseLRM** — used for distances up to 220 m on FDDI-grade multimode fiber.

- **10GBaseER** — used for extended ranges of up to 40 km over single-mode fiber.

- **10GBaseLX4** — supports distances between 240 m and 300 m over multimode fiber using four separate laser sources operating on unique wavelengths. Also supports distances of 10 km over single-mode fiber.

802.3an amendment

The IEEE 802.3an amendment specifies 10-gigabit Ethernet over twisted pair:

- **10GBaseT** — provides 10 Gbps over twisted pair using Category 6 or Category 7 cable and RJ-45 connectors. With Cat 6 cabling, the maximum cable length is 56 m. An augmented Category 6 cable specification "6a" designed to reduce crosstalk between UTP cables is expected to extend the length to 100 m. Maximum cable length for Cat 7 is 100 m.

IEEE 802.5 — Token Ring

The token-ring network is specified in the IEEE 802.5 definition. Token ring was initially developed by IBM for its mainframe environment, and the IEEE 802.5 standard complies with the corporation's original development.

NOTE:
Cat 7 cable is being designed for home use. It runs at 600 MHz, and because it can support cable TV, it will eventually replace coaxial cable.

OBJECTIVE:
3.2.3: Ethernet vs. Token Ring

NOTE:
Token-ring use has become less common with the growth of star-topology Ethernet.

IEEE 802.5 access method

token passing
The LAN access method used by token ring networks. A data frame, or token, is passed from one node to the next around the network ring.

Multistation Access Unit (MAU)
The network device that is the central connection point for token-ring networks.

Whereas Ethernet uses the CSMA/CD access method, token-ring networks use the **token passing** access method. Instead of sending broadcasts, as Ethernet does, a token-ring network passes a token in one direction around the network. Each node processes the token to determine the destination. The node accepts the packet or places it back on the network ring. One or more tokens can circle the ring. With token passing, collisions do not occur; it is similar to a one-way street without cross traffic.

The IEEE standard does not specify a wiring standard, but IBM token-ring networks use twisted-pair wire. Data rates of 4 or 16 Mbps are possible with token-ring networks. Token-ring networks appear to use the star topology, but actually use a hub-like device called a **Multistation Access Unit (MAU)** to form a ring. You learned about MAUs earlier in this lesson.

The MAU creates the ring using internal connections, as shown in Figure 1-35.

NOTE:
Each MAU has Ring In and Ring Out connectors for connecting to other MAUs. Ring Out connects to Ring In on the next MAU in the ring until a complete ring is created. If a MAU is not connected to other MAUs, Ring In and Ring Out are connected internally to complete the ring.

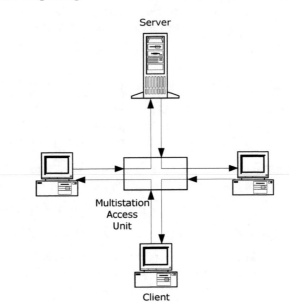

Figure 1-35: Token-ring network with MAU

The failure of one node in a ring topology can cause the network to fail. Therefore, MAUs can identify and bypass faulty nodes and network segments so the network can continue to function.

IEEE 802.11 — wireless Ethernet

The 802.11 specification was introduced in 1997, and standardizes wireless LAN equipment and speeds. Such equipment is often called wireless Ethernet equipment, and has become popular in homes, small businesses and large enterprises.

IEEE 802.11 wireless specifications

NOTE:
You should already understand the media required for creating a wireless Ethernet network.

Following is a summary of the most common wireless Ethernet specifications:

*   **802.11 (WiFi)** — the original specification for wireless networking. Initially provided for data rates of 1 Mbps or 2 Mbps in the 2.4-GHz band using either FHSS or DSSS. At one time, the term WiFi applied only to products using the 802.11b standard, but today it applies to products that use the 802.11 standard. The 802.11 specifications are part of an evolving set of wireless network standards known as the 802.11 family.

The particular specification under which a wireless network operates is called its flavor.

NOTE:
Following are additional IEEE 802.11 specifications:

802.11c — specifies the use of MAC bridges, which are used to connect networks.

802.11d — for international wireless networks.

802.11e — quality of service standards for backbone networks. Can be used in 802.11a and 802.11b networks.

802.11f — standardizes WAP communication between different vendors.

802.11h — allows wireless networks to use the 5-GHz band, making them acceptable in Europe.

802.11i — specifies additional security measures.

- **802.11a** — operates at up to 54 Mbps in the 5-GHz band. 802.11a uses OFDM for transmitting data. It also offers stronger encryption and more authentication features than 802.11b, and includes Forward Error Correction (FEC) to guard against data loss. 802.11a offers the same speed as 802.11g but offers higher capacity. 802.11a networks also allow the use of different channels, which helps avoid conflicts. The 802.11a standard was ratified after 802.11b and is not backward-compatible with 802.11b or 802.11g.

- **802.11b** — although not the first wireless standard, traditionally the most popular implementation. Operates at 11 Mbps (but will fall back to 5.5 Mbps, then to 2 Mbps, then to 1 Mbps if signal quality becomes an issue) in the 2.4-GHz band. Uses DSSS only. Because it operates in the 2.4-GHz band, it is subject to interference from microwave ovens, cordless phones and Bluetooth devices, which also operate in this band. The 802.11b standard also uses weak encryption and authentication, but is inexpensive and easy to install.

- **802.11g** — operates at speeds of up to 54 Mbps in the 2.4-GHz band. Backward-compatible with 802.11b. An 802.11g network card will work with an 802.11b access point, and an 802.11g access point will work with an 802.11b network card but only at speeds up to 11 Mbps. To achieve 54-Mbps throughput, you must use 802.11g network cards and access points. The 802.11g standard uses OFDM or DSSS. These networks provide security features similar to those provided by 802.11a networks.

IEEE 802.11 access method

The access method for the IEEE 802.11 specifications is **Carrier Sense Multiple Access/Collision Avoidance (CSMA/CA)**. CSMA/CA specifies that each node must inform other nodes of an intent to transmit. When the other nodes have been notified, the information is transmitted. This arrangement prevents collisions because all nodes are aware of a transmission before it occurs.

IEEE 802.12 — 100VG-AnyLAN

The 100VG-AnyLAN proposal was originally developed by AT&T and Hewlett-Packard, and is managed by the IEEE 802.12 committee. IEEE 802.12 is usually referred to by its wiring standard, 100VG-AnyLAN.

IEEE 802.12 access method

A key fact about 100VG-AnyLAN is that it does not support CSMA/CD. Instead, it supports an access method called **demand priority**, in which the hub simultaneously arbitrates when and how systems can access the network. It supports different levels of priority, so it can guarantee that time-sensitive applications (such as real-time video) get the access they need.

This scheme reduces the possibility of nodes competing for access because the hub determines which stations get access. If multiple transmission requests arrive at the hub, the transmission with the highest priority is serviced first. If two stations request the same priority at the same time, both are serviced in alternating turns.

The demand priority access method used in 100VG-AnyLAN may be an advantage for some customers because it provides a way to guarantee priority for some LAN traffic types. In addition, transmissions sent through the hub are not broadcast to other stations, thereby preventing the possibility of monitoring by eavesdroppers.

Carrier Sense Multiple Access/Collision Avoidance (CSMA/CA)
The LAN access method used by the IEEE 802.11 wireless specification and Apple LocalTalk.

demand priority
The LAN access method used by 100VG-AnyLAN networks. By prioritizing transmissions, hubs specify how and when nodes can access the network.

The 100VG-AnyLAN standard can use many different cables for its wiring standard (hence the term "AnyLAN"). For instance, it can use Category 3, 4 or 5 UTP, STP or fiber-optic cable.

In the following lab, you will research IEEE LAN standards. Suppose that your IT supervisor has asked for the latest information on IEEE 802.12. Where would you find this information on the Web?

Lab 1-2: Researching IEEE LAN standards

In this lab, you will use your favorite search engine to find more information about various IEEE LAN standards.

1. Open your Web browser and access your favorite search engine.

2. Enter a text string for a LAN standard — for example, "IEEE 802.3ab" — and explore the various results.

3. Search for several LAN standards to gain a better understanding of the concepts, principles and speed ratings.

4. Close your browser.

Remember that information about standards and new technologies can be found all over the Web. Spend some time researching this information.

Additional LAN Standards

This section will discuss two LAN standards not included with the IEEE standards. These standards are either proprietary or standardized by another organization. They are:

- Apple LocalTalk.
- Fiber Distributed Data Interface (FDDI).

Apple LocalTalk

NOTE:
Apple computers support Ethernet networking through EtherTalk, and token-ring networking through TokenTalk.

LocalTalk is a network type used by Apple. Although not an IEEE standard, LocalTalk is important because it uses CSMA/CA. As you learned earlier, CSMA/CA specifies that each node must inform other nodes of an intent to transmit. After the other nodes have been notified, the information is transmitted. This arrangement prevents collisions because all nodes are aware of a transmission before it occurs.

Fiber Distributed Data Interface (FDDI)

FDDI (pronounced "fiddy") is a high-speed LAN standard. It was developed by the X3T9.5 American National Standards Institute (ANSI) accredited standards committee. Like the IEEE 802.5 Token Ring standard, FDDI is token-based.

The standard specifies the MAC sublayer of the data link layer, as well as the physical layers for a 100-Mbps counter-rotating, token-ring, fiber-optic LAN.

municipal area network (MAN)
A network used to communicate over a city or geographic area.

FDDI uses two counter-rotating rings to provide redundancy and allow the network to function if one ring fails. FDDI functions well over distances of up to 200 kilometers (with a single ring) with as many as 1,000 stations connected. In a dual-ring topology, each ring is limited to 100 kilometers. Because it is often used to cover a city or a specific geographic area, a FDDI network can be classified as a **municipal area network (MAN)**.

FDDI supports both synchronous and asynchronous traffic (which will be discussed shortly). A FDDI network is illustrated in Figure 1-36.

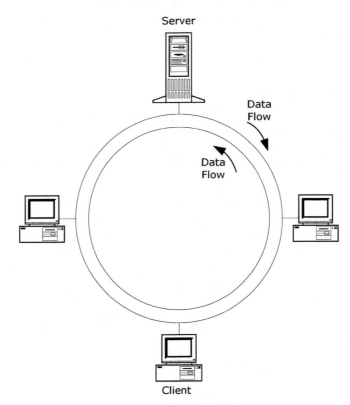

Figure 1-36: FDDI network

To summarize access methods, IEEE 802.3 and Ethernet use CSMA/CD, LocalTalk and wireless networks use CSMA/CA, token-ring networks use a token-based method, and 100VG-AnyLAN networks use demand priority.

WAN Standards

In recent years, WAN technology has progressed quickly because telecommunication companies have invested in bandwidth. These WAN technologies include X.25 and fast packet switching, frame relay and ATM.

NOTE:
Cost is one of the major limiting factors in WAN connection method use.

Advanced Research Projects Agency Network (ARPANET)
A computer network, funded by ARPA, that served as the basis for early networking research and was the backbone during the development of the Internet.

X.25

X.25 developed from the **Advanced Research Projects Agency Network (ARPANET)** 1822 protocol, which was the original ARPANET packet-switching scheme. X.25 became an ITU standard in 1976. It is currently used for automated teller machine transactions, credit card verifications and many other point-of-sale transactions. X.25 operates at 56 Kbps or slower. Newer packet-switching technologies can outperform X.25, but it is still used worldwide. X.25 ensures error-free data delivery by checking errors at many points along the data path.

Fast packet switching

Fast packet switching refers to two different types of transmissions through mesh-type switching networks. With fast packet switching, tasks such as error correction, packet sequencing and acknowledgments are not performed by the network. Fast packet switching is the responsibility of end systems; because the network has less overhead associated with processing packets, it can move information quickly.

Eliminating error correction at the lower layers greatly improves performance. Fast packet-switching technology is implemented at the MAC sublayer of the data link layer, in contrast to X.25, which is implemented at the network layer.

Frame relay and ATM are examples of fast packet-switching technologies.

Frame relay

Frame relay is a fast packet-switching technology that uses fiber-optic and digital cabling. It uses variable-length packets and allows high-speed connections using shared network facilities. It does not extensively support error checking and acknowledgments, as X.25 does. As the name implies, frame relay is a relay service, whereas X.25 is a packet service.

If your company wants to join a frame relay network, your local telephone company must connect your office to a frame relay port, or Point of Presence (POP). The POP must be a frame relay service provider. A frame relay port is created for your company, giving it access to the frame relay network. Figure 1-37 illustrates a frame relay network, with several locations attached.

NOTE:
The cloud in this graphic represents the frame relay connections and is not meant to imply the Internet.

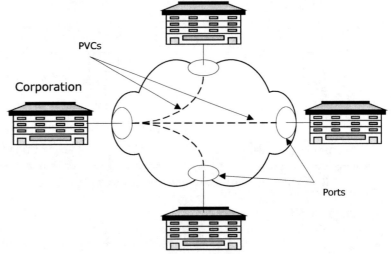

Figure 1-37: Frame-relay packet switching

Frame relay networks use Permanent Virtual Circuits (PVCs). These logical, dedicated, end-to-end connections are used for data transfer. After a PVC is established, it exists until the transaction, transmission or service is terminated. Therefore, frame relay is a software-based network because it shares the physical network with other frame relay networks.

Frame relay uses "bandwidth on demand," meaning that frame relay customers can choose the amount of bandwidth they need. Each frame relay port has its own port speed, usually at a transmission rate ranging from 64 Kbps to 1.544 Mbps. Frame relay is implemented at the MAC sublayer of the data link layer.

Asynchronous transfer mode (ATM)

ATM uses fixed-sized cells (instead of frame relay's variable-length packets) and PVCs to support data as well as real-time video and voice. ATM can be used by both LANs and WANs, but it is most commonly used as an Internet backbone. The ATM protocol is defined by the ITU and the specialized ATM Forum.

ATM is referred to as a cell relay technology because it organizes data into 53-byte fixed-length cells. These cells are transmitted and segmented depending on the type of data sent. For example, bandwidth is allocated depending on the application class being used.

Because ATM uses fixed-length cells, it is faster than frame relay. Switching devices need not locate the beginning and end of each cell: These cells are all the same size.

Although ATM typically operates at speeds ranging from 155 Mbps to 622 Mbps, it has a potential throughput rate of 1.2 Gbps. FDDI and T3 technology are implementing ATM elements. However, not all media support ATM capabilities. Like frame relay, ATM is implemented at the MAC sublayer of the data link layer.

T-Carrier System

NOTE:
You need to know the T-carrier bandwidths.

The T-carrier system is a North American digital transmission format that provides dedicated and private-line services for digital voice and data transmission at rates of up to 45 Mbps. T-carrier services are usually used to connect a LAN to a WAN, such as a company network to the Internet or to a frame relay network.

Table 1-7 shows common T-carrier system data transfer rates.

Table 1-7: T-carrier transfer rates

T-Carrier	Data Transfer Rate
T1	1.544 Mbps
T2	6.312 Mbps
T3	44.736 Mbps
T4	274.176 Mbps

A single 64-Kbps line is known as a DS0 line. A T1 line supports 24 DS0 channels. Each of the 24 channels in a T1 circuit can carry voice or data transmission. In Japan, the J-carrier system is used. This system has the same speeds as the T-carrier system.

Fractional T1

Fractional T1, also called FT1, allows customers to lease the 64-Kbps channels individually instead of the full T1 line.

Connecting a T1 line to a LAN

To connect a T1 line to a LAN, you need the following systems:

- **CSU** — the first point of contact for the T1 wires; it diagnoses and prepares the signals on the line for the LAN.

- **DSU** — connects to the CSU and converts LAN signals into T1 signaling formats.

- **Multiplexor** — provides a mechanism to load multiple voice and data channels into the digital line.

- **Router** — provides the interface between the LAN and the T1 line.

E-Carrier System

NOTE:
Be careful not to confuse the T-carrier and E-carrier bandwidths.

The E-carrier system is a European digital transmission format similar to the North American T-carrier system. Each transmission speed is a multiple of the E1 format, which operates at 2.048 Mbps. Table 1-8 lists the five E-carrier speeds.

Table 1-8: E-carrier transfer rates

E-Carrier	Data Transfer Rate
E1	2.048 Mbps
E2	8.448 Mbps
E3	34.368 Mbps
E4	139.264 Mbps
E5	565.148 Mbps

E-carrier and J-carrier lines use the same equipment to connect LANs (for example, CSU/DSUs and multiplexors).

SONET/SDH

Synchronous Optical Network (SONET) is a high-speed fiber-optic system that is used by
telecom companies and carriers. The European counterpart is the Synchronous Digital
Hierarchy (SDH). SONET/SDH is primarily used for network backbones, such as the Internet
backbone, because of its ability to transmit at high speeds (for example, 39.813 Gbps).

Synchronous Optical Network (SONET)
High-speed fiber-optic system used as a network and Internet backbone. The European counterpart is the Synchronous Digital Hierarchy (SDH).

OCx
Optical carrier levels; defines the transmission speeds used in SONET/SDH.

SONET implements a ring architecture with at least two data paths. If one path fails, the
system uses the other path. Because of this feature, SONET/SDH is called a self-healing
ring architecture. It uses TDM to simultaneously transmit multiple data streams.

Optical carrier (OC) refers to the optical signal, which defines the transmission in the
SONET/SDH specification. The optical carrier levels are often called **OCx.**

In SDH, the term Synchronous Transport Module (STM) is used to describe the
bandwidth provided. Table 1-9 provides common SONET and SDH data transfer rates.
Notice the absence of an equivalent for OC-1 in SDH.

Table 1-9: SONET/SDH system data rates

SONET Service	Data Transfer Rate	SDH Service	Data Transfer Rate
OC-1	51.84 Mbps	**No Equivalent**	N/A
OC-3	155.52 Mbps	STM-1	155.52 Mbps
OC-12	622.08 Mbps	STM-4	622 Mbps
OC-48	2488.32 Mbps	STM-16	2.488.32 Gbps
OC-192	9953.28 Mbps	STM-64	9.953 Gbps
OC-768	39813.12 Mbps	STM-256	39.813 Gbps

Case Study

Choosing Protocols

Elena is a networking consultant. Three clients have asked her which protocol(s) would be best to implement their changing network requirements.

Client 1 is currently using IPX/SPX. The client uses the network to access a database, receive e-mail and transfer files. This client now wants to use a P2P application, browse the Web and check Internet e-mail (SMTP and IMAP). Client 1 wants Elena to recommend a new protocol that will enable him to create a WAN.

Client 2 has asked Elena to configure 10 Windows XP Professional systems to use IPX/SPX so that they can communicate with NetWare servers that have existed since 1996. Elena installed NWLink on the XP systems, yet they cannot communicate with the NetWare servers. These Windows XP systems can, however, communicate with one another.

Client 3 is designing a new network that will include Windows 2003 and Linux servers. All the servers will need to support Windows 2003, UNIX, Linux and Macintosh clients. The network will be implemented as a WAN with more than 2,000 nodes located in different areas of the United States. All systems will need to access the Internet. Client 3 wants Elena to install any and all necessary protocol(s).

*   *   *

For Client 1, Elena recommended TCP/IP. This protocol supports routing and can be used with other protocols that the client wants to use. Although P2P applications may exist for IPX/SPX, this type of application is more plentiful for TCP/IP.

For Client 2, Elena checked the frame type on the older system and adjusted the frame type setting on the XP systems.

For Client 3, Elena installed TCP/IP as the only protocol. All servers and clients listed support TCP/IP. Also, the fact that the network will be implemented as a WAN means that a routable protocol is required.

*   *   *

Consider Elena's solutions. Are they effective? What alternatives, if any, might also work?

Version 1.2

Lesson Summary

Application project

Does your company use both LAN and WAN technologies? To your knowledge, is your network an Ethernet, token ring, fast Ethernet, 100VG-AnyLAN or gigabit Ethernet? Could any of the technologies you learned in this lesson improve your current network's performance?

The costs of using fiber optics and switches are becoming more affordable for many organizations. Do you think these technologies might soon completely replace traditional hubs, bridges, routers and copper wire-based networks? Visit the Cisco Web site (*www.cisco.com*) and identify products discussed in this lesson, such as bridges, routers and switches. Next, access the Nortel Networks Web site (*www.nortelnetworks.com*) and identify its competing products. Search the Internet to locate several other companies that offer LAN and WAN devices. Locate pricing information for an Ethernet 16-port 10/100 switch. How does it compare with the price of a 16-port 10/100 hub? Are the additional network speed and manageability worth the price difference?

Skills review

In this lesson, you learned the basic networking concepts and you learned about networking models. You also learned about basic networking categories, and studied basic network topologies: bus, star, ring, hybrid and mesh. You also received an overview of the major networking operating systems.

You learned about the OSI reference model; packet creation; and the application-layer, transport-layer and network-layer protocols. You learned the fundamentals of key network protocols, such as TCP/IP, IPX/SPX and NetBEUI, and should now have a basic understanding of how to bind a protocol to a NIC.

You also acquired a basic understanding of LANs and WANs and studied the communication devices involved, including NICs, repeaters, hubs, bridges, routers, switches and CSU/DSUs. Transmission media types were introduced, such as twisted-pair, coaxial and fiber-optic cable, as well as wireless media. You also studied transmission types and learned about network standards, such as IEEE LAN standards, LocalTalk, FDDI and WAN technologies.

Now that you have completed this lesson, you should be able to:

✓ Identify and describe the functions of servers, workstations and hosts.

✓ Identify major network operating systems and their respective clients.

✓ Discuss packets and describe packet creation, and explain the Open Systems Interconnection (OSI) reference model.

✓ Compare, contrast and discuss the functions of network protocols, including TCP/IP.

✓ Describe the basics of local area networks (LANs) and wide area networks (WANs).

✓ Identify and describe the function of network access points (NAPs).

✓ Describe transmission media and types, including cabling, asynchronous and synchronous, simplex, half duplex, full duplex, baseband and broadband.

✓ Identify network architectures, and describe basic network topologies and carrier systems (for example, T and E carriers).

Lesson 1 Review

1. What is the purpose of a Network Operations Center (NOC)?

    _____

    _____

    _____

    _____

    _____

    _____

2. Your company is using P2P technology to distribute software. Where is this software stored?

    _____

3. Name three products that are often called flavors of UNIX.

    _____

    _____

4. What three elements are common to all networks?

    _____

5. List the seven OSI/RM layers, beginning with Layer 7.

    _____

6. Why is it important for operating system vendors to consider the OSI/RM when developing networking software?

    _____

    _____

7. What is the difference between routable and nonroutable protocols?

    _____

    _____

    _____

8. What is a hub, and what is its function in a network?

    _____

    _____

9. Name the two types of twisted-pair cable, and the two varieties of wire available for each.

_____

_____

10. What are the two major types of fiber-optic cable?

_____

11. A network administrator suspects a security problem on a wireless network, and has changed the SSID on the WAP. How will existing wireless network clients be affected?

_____

_____

_____

Lesson 1
Supplemental Material

This section is a supplement containing additional tasks for you to complete in conjunction with the lesson. These elements are:

- **Activities**
  Pen-and-paper activities to review lesson concepts or terms.

- **Optional Labs**
  Computer-based labs to provide additional practice.

- **Lesson Quiz**
  Multiple-choice test to assess knowledge of lesson material.

Activity 1-1: Identifying network topologies

The ability to recognize common network topologies is important. Identify each of the network topologies represented in the following graphics.

1.

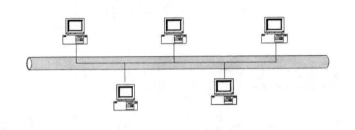

2.

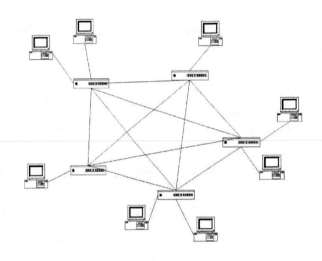

3.

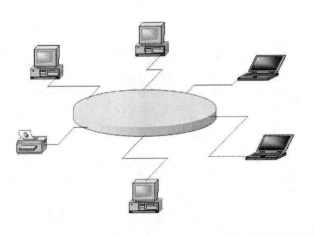

4.

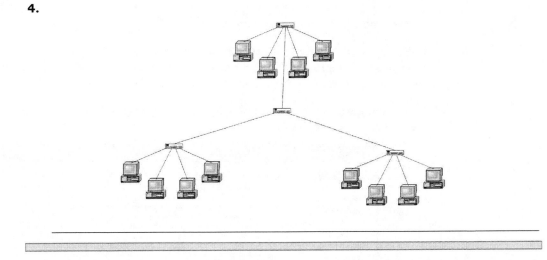

 Optional Lab 1-1: Using a P2P network

In this optional lab, you will use a P2P network to search for and download files.

1. If necessary, first install the Java 2 Runtime Environment. (If your system already has a recent version of Java installed, you can skip to Step 4.) Open **Windows Explorer** and navigate to the C:\CIW\Network\LabFiles\Lesson01 folder and double-click **jre-1_5_0_06-windows-i586-p.exe** to display the Java Installation wizard.

2. Follow the instructions to install Java on your computer. Specify a **Typical** installation when given the choice between a Typical or Custom installation.

3. If prompted, restart your computer to complete the installation of the Java 2 Runtime Environment.

4. In **Windows Explorer**, navigate to the C:\CIW\Network\LabFiles\Lesson01folder, double-click **phex_3.0.2.100.exe** and follow the instructions to install Phex.

    Note: You can visit the Phex home page (www.phex.org/mambo/) for tips, instructions and user guides about using Phex.

5. Launch **Phex**, if necessary, and click **OK** to close the Respect Copyright warning. When the Configuration Wizard appears, click **Next** to begin the basic configuration process. The Configuration Wizard guides you through setting up the minimum specifications — your connection type and speed, your folders for downloading files, and your folder(s) for sharing files with other users.

6. On the Bandwidth Settings screen, display the **Connection Type And Speed** drop-down list, select the connection type appropriate to your system, then click **Next**. Phex uses the connection type and speed setting to calculate how many minutes may be required for any given download or upload.

7. The Download Directories screen suggests default directories for storing incomplete and completed download files. Accept these default directories by clicking **Next**.

8. The Shared Files screen allows you to specify directories where you will store files that you want to share with other users on the Gnutella network. Click the **Add Folder** button to open the Select Directory To Share dialog box. Click the **Desktop**

icon, click the **Create New Folder** icon, type *For_P2P* and then press **ENTER** to create a new folder on the Desktop.

9. Select the **For_P2P** folder in the list box, then click the **Select** button to specify this new folder as the folder you will use for sharing files. Click **Next**, then click **Finish**. You can also configure Phex using the Options dialog box.

10. If your computer is behind a firewall, select **Settings | Options** to open the Options dialog box, as shown in Figure OL1-1.

Figure OL1-1: Phex Options dialog box

11. Click **Firewall/Proxy** under the General Settings heading, and enter the firewall or proxy settings appropriate to your system. Click **Apply**, and then click **OK**.

    *Note: If you are using the Windows XP SP2 firewall, display the Windows Firewall dialog box (**Start | Control Panel | Windows Firewall**). Click the **Exceptions** tab, then click the **Add Program** button. Scroll through the **Add A Program** dialog box, and click **Phex 3.0.2.100**. Click **OK** twice, then close the Control Panel.*

    Note: You may still experience difficulty connecting if you are behind a firewall.

12. Quit and then restart Phex. Phex will attempt to connect to one of the Gnutella network hosts in its database; IP addresses are loaded and tried sequentially. Any connection that displays in green is a functioning connection.

13. After your Phex client has established a functioning connection, you can search for and download files.

14. Click the **Search** tab. Click in the **Type Your Keywords Here** list box, type *linux*, then press **ENTER**. Phex will begin to search the Gnutella network. Your search results should resemble Figure OL1-2.

Figure OL1-2: Search results in Phex

Warning: Do not search for or download copyrighted material (for example, music files from your favorite band). Downloading copyrighted material is illegal.

15. When you find a file you want to download, right-click the file name in the list box, then click **Download** to add the file to your download queue. Downloading occurs in the background.

16. When you are finished, quit Phex.

Did you think that this P2P client was easy to use? Did you find many results for search terms?

In this optional lab, you used a P2P client to search the Gnutella network.

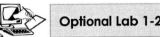

Optional Lab 1-2: Reviewing network operating systems

NOTE:
The answers provided with this lab assume that your system is set up using the instructions provided in the Course Setup Guide and System Requirements section. If a different setup has been used, your answers may vary.

The purpose of this optional lab is to introduce you to some fundamental information about the network configurations being used in this course.

1. Restart your system and watch the startup process. Your operating system will be identified during startup. What operating system are you running? Is it a network client or a network operating system? Write your responses in the space provided:

   _____

   _____

   _____

2. Select **Start | Control Panel**, then click the **Switch To Classic View** hyperlink (if necessary) to display the classic Windows 2000 interface.

3. Double-click the **System** icon to display the System Properties dialog box.

4. Click the **Computer Name** tab. Is your computer configured as a member of a workgroup?

   _____

5. Close all windows and return to your Desktop.

Even though operating systems such as Windows XP Professional are technically considered a network operating system, they can also be deployed in a peer-to-peer (or workgroup) network environment. When deployed in a workgroup, the server is typically referred to as a "stand-alone server."

Optional Lab 1-3: Implementing a wireless network

NOTE:
This optional lab requires a WAP and two wireless NICs.

In this optional lab, you will implement a wireless network.

1. Obtain a WAP.

2. Obtain two wireless NICs.

3. Configure the WAP to use a SSID such as ciw-certified (lowercase, as SSIDs are case-sensitive). Do not configure the WAP to use encryption at this point.

4. Configure the wireless NICs to use infrastructure mode. Do not enable encryption on the NICS.

5. Configure the NICs to use the same SSID as the WAP.

6. You should now have basic connectivity. Troubleshoot the connection if problems occur. Troubleshooting tools can include:

   • Verifying settings in the software that configures the WAP.

   • Verifying settings in the software that configures each NIC.

7. Plug the WAP into a standard hub and try to get the wireless systems to communicate with standard wired clients. If the hub is attached to a router with Internet access, try to configure the wireless systems to communicate on the Internet (set a default gateway).

In this lab, you configured a wireless network.

Lesson 1 Quiz

1. You are designing a network for a company with 100 employees and must decide on a network topology. The company's stock price is rising dramatically and management has decided to double the company's size in the next two months. You must design and implement the network in the next week. Which of the following network topologies will best allow you to expand the network after the initial implementation with minimal disruption to the company?

   a. Star
   b. Star bus
   c. Ring
   d. Hybrid

2. A server is:

   a. a computer connected to a mainframe.
   b. a computer that acts as a mainframe.
   c. a computer that shares resources with other computers on a network.
   d. a "front-end" computer.

3. Which of the following is a transport layer protocol?

   a. HTTP
   b. SPX
   c. SMB
   d. IP

4. What is a packet?

   a. A protocol that enables information to be sent across a network
   b. Another name for an e-mail message
   c. A protocol that sends e-mail messages
   d. A fixed piece of information sent across a network

5. Which OSI layer is responsible for reliability of the data sent between hosts?

   a. Transport layer
   b. Presentation layer
   c. Network layer
   d. Application layer

6. Which of the following protocols has been adopted as the official protocol for data transmission on the Internet?

   a. IPX/SPX
   b. NetBEUI
   c. TCP/IP
   d. NetBIOS

7. A local area network (LAN) is:

   a. a group of computers connected over an expansive geographic area.
   b. another name for a peer-to-peer network.
   c. a group of computers connected within a confined geographic area.
   d. another name for a server-based network.

8. A network access point (NAP) is:

   a. a junction between a small network and a larger, high-speed network (an Internet backbone).
   b. a junction between one Internet backbone and another.
   c. a connection point between two or more computers in a WAN.
   d. a connection point between two or more computers in a LAN.

9. What type of cable is recommended when wiring for 100BaseTX?

   a. Four pairs of Category 1 UTP
   b. Four pairs of Category 3 UTP
   c. Two pairs of Category 5 UTP
   d. Two-channel fiber optic

10. What is logical topology?

    a. The actual path a signal takes across a network
    b. The study of a signal's path across a single network
    c. The study of a signal's path across several networks
    d. The path a signal takes, as designated by the design of the network (also called physical topology)

11. Wireless networks are specified in which of the following IEEE standards?

    a. IEEE 802.11
    b. IEEE 802.3
    c. IEEE 802.5
    d. IEEE 802.12

Lesson 2:
TCP/IP Suite and
Internet Addressing

Objectives

By the end of this lesson, you will be able to:

- Define and describe the Internet architecture model and various Internet protocols.

- Describe the purpose of Requests for Comments (RFCs).

- Explain the routing process, including static versus dynamic routing, and interior versus exterior routing protocols.

- Compare and contrast Routing Information Protocol (RIP) with Open Shortest Path First (OSPF).

- Describe port numbers and their functions, including well-known and registered port numbers.

- Explain IP addressing, address classes, default subnet masks and the use of private IP addresses.

- Identify the usefulness of IPv6.

- Define the TCP/IP properties needed to configure a typical workstation.

- Describe various diagnostic tools for troubleshooting TCP/IP networks.

Pre-Assessment Questions

1. Which of the following protocols in the TCP/IP suite is categorized as an application-layer protocol?

   a. PPP
   b. TCP
   c. UDP
   d. FTP

2. What is the port number most often associated with HTTP?

   a. 21
   b. 25
   c. 80
   d. 443

3. What is a network analyzer?

   _____

OBJECTIVE:
3.1.5: TCP/IP

NOTE:
Remember that
TCP/IP is considered
the *de facto*
standard for LAN
and WAN
implementations. A
complete
understanding of
TCP/IP concepts is
critical.

Introduction to TCP/IP

TCP/IP allows computers from different vendors with various operating systems and capabilities (from mainframes to desktop computers) to communicate. Since its implementation in 1983 by the major networks that made up the Internet, TCP/IP has far exceeded expectations. Today, it is the most widely used networking protocol suite in the world, and is the language of communication on the Internet.

For one computer to communicate with another computer over a TCP/IP network, it must know the other computer's Internet address. Each computer, or node, has its own 32-bit Internet address, called an Internet Protocol (IP) address. The IP address uniquely identifies and distinguishes a node from any other node on the Internet.

This lesson will discuss the Internet architecture, common protocols used on the Internet, and Request for Comments (RFC) documents that define and reference Internet protocols. It will also cover IP addressing, address classes, addressing rules, reserved addresses and subnet masks. The lesson will conclude with a discussion of diagnostic tools used to troubleshoot TCP/IP networks.

Internet Architecture

Similar to other networking models, the Internet architecture divides protocols into layers. Each layer is responsible for specific communication tasks. The Internet architecture consists of four layers, each coinciding with layers in the OSI/RM. Figure 2-1 illustrates the Internet architecture, and Table 2-1 displays the OSI/RM and the Internet architecture equivalents. Please note that several Internet architecture models exist, each slightly different from the others. A four-layer version was selected for this course.

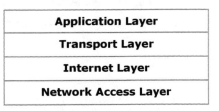

Application Layer
Transport Layer
Internet Layer
Network Access Layer

Figure 2-1: Internet architecture

Table 2-1: OSI/RM and Internet architecture layer equivalents

OSI/RM Layer	Internet Architecture Equivalent
Application	Application
Presentation	
Session	Transport
Transport	
Network	Internet
Data Link	Network Access
Physical	

Network access layer

NOTE:
Refer back to the OSI/RM to ensure that you have a firm understanding of that model.

The network access layer of the Internet architecture corresponds to the physical and data link layers of the OSI reference model. The network access layer accepts higher-layer datagrams and transmits them over the attached network, handling all the hardware details of interfacing with the network media. This layer usually consists of:

- The operating system's device driver.

- The corresponding network interface card.

- The physical connections.

For Ethernet-based LANs, the data sent over the media are called Ethernet frames, which range in size from 64 to 1,518 bytes (1,514 bytes without the Cyclical Redundancy Check).

Internet layer

The Internet layer of the Internet architecture corresponds to the network layer of the OSI model. It is responsible for addressing and routing packets on TCP/IP networks. A packet received from the transport layer is encapsulated in an IP packet. Based on the destination host information, the Internet layer uses a routing algorithm to determine whether to deliver the packet locally or send it to a default gateway.

Following are the protocols used at the Internet layer:

- Internet Protocol (IP)

- Internet Control Message Protocol (ICMP)

- Internet Group Management Protocol (IGMP)

- Address Resolution Protocol (ARP)

- Reverse Address Resolution Protocol (RARP)

Transport layer

NOTE:
The Internet-layer, transport-layer and application-layer protocols are discussed in more detail later in this lesson.

The transport layer of the Internet architecture corresponds to the transport and session layers of the OSI/RM. The transport layer accepts application-layer data and provides the flow of information between two hosts using the following two different transport protocols:

- Transmission Control Protocol (TCP)

- User Datagram Protocol (UDP)

The transport layer also divides the data received from the application layer into smaller pieces, called packets, which you were introduced to earlier. Each packet is passed to the Internet layer.

NOTE:
Unlike most other connectionless protocols, UDP does support error checking through CRC.

The transport layer is also known as the host-to-host layer, the end-to-end layer, or the source-to-destination layer.

Application layer

The application layer of the Internet architecture corresponds to the presentation and application layers of the OSI/RM. The application layer interacts with the transport-layer protocols to send or receive data.

Users can invoke application programs and protocols, including **Telnet**, File Transfer Protocol (FTP), Simple Mail Transfer Protocol (SMTP) and Simple Network Management Protocol (SNMP), for access to nodes on the Internet.

 The application layer is also called the process layer.

Requests for Comments (RFCs)

Requests for Comments (RFCs) are published documents of interest to the Internet community. They include detailed information about standardized Internet protocols, such as IP and TCP, and those in various stages of development. They also include informational documents regarding protocol standards, assigned numbers (for example, port numbers), host requirements (for example, data link, network, transport and application OSI layers) and router requirements.

RFCs are identified by number. The higher the number, the more recent the RFC. Be sure you are viewing the most recent RFC during your research. A recommended RFC reference site is located at *www.rfc-editor.org/rfc.html.*

If an RFC has been updated, the index listing (in other words, the RFC editor query results) will state the replacement RFC number.

Protocol states

Before a protocol becomes a standard, it passes through four maturity-level protocol states: experimental, proposed, draft and standard. If a protocol becomes obsolete, it is classified as historic. To progress through the steps, the protocol must be recommended by the Internet Engineering Steering Group (IESG) of the Internet Engineering Task Force (IETF).

Maturity-level protocol states

Following are descriptions of the four maturity-level protocol states:

- **Experimental** — protocols that should only be used in a laboratory (or experimental) situation. They are not intended for operation on systems other than those participating in the experiment.

- **Proposed** — protocols that may be considered for future standardization. Testing and research are encouraged, optimally by several groups. These protocols will probably be revised before progressing to the next stage.

- **Draft** — protocols being seriously considered by the IESG to become Internet standards. Testing is encouraged, test results are analyzed and feedback is requested. All feedback should be sent to the IESG. Changes are often made at the draft stage; the protocol must then return to the proposed stage.

- **Standard** — protocols determined by the IESG to be official standard protocols on the Internet. Standard protocols are of two types: those that apply to the entire Internet, and those that apply only to certain networks.

Additional protocol states

Following are descriptions of additional protocol states:

- **Historic** — protocols that have been replaced by more recent ones or that never received enough interest to develop. Historic protocols are highly unlikely to become Internet standards.

- **Informational** — protocols developed outside the IETF/IESG (for example, protocols developed by vendors or by other standardization organizations). These protocols are posted for the benefit of the Internet community.

RFC STD 1 ·

Documents at the draft stage usually become standards after a lengthy review process. The IETF recognizes the importance of remaining aware of draft RFCs that become standards. To ensure that everyone can readily discover when an RFC becomes a standard, the IETF has created the STD 1 document (often known as STD 0001). The STD 1 document is a live document (in other words, one that is being continually updated). Whenever an RFC becomes a standard, the STD 1 document is updated, often on a quarterly basis. You can obtain the STD 1 document at the RFC Editor site at *www.rfc-editor.org*. Search for the number 1, and you will find the latest STD 1 document. The actual document is published as a new RFC (for example, RFC 3300) whenever enough changes warrant an update.

Internet Protocols

NOTE:
Activity 2-1:
Reviewing TCP/IP
protocols provides additional practice in identifying TCP/IP protocols.

Each layer of the Internet architecture involves protocols. The next section briefly describes common protocols, by layer, used on the Internet. Each protocol is listed with its respective RFC(s). Figure 2-2 illustrates these relationships within the Internet architecture. These protocols will be discussed in detail throughout the course.

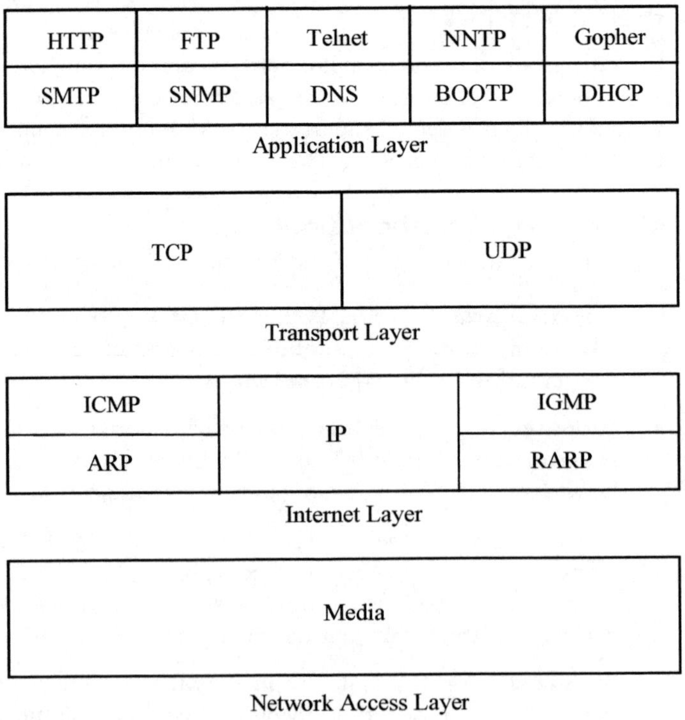

HTTP	FTP	Telnet	NNTP	Gopher
SMTP	SNMP	DNS	BOOTP	DHCP

Application Layer

TCP	UDP

Transport Layer

ICMP		IGMP
ARP	IP	RARP

Internet Layer

Media

Network Access Layer

Figure 2-2: Internet protocols and Internet architecture

Network access layer

The protocols used at the network access layer can vary considerably, depending on which technologies are responsible for placing data on the network media and pulling data off. Examples of these technologies include:

- **LANs** — Ethernet, Token Ring and FDDI.

- **WANs** — frame relay, serial lines and ATM.

Internet layer

The following protocols are used at the Internet layer of the Internet architecture:

- **Internet Protocol (IP)** — the basic data-transfer method used throughout the Internet. It is responsible for IP addressing, and performs the routing function, which selects a path to send data to the destination IP address. IP is defined in RFC 791.

- **Internet Control Message Protocol (ICMP)** — the troubleshooting protocol of TCP/IP. It allows Internet hosts and gateways to report errors through ICMP messages. If a problem occurs on a TCP/IP network, an ICMP message will probably be generated. ICMP is specified in RFC 792.

- **Internet Group Management Protocol (IGMP)** — used for multicasting, in which one source sends a message to a group of subscribers (multicast groups). For multicast delivery to be successful, members must identify themselves and the groups that interest them to local multicast-enabled routers. IGMP allows users to join and maintain membership in multicast groups. IGMP is defined in RFC 1112.

- **Address Resolution Protocol (ARP)** — translates Internet addresses to physical addresses. For example, it uses your IP address to discover your computer's Ethernet address. ARP is specified in RFC 826.

- **Reverse Address Resolution Protocol (RARP)** — performs the reverse function of ARP. It uses a node's hardware address to request an IP address. RARP is generally used for diskless workstations and X terminals. RARP is defined in RFC 903.

Transport layer

The following protocols are used at the transport layer of the Internet architecture:

- **Transmission Control Protocol (TCP)** — provides session management between the source and destination systems. It ensures that data is delivered, that it is in sequence and that no duplicate data is sent. Two computers must contact each other through a TCP connection (in other words, a session must be established) before transferring data. TCP is defined in RFC 793.

- **User Datagram Protocol (UDP)** — provides a simple datagram form of communication. One UDP packet is created for each output operation by an application, and a session is not necessary. UDP does not provide congestion control, use acknowledgments, retransmit lost datagrams or guarantee reliability, as does TCP. UDP is defined in RFC 768.

Application layer

The following protocols are used at the application layer of the Internet architecture:

- **Hypertext Transfer Protocol (HTTP)** — used to transport HTML documents (Web pages) across the Internet. HTTP requires a client program on one end (a browser) and a server on the other, both running TCP/IP. HTTP establishes a Web server connection and transmits HTML pages to a client browser. HTTP 1.0 establishes a new protocol connection for each page requested, which creates unnecessary Internet traffic. HTTP 1.1 uses persistent connections, which allow multiple downloads with one connection. Both the client and the server must support HTTP 1.1 to benefit. HTTP is defined in RFCs 1945 and 2616.

- **File Transfer Protocol (FTP)** — a system for transferring files between computers on a TCP/IP network. FTP offers an efficient and quick way to transfer files because it does not have the overhead of encoding and decoding data, such as sending files as e-mail attachments. FTP is specified in RFC 959.

- **Trivial File Transfer Protocol (TFTP)** — used for initializing diskless systems. It works with the BOOTstrap Protocol (BOOTP). TFTP uses UDP, whereas FTP uses TCP. Because TFTP is simple and small, it can be embedded in read-only memory (ROM), which is ideal for diskless workstations or routers seeking configurations upon initialization. TFTP is specified in RFC 1350.

- **Telnet** — a terminal emulation protocol developed for ARPANET. It allows a user at one site to log on and run programs from a remote system. Telnet is specified in RFC 854.

- **Network News Transfer Protocol (NNTP)** — allows sites on the Internet to exchange Usenet news articles, which are organized into topics such as "programming in C++" or "international trade issues." To use newsgroups, you must have access to an NNTP server with which you are authorized to read and post news. NNTP is specified in RFC 977.

- **Gopher** — a menu-based program used to find resources on the Internet. It is very similar in concept and practice to today's Web. Users follow links from site to site in search of information. It was one of the first tools developed to pull the Internet together so users could access the entire Internet rather than just one site. Gopher servers have been largely replaced by Web servers. Gopher is specified in RFC 1436.

- **Simple Mail Transfer Protocol (SMTP)** — the Internet standard protocol for transferring e-mail messages from one computer to another. It specifies how two mail systems interact. SMTP is often used with Post Office Protocol version 3 (POP3), which is a standard Internet mail service that uses SMTP. POP3 stores incoming e-mail until users authenticate and download it. POP3 is defined in RFC 1939 and STD 53. SMTP is specified in RFC 821. POP3 is not considered part of the TCP/IP suite, but is integral to e-mail use.

- **Simple Network Management Protocol (SNMP)** — used for managing TCP/IP networks. It is a standardized management scheme that vendors can support. Thus, all SNMP-compliant network devices can be centrally managed by an SNMP manager. SNMP also offers low resource requirements, portability and wide acceptance. SNMP is specified in RFC 1157.

fully qualified domain name (FQDN)
The complete domain name of an Internet computer, such as www.CIW-certified. com.

- **Domain Name System (DNS)** — a mechanism used on the Internet to translate host computer names into Internet (IP) addresses. It is one of the most universal methods of centralized name resolution. For example, when a user requests the **fully qualified domain name (FQDN)** www.companyname.com, DNS servers translate the name into the IP address 201.198.24.108. DNS is defined in RFCs 1034 and 1035.

- **BOOTstrap Protocol (BOOTP)** — an alternative to RARP. Additionally, it provides a method for diskless workstations and X terminals to determine their IP addresses. A single BOOTP message specifies many items needed at startup, including the diskless computer's IP address, the address of a gateway (router) and the address of a particular server (such as a DNS server). BOOTP is specified in RFC 951.

- **Dynamic Host Configuration Protocol (DHCP)** — based on BOOTP. It is designed to assign Internet addresses to nodes on a TCP/IP network during initialization. It can also assign the address of a gateway (router) and the address of a particular server. Like BOOTP, it saves administrators a great deal of time because client systems do not require manual TCP/IP configuration. DHCP is defined in RFC 2131.

Demultiplexing

Demultiplexing is the method that a destination computer uses to process the incoming packet. Figure 2-3 illustrates the demultiplexing process. Please refer to this diagram throughout the course.

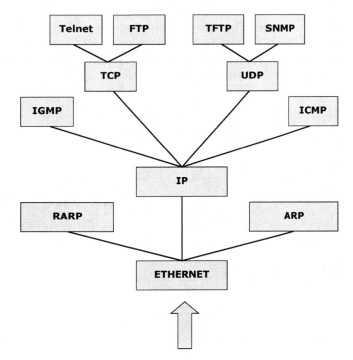

Figure 2-3: Demultiplexing of protocols

Introduction to Routing

OBJECTIVE:
3.2.4: Routing
processes

NOTE:
Refer to Lesson 1 if
you need to review
the OSI/RM.

Routing is an extremely important function of IP. It is the process of choosing a path over which to send packets. The device that performs this task is called a router, which forwards packets from one physical network to another. (You were introduced to routers earlier in the course.) Your knowledge of IP will enable you to see the correlation between IP and routing.

The Internet layer, or OSI/RM network layer (Layer 3), performs the routing function. A packet, or datagram, carries sufficient information for routing from the originating host to the destination host using the IP address. Packets may traverse several networks before reaching their destination host.

Packets are routed transparently, and not necessarily reliably, to the destination host. The term "transparent," when applied to routing, means that after the routing hardware and software are installed, changes are undetectable by users because the routing process is largely automated. The complexity of routing is not visible to the user. The transport or application layer is responsible for reliability, which ensures that the data arrives at the other end.

Routing can be summarized as:

- The process that determines the path that packets will travel across networks.

- One of the most important IP functions.

Routing can be divided into two general classifications: direct and indirect.

Direct routing

NOTE:
Packets having a source and destination on the same network are typically not referred to as being routed because no router is involved. Any router attached to the network will ignore local packets.

If two computers on the same physical network need to communicate, the packets do not require a router. The computers are considered to be on the same local network. In an IEEE 802.3/Ethernet TCP/IP network, the sending entity encapsulates the packet in an Ethernet frame, binds the destination Internet address to an Ethernet address, and transmits the resulting frame directly to its destination. This process is referred to as direct routing. ARP is an example of a direct routing protocol.

The destination system is on the same physical network if the network portions of the source and destination addresses are the same.

Indirect routing

NOTE:
Indirect routing is commonly referred to as "routing."

If two computers that are not on the same physical network need to communicate, they must send the IP packet to a router for delivery. They are located on remote networks. Whenever a router is involved in communication, the activity is considered indirect routing.

Routing process

Routing involves the following two key elements:

NOTE:
You need a general understanding of how routing works, but you do not need the details of how to manually manage a routing table.

- The host must know which router to use for a given destination; the router is determined by the default gateway. The default gateway is the IP address of the router on your local network; this router will route the packet to the destination network.

- The router must know where to send the packet; the destination is determined by the router's routing information table.

Routing information table

hop
One link between two network devices; the number of hops between two devices is considered a hop count.

A routing information table is a database maintained by a router. The table contains the location of all networks in relation to the router's location. When a packet arrives at the router, the router examines the packet's destination network, and then checks its own routing information table. It determines the next router to which to send the packet, and forwards the packet to that router. This part of the journey is considered a **hop**. In some cases, the destination network is attached to the router, in which case the packet has reached its destination network. Figure 2-4 illustrates a simplified routing information table that will help you understand the basic process.

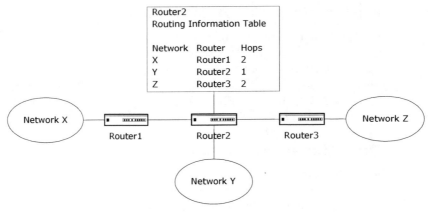

Figure 2-4: Routing information table

OBJECTIVE:
3.2.4: Routing
processes

Static vs. dynamic routing

Static routers contain routing information tables that must be built and updated manually. If a certain route does not exist in the static routing information table, the router will be unable to communicate with that network.

A dynamic router communicates with other dynamic routers to calculate routes automatically using routing protocols such as Routing Information Protocol (RIP) and Open Shortest Path First (OSPF). Dynamic routers can exchange information about routes of known networks. When a route changes, the routers automatically update themselves by recalculating routes.

Routing Protocols

Earlier, routing was defined as the process of selecting a path on which data will travel across networks. Routing also requires routing protocols, which determine how routers share information and how they report routing information table changes to one another. Routing protocols enable networks to dynamically change without the need to enter static routing information table entries for each adjustment.

OBJECTIVE:
3.2.4: Routing
processes

Interior vs. exterior protocols

Following are the two basic types of routing protocols:

- **Interior routing protocols** — used within an organization's network. Examples are RIP, RIP version 2 (RIPv2) and OSPF.

- **Exterior routing protocols** — used outside an organization's network. Exterior Gateway Protocol (EGP) and Border Gateway Protocol (BGP) are examples of such protocols (further discussion of exterior routing protocols is beyond the scope of this course).

An autonomous system is managed by a single organizational entity, which includes all networks and routers managed by that entity. If routers belong to different autonomous systems and they exchange routing information, the routers are considered exterior gateways. Routers within an autonomous system are called interior gateways.

Routing Information Protocol (RIP)

RIP is commonly implemented on small to medium-sized LANs. RIP maintains only the best route to a destination. Old route information is replaced by new route information, causing network topology changes that are reflected in routing update messages. Routing update messages cause routers to update their tables and propagate the changes. Two versions of RIP are used: RIPv1 (RFC 1058) and RIPv2 (RFC 2453). RIPv2 retains RIP's simplicity, but is more efficient.

Open Shortest Path First (OSPF)

A disadvantage of RIP is that routes are selected on the basis of the closest path (fewest hops) between the source system and the destination system. No emphasis is placed on factors such as available bandwidth, multiple connections or security.

The OSPF routing protocol is an interior gateway routing protocol that overcomes many of RIP's shortcomings. OSPFv2 (RFC 2328) has recently become an Internet standard protocol.

OSPF contains the following practical features:

- **Routing information table updates** — Updates occur when necessary, rather than at regular intervals. This irregular frequency reduces traffic on the network and saves bandwidth.

- **Various types of service routing** — OSPF makes it possible to install multiple routes to a given destination. Each route can be defined on the basis of a service, such as high bit rate and/or security.

- **Load balancing** — If multiple routes exist to a given destination and all routes cost the same, OSPF distributes traffic evenly over all routes.

- **Network areas** — OSPF provides the ability to partition a network into areas, allowing growth and organization. Each area's internal topology is hidden from other areas.

- **Authenticated exchanges** — All exchanges between routers using OSPF are authenticated. OSPF allows the use of various authentication schemes. This arrangement is important because only trusted systems should propagate routing information.

- **Defined route support** — OSPF allows the definition of host-specific or network-specific routes.

Port Numbers

After an IP packet has arrived at the destination host using the IP address (you will learn about IP addressing later in the course), the packet is passed to the transport layer. The transport layer determines which service the packet is using by examining the packet's destination port number.

TCP and UDP headers contain both source and destination port numbers. These port numbers are addresses by which processes can be identified. Each port number is a 16-bit integer value that identifies a communication channel to a specific user process. For example:

- FTP = port 21.

- HTTP = port 80.

- DNS = port 53.

- SMTP = port 25.

NOTE:
Assuming a default installation, the Windows 98/Me *systemroot* folder is the C:\Windows folder. The Windows NT/2000 *etc* folder by default is at C:\WINNT\System32\Drivers\etc.

To view many of the services and the ports associated with them, examine the services file located in the *etc* directory for Windows NT/2000 or UNIX. For Windows XP the path is C:\Windows\System32\etc. You can also review the *systemroot* directory for Windows 95/98/Me for the services file. The purpose of the services file is to map port numbers to the actual name of the service associated with that port. In addition, you can visit the RFC Editor site at *www.rfc-editor.org* to review the latest database entries. At one time, RFC 1700 contained the latest entries. According to RFC 3232, RFC 1700 is obsolete, and has now been replaced by an online database. The entity responsible for assigning port numbers was at one time the Internet Assigned Numbers Authority (IANA). Today, however, this responsibility has been given to the Internet Corporation for Assigned Names and Numbers (ICANN).

NOTE:
The URL for IANA's current assignments (www.iana.org/assignments/port-numbers) may change over time. Remember that the ICANN is now responsible for assigning port numbers. The URL for the ICANN is www.icann.org.

As of this writing, the current port assignments list is at the following location: *www.iana.org/assignments/port-numbers*. To search the entire database, go to the IANA Protocol Numbers and Assignment Services page at *www.iana.org/numbers.html*.

Classifying port numbers

According to IANA, the following three ranges of port numbers exist:

- **Well-known** — ports between 0 and 1023

- **Registered** — ports between 1024 and 49151

- **Dynamic (private)** — ports between 49152 and 65535

Although port 0 is rarely used, it is still a designated port. Many references tend to refer to ports 1 through 1023. Also, many references tend to use the term "well-known" for all ports ranging from 0 to 1023. They also tend to use the terms "dynamic" or "ephemeral" for any port ranging from 1024 to 65535.

Following is a discussion of each range.

Well-known port numbers

Also called reserved port numbers, well-known port numbers range from 0 to 1023 and are controlled by the ICANN (previously the IANA). Well-known port numbers are used by TCP and UDP to identify well-known services that a host can provide. No process is allowed to bind to a well-known port unless its effective user ID is 0 (a user account with unlimited access privileges, such as root [UNIX], superuser [UNIX], supervisor [NetWare] or administrator [Windows NT/2000]).

Registered port numbers

Registered port numbers range from 1024 to 49151 and are considered nonprivileged. Therefore, any process can use them. Administrative permissions are not required. ICANN registers these port numbers and IANA's Web site lists them, but ICANN does not formally assign them in the same manner as well-known ports. These ports are often used by specific services as contact ports. Contact ports are often necessary when a server must communicate with a remote system.

Ephemeral (short-lived or transitional) port numbers are unique port numbers typically assigned to client processes. The server process determines the ephemeral port number from the TCP or UDP header, and thereby knows the process with which to communicate at the remote system.

NOTE:
See **Optional Lab 2-1: Viewing port number assignments.**

IANA allows companies to petition ICANN and IANA to create either a well-known or a registered port number for a specific service. See the following URL for more information: www.iana.org/numbers.html.

Dynamic port numbers

Also called private ports, dynamic port numbers range from 49152 to 65535, and are not controlled or registered in any way by ICANN. Client-side applications open these ports randomly when accessing remote systems.

Internet Addressing

OBJECTIVE:
3.3.1: Unique IP addressing

To ensure that each user on the Internet has a unique IP address, the ICANN issues all Internet addresses. The previous controlling organization, the IANA, was funded and overseen by the U.S. government. The ICANN is a private, non-governmental organization that performs the same tasks, such as Internet address space allocation. To learn more about the ICANN, visit *www.icann.org*.

NOTE:
Each system used to communicate on the Internet will have an address unique to the Internet. When communicating on a private intranet, the system's address must be unique to the LAN, but is not necessarily valid on the Internet.

Most Internet addresses contain a network portion and a host portion. The network portion precedes the host portion:

network portion, host portion

Internet addresses are specified by four fields, separated by periods:

field1.field2.field3.field4

Each field represents one byte of data. Internet addresses are typically written in dotted decimal notation. Each field has a value ranging from 0 to 255, as demonstrated by the following Internet address:

208.157.24.111

In the preceding example, the network portion is 208.157.24, and the host portion is 111.

Subnet Mask

Each system in a TCP/IP network must be configured with an IP address and a subnet mask. As you have already seen, the IP address is expressed in a four-part dotted decimal format, such as:

192.162.102.221

The subnet mask determines which part of the address is used as the network address and which is used to identify a specific host on the network. For example, your subnet mask might resemble the following:

255.255.255.0

The network address identifies a general location on the network and the host address identifies a specific system. You can compare these elements to the address on a letter. The network address works like the city and state address, identifying a general location. The host address is analogous to the street name and house number, identifying a specific location.

NOTE:
A router still sees the address as consisting of a network portion and host portion only. The concept of a subnetwork portion is a convenient concept for teaching custom subnetting, which is an advanced procedure not covered in this course.

Subnet masks serve the following two main purposes:

- Distinguishing the network and host portions of an IP address

- Specifying whether a destination address is local or remote

First, the subnet mask distinguishes network and host portions of an IP address. Because the system does not know which bits in the host field should be interpreted as the subnetwork part of the Internet address, it refers to the subnet mask. The subnet mask tells the system which bits of the Internet address should be interpreted as the network, subnetwork and host addresses.

NOTE:
All TCP/IP network-connected devices will be configured with at least an IP address and subnet mask.

Subnet masks also specify whether a destination address is local or remote. Note that the subnet mask is used to "mask" the network address, so only the host address remains. In routing, this masking is extremely important. It allows a computer to determine whether a destination address is intended for a computer on the same (local) network, or a different (remote) one.

If the destination address is on the same network, the information can be transmitted locally. If the destination address is on a different network, the information must be sent to a router, which can locate the remote network.

The subnet mask identifies whether the destination address is local or remote through a process called ANDing.

ANDing

OBJECTIVE:
3.3.4: Subnet masks

The network portion of an Internet address can be determined by using the Boolean AND operation with the Internet address and the subnet mask. This process is internal to TCP/IP, but its function is important.

NOTE:
With regard to ANDing, you only need to understand that systems automatically AND the subnet mask and the IP address to determine whether an address is local or remote.

When the computer is initialized, it uses the ANDing function with its local IP address and local subnet mask. Whenever it sends information to a destination address, it uses the ANDing function again with the destination address and the local subnet mask. If the value matches the initial ANDing function result, it is a local destination. If the value is different, it is a remote address.

To use the ANDing function, convert your local IP address and subnet mask into binary form. For the following example, your IP address is 131.226.85.1 and your subnet mask is 255.255.0.0.

Calculate each corresponding bit using the following rules:

- 1 and 1 = 1

- Any other combination = 0

When your computer initializes, the ANDing process calculates the following result:

Local IP address	10000011 11100010 01010101 00000001
Local subnet mask	11111111 11111111 00000000 00000000
First ANDing result	10000011 11100010 00000000 00000000

By converting the ANDing result to decimal value, the process reveals that the network portion of the address is 131.226.

Your computer uses the ANDing result from the initialization process to determine whether all future destination addresses are local or remote. For example, you are sending information to the destination address 131.226.50.4.

Destination IP address	10000011 11100010 00110010 00000100
Local subnet mask	11111111 11111111 00000000 00000000
Second ANDing result	10000011 11100010 00000000 00000000

The network address found is 131.226. Compare the first and second ANDing results. Because they are the same, the data is sent locally, and the router will not be used. If they were different, the data would be sent through a router to the remote network.

Internet Address Classes

OBJECTIVE:
3.3.2: IP address classes

NOTE:
Ensure that you understand these address classes; be able to recognize class A, class B and class C addresses.

Without a classification system, the 3,720,314,628 possible Internet addresses would have no structure. To provide structure, IP addresses are categorized into classes. Classes can be determined by looking at the first byte of an Internet address.

Internet addresses are divided into five classes: A, B, C, D and E. The IP address range for each class is shown in Table 2-2. The characteristics of each class are detailed in this section.

Table 2-2: IP address classes

Address Class	IP Address Range
Class A	0.0.0.0 to 127.255.255.255
Class B	128.0.0.0 to 191.255.255.255
Class C	192.0.0.0 to 223.255.255.255
Class D	224.0.0.0 to 239.255.255.255
Class E	240.0.0.0 to 247.255.255.255

Class A

Class A addresses typically use the first byte for the network portion and the last three bytes for the host portion. Class A addresses range from:

0.0.0.0 to 127.255.255.255

The first byte can range from 1 to 126 (0 is a special-case source address and 127 is a reserved loopback address, which you will learn about later in this lesson). Class A addresses provide the potential for 126 networks with 16,777,214 hosts each.

The following is an example of a class A address (the first byte is the network address):

121.1.1.32

Class B

Class B addresses typically use the first two bytes for the network portion and the last two bytes for the host portion. Class B addresses range from:

128.0.0.0 to 191.255.255.255

The first byte can range from 128 to 191. Class B addresses provide the potential for 16,384 networks with up to 65,534 hosts each.

The following is an example of a class B address (the first two bytes are the network address):

168.100.1.32

Class C

NOTE:
You will probably work exclusively with class C addresses unless you are using reserved IP addresses on a private network.

Class C addresses typically use the first three bytes for the network portion and the last byte for the host portion. Class C addresses range from:

192.0.0.0 to 223.255.255.255

The first byte can range from 192 to 223. Class C addresses provide the potential for 2,097,152 networks with up to 254 hosts each.

The following is an example of a class C address (the first three bytes are the network address):

205.96.224.32

Class D

NOTE:
A host can have a unique class A, class B or class C IP address and still be identified by a class D address for multicasting.

Class D addresses support multicasting (which was introduced earlier). With multicasting, a packet is targeted to a group that is identified by a network address only. No host portion exists in the address. The first byte can range from 224 to 239. The following is an example of a class D address (all four bytes are the network address):

230.5.124.62

Class E

Class E addresses are reserved for future use. The first byte can range from 240 to 247.

OBJECTIVE:
3.3.4: Subnet masks

Default subnet masks for IP address classes

NOTE:
See **Activity 2-3: Determining default subnet masks**.

As you have already learned, all hosts with an IP address also use a subnet mask that helps a system determine the network to which it belongs. The simplest type of subnet mask is the default subnet mask. By default, each 8-bit field is turned on (255 — all binary ones) or off (0 — all binary zeros), depending on the address class (A, B or C).

Table 2-3 describes the three IP address classes in common use, as well as their standard subnet masks. Class D and E addresses do not have hosts, and therefore do not require subnet masks.

Table 2-3: Standard IP classes and subnet masks

Class	Address Range	Standard Subnet Mask
Class A	1.0.0.0 to 126.0.0.0	255.0.0.0
Class B	128.0.0.0 to 191.0.0.0	255.255.0.0
Class C	192.0.0.0. to 223.0.0.0	255.255.255.0

For more information about class A, B and C IP addresses, consult RFCs 790 and 1366, as well as the following sites:

- *www.networkcomputing.com/netdesign/ip101.html*

- *www.darril.net/classful.aspx*

Private IP addresses

Many companies and organizations do not use standard IP address ranges that can be used on the Internet. To save money, these companies purchase only a limited number of Internet-addressable addresses, and then use private IP addresses.

The ICANN suggests that companies use private IP addresses on their networks if either of the following situations is applicable to them:

- The host does not require access to other enterprise or Internet hosts.

- The host's Internet needs can be handled by mediating gateways (for example, application-layer gateways). For example, the host may require only limited Internet services, such as e-mail, FTP, newsgroups and Web browsing.

Table 2-4 provides a list of private IP addresses.

Table 2-4: Private IP addresses

Class	Private IP Address Range	Subnet Mask	CIDR Notation
Class A	10.0.0.0 to 10.255.255.255	255.0.0.0	10/8
Class B	172.16.0.0 to 172.31.255.255	255.240.0	172.16/12
Class C	192.168.0.0 to 192.168.255.255	255.255.0.0	192.168/16

Notice that the class B and class C ranges do not use standard subnet masks. Frequently, systems administrators will use standard class B and class C subnet masks, but this is not specifically recommended by RFC 1918.

Notice also that Table 2-4 includes CIDR notation, which will be discussed shortly.

Private IP addresses and Network Address Translation (NAT)

The IP address ranges indicated in the preceding table are called private IP addresses because they have no global meaning and cannot be sent across Internet routers. Internet routers are expected to reject (filter out) routing information about them (the rejection will not be treated as a routing protocol error). However, private network addresses can be sent across company routers. In order for computers with these IP addresses to use the Internet, they must use Network Address Translation (NAT). NAT allows a router or firewall to alter the IP packet and replace the private IP address with one that can be routed across the Internet. You can also use a proxy server, which will act as a mediator between the private network and all other public networks.

The benefits of using private network addresses include the following:

- Conservation of globally unique IP addresses when global uniqueness is not required.

- More flexibility in enterprise design because of large address space.

- Prevention of IP address clashes when an enterprise gains Internet connectivity without receiving addresses from the ICANN.

Classless Interdomain Routing (CIDR)

OBJECTIVE:
3.3.5: Classless
Interdomain Routing
(CIDR)

Today, IP addresses are no longer assigned based on address classes. They are assigned according to specific ranges of addresses. Each range given will be assigned a specific subnet mask presented in Classless Interdomain Routing (CIDR) notation. CIDR notation has the following format:

address block/prefix

In this format, the address block is given, and a number is given for the prefix. The prefix designates the number of bits used by the subnet mask. For example, a range of addresses from 55.66.77.88 to 55.66.88.99 with the subnet mask of 255.255.255.0 would be noted as follows:

55.66.77.88-55.66.88.99/24

Notice in the preceding example that what would previously have been considered a class A IP address can be used with a class C subnet mask. This capability enables the ICANN to assign a custom subnet mask to any range of addresses. Using CIDR notation in this way allows the conservation of IP addresses because the ICANN can assign a specific number of addresses instead of a set range.

Internet Protocol Version 6 (IPv6)

OBJECTIVE:
3.3.6: IPv6 concepts

With Internet use growing so rapidly, the current addressing scheme is in danger of depleting the limited number of available IP addresses. It is also creating unmanageable routing tables for the Internet's backbone routers. Although this course assumes the use of IP version 4 (IPv4), which is the standard version of IP, IPv4 has several shortcomings, including the following:

- **Limited address space** — IPv4, the current version, provides enough addresses for slightly more than 4.2 billion address assignments. Although this number seems large, it does not provide enough IP addresses to support all the IP-enabled devices that will be used in the future. Consider the fact that networked computers, cell phones, PDAs and other devices that must be Internet-enabled all use IP addresses.

encryption
A security technique
designed to prevent
access to
information by
converting it into a
scrambled
(unreadable) form
of text.

- **Lack of security** — IPv4 does not provide native **encryption** or authentication mechanisms, which has enabled unscrupulous individuals and groups to wage attacks and gain unauthorized access to sensitive information.

- **Speed problems** — IPv4 is highly dependent on network routers to break down transmissions, which can increase network traffic and slow transmission speed.

- **Configuration problems** — IPv4 address configuration can be automated, but the process must still be simplified.

IP version 6 (IPv6) solves these problems and will allow the Internet to function effectively well into the future. Not only does it solve addressing and routing-table problems, but it also improves the protocol. For example, it is more efficient and requires less administrative overhead than IPv4.

NOTE:
Following is a hierarchical list of large number measurements, complete with North American powers:
million (10^6)
billion (10^9)
trillion (10^{12})
quadrillion (10^{15})
quintillion (10^{18})
sextillion (10^{21})
septillion (10^{24})
octillion (10^{27})
nonillion (10^{30})
decillion (10^{33})
undecillion (10^{36}).

IPv6 provides a practically unlimited number of IP addresses because it uses a 128-bit address. As a result, it provides 340 undecillion addresses. Whereas 4 billion addresses would be 4 multiplied by 10^9, 340 undecillion addresses would be 340 multiplied by 10^{36}, which allows for a significantly larger address pool.

IPv6 is less dependent than IPv4 on routers, which helps reduce the likelihood that routers will become overburdened (in other words, congested). For more information about IPv6, visit the IPv6 Information Page (*www.ipv6.org*).

IPv6 may be implemented between 2005 and 2015, depending on how fast current IP addresses are used. IPv6 and IPv4 will probably coexist, and IPv4 will be part of Internet use for several more generations.

Movie Time!

Watch the following CIW v5 Foundations Movie to learn even more about this topic.

Devices, Routing and Protocols (approx. playing time: 06:00)

All movie clips are © 2007 LearnKey, Inc.

System Configuration and IP Addresses

OBJECTIVE:
3.2.5: TCP/IP
network addressing

Systems can be configured to use IP addresses in the following two ways:

- **Static address assignment** — The systems administrator manually enters IP address information.

- **Automatic address assignment** — The systems administrator configures a client to obtain IP address information automatically from a server. This method uses DHCP (which you learned about earlier) and Automatic Private IP Addressing (APIPA).

You will learn more about DHCP and APIPA shortly.

Default gateway

OBJECTIVE:
3.2.5: TCP/IP
network addressing

Most IP-enabled systems are also configured with a default gateway, which is an IP address that specifies a routing device (for example, a router or firewall). After a network host is configured with a default gateway, the host will be able to communicate with a remote network, if permitted by the routing device. A default gateway is often referred to simply as a gateway.

Loopback address

NOTE:
Testing the loopback address with the ping utility verifies that the computer's TCP/IP stack has loaded and initialized properly. In other words, TCP/IP is working.

The loopback address 127 cannot be used as an Internet address. Any IP address that begins with 127 is a loopback address (12.7.0.0.0 to 127.255.255.255). This address allows a client and server on the same host to communicate with each other. The loopback address is ideal for testing and troubleshooting. For example, if your computer hosts a Web server and you type http://127.0.0.1 in your Web browser's address text box (as a client), you will access the Web site. The loopback address can also be used to test local TCP/IP functionality by using the `packet Internet groper (ping)` program, which you will learn about shortly.

hosts file
A file that contains mappings of IP addresses to host names.

For UNIX and Windows NT/2000 systems, the loopback address is listed in the **hosts file** and is typically 127.0.0.1 with the assigned name localhost.

Broadcast address

Broadcast addresses send messages to all network hosts, and are used only as destination addresses. The network and/or host portions of an IP address cannot use the broadcast address 255 (all binary ones). Following are the four broadcast address types:

- **Limited broadcast (255.255.255.255)** — This type is used for configuring hosts when they start up. For example, a computer without an IP address can broadcast this address to obtain an IP address (from a DHCP or BOOTP server, for example).

- **Net-directed broadcast (netid.255.255.255)** — This type is used to broadcast to all hosts in a network. For example, if the network portion of your IP address is 192.34.200 and the host portion is 12, your computer can broadcast messages to all network hosts by using the destination address 192.34.200.255.

- **Subnet-directed broadcast** — If a network is divided into several subnets, a broadcast can be limited to the hosts within a subnet. You will learn about subnets later in this lesson.

- **All-subnets-directed broadcast** — If a network is divided into several subnets, a broadcast can be sent to all hosts within all network subnets. This type of broadcast is obsolete; multicasting (see class D addresses) is preferred.

Network and special-case source addresses

NOTE:
See **Activity 2-2: Determining classes and valid IP addresses.**

The network and/or host portions of an IP address can contain zeros, but the entire network or host portion of the address cannot be entirely zeros. For instance, the class C address 198.168.3.0 is a network address, and cannot be assigned to a node.

The special-case source IP address of a computer is all zeros (0.0.0.0) when it initializes and requests an IP address (from a DHCP or BOOTP server, for example). Although the computer broadcasts the request for the IP address, its source address is initially 0.0.0.0, until it is assigned a network IP address. The special-case source address can also specify a host on the network during initialization. For instance, the network portion of a class C address can be all zeros, and the host portion can be 11, which is 0.0.0.11. These addresses cannot be used as valid IP addresses for a node.

Normal TCP/IP workstation configuration

OBJECTIVE:
3.2.5: TCP/IP network addressing

OBJECTIVE:
3.6.1: Troubleshooting IP-enabled systems

NOTE:
A default gateway is required only in routed networks.

A network host must have at least an IP address and a subnet mask to communicate on a network. WAN communication requires at least an IP address, a subnet mask and a default gateway. Following are the basic configuration parameters for a workstation on a TCP/IP network:

- **IP address** — the 32-bit IP address that is unique to your workstation on the network. If you enter the IP address manually, it is considered a static IP address.

- **Subnet mask** — the 32-bit number used to distinguish the network and host portions of your IP address; also used to calculate whether a destination address is local or remote.

- **Default gateway** — the local computer's IP address (usually a router). If your computer calculates that a destination address is remote, your computer will send the packet to the default gateway. The router will send the packet to the remote network.

NOTE:
If a system is configured as a DHCP client, it will receive its IP address, subnet mask and default gateway from the DHCP server.

- **DHCP client** — If you are a DHCP client, your TCP/IP configurations will automatically be sent to your computer when you initialize your system, which is the easiest way to configure clients on a network. Obtaining an IP address from a DHCP server is the alternative to entering a static IP address.

TCP/IP services

Table 2-5 lists some of the TCP/IP services you may encounter when working with systems on a TCP/IP network.

Table 2-5: TCP/IP services

Term	Description
Domain Name System (DNS) service	A name resolution service. The primary means of resolving names on a network. Resolves names to IP addresses. A system can query a DNS server with a host name and receive the host's IP address as a response. A DNS server may also be configured to provide a host name when queried with an IP address.
Windows Internet Naming Service (WINS)	A legacy name resolution service. A system can query a WINS server with a NetBIOS name and receive the host's IP address. Windows family systems default to using NetBIOS names as computer names. WINS resolution is required only in a routed network environment, if DNS is not being used. All Windows systems contain a limited name resolution service that runs automatically and does not require configuration. However, this service does not work across routers.
Dynamic Host Configuration Protocol (DHCP) service	Supports automated TCP/IP host configuration. When a DHCP client starts up, it will send a query requesting configuration information. It will be given an IP address and subnet mask and may be given additional configuration information such as a primary DNS server IP address.
Automatic Private IP Addressing (APIPA)	If a modern Windows client fails to obtain an address from a DHCP server, the client will use APIPA, which causes a private IP address (an address that cannot be used on the Internet) to be assigned to the adapter. If you see a system with an IP address that begins with 169.254 and has a subnet mask of 255.255.0.0, assume that the address was assigned through APIPA.

When configuring a system for use on a TCP/IP network, you may be required to enter the IP address for one or more DNS servers, one or more WINS servers, or both. You do not need to provide the IP address for a DHCP server, but you must identify any systems that will be receiving their IP addresses and other configuration information through DHCP.

The hosts and lmhosts files

As mentioned earlier, the hosts file maps DNS host names to IP addresses. It is installed whenever you install the TCP/IP suite (or stack). You can edit this file and create entries using the following syntax:

```
IPAddress        hostname
```

For example, if you want to create a manual host entry for a system with the IP address 192.168.2.4 so that it had the name of james, you must enter the following:

```
192.168.2.4     james
```

The lmhosts file stands for "LAN manager hosts," and maps NetBIOS names to IP addresses; it is the manual equivalent of a WINS entry. A simple lmhosts file entry is identical to a hosts file entry. However, the lmhosts file allows several additional values, including:

- **#PRE** — allows the system to preload the name into its cache for more efficient name resolution.

- **#DOM** — specifies the name of a domain in which the named system is located.

For Microsoft systems, both the hosts and the lmhosts files reside in the following locations:

- Windows 9x/Me: %systemroot%\

- Windows NT/2000/XP: %systemroot%\systeme32\etc\drivers\

Your Windows systems may read entries in these files before consulting the DNS or WINS server. So if you experience a problem in name resolution, read these files to ensure that they do not contain conflicting information.

Name resolution configurations

You can configure your computer to use name resolution systems, including DNS, WINS or both. Following are several important configuration parameters:

- **Host name** — If you use DNS, you must specify the name of your computer, which is the host name. Your computer will be identified by this name (for example, student11) on the network.

- **Domain name** — If you use DNS, you must specify the domain name (for example, yourcompany.com) to which your computer belongs.

- **DNS server** — If you use DNS, you must identify the DNS servers that will provide you with the DNS service.

- **NetBIOS name** — On a Windows network, the NetBIOS name is the computer name. Microsoft Windows uses NetBIOS names for computer identification on a network.

- **WINS server** — As discussed earlier, WINS is a Microsoft name resolution protocol that maps NetBIOS names (instead of host names) to IP addresses. If your network uses WINS, you must identify the servers that will provide you with WINS. WINS uses the NetBIOS name of your computer.

DHCP

As you learned earlier, DHCP assigns IP addresses automatically on a TCP/IP network. Because DHCP automatically assigns IP addresses, it has become a central part of large-enterprise LANs and WANs. DHCP can save a great deal of time for the IT department because IT personnel are not required to manually configure each computer on the network.

DHCP assigns more than just an IP address, subnet mask and default gateway. It can also assign DNS server information, WINS server information, and almost any other TCP/IP configurations needed by network clients.

With DHCP, a client system receives its TCP/IP configurations automatically at startup. DHCP assigns these configurations on a lease basis. The lease contains all the TCP/IP configurations for a system. For example, the leased IP address your computer receives may expire after 24 hours. After the address expires, it can be leased to another computer on the network or renewed by the same computer. If the client system is removed from one network and connected to another, it will automatically relinquish its old lease and be assigned a new one when connected to the new network.

In Windows 95/98/Me, you can release and renew your DHCP TCP/IP configurations by selecting the Start menu, selecting Run, then typing `winipcfg` in the Open text box. To release the current DHCP configuration, click the Release button. To renew your DHCP configurations, click the Renew button. Your lease will be renewed, or you will receive a new lease that contains a different IP address.

The DHCP server has a pool of IP addresses that it can assign to network computers. This pool of addresses consists of a range of IP addresses that the network administrator enters into the DHCP server. The DHCP server then distributes these addresses to the network computers. The addresses might be private IP addresses or addresses assigned to the company from an ISP.

DHCP is based on BOOTP, an older protocol that assigned diskless workstations, or "dumb terminals," IP addresses and other parameters. DHCP is more powerful than BOOTP because it allows reusable addresses and additional configuration options. DHCP users can communicate with BOOTP systems.

Diagnostic Tools for Internet Troubleshooting

OBJECTIVE:
3.6.2: Diagnostic troubleshooting tools

Now that you are familiar with IP addresses, you can learn how certain diagnostic tools use IP addresses to discover information within a TCP/IP network. This section will introduce tools that are used regularly by system administrators to troubleshoot TCP/IP networks. Use the following TCP/IP commands and tools to assist with general network troubleshooting:

NOTE:
You may be unable to use these tools outside the local network if you are behind a firewall.

You need to understand the basic capabilities of each utility and when it should be used, and be able to recognize the command's output.

- `ping`

- `tracert` and `traceroute`

- `route`

- `netstat`

- `nbtstat`

- `ipconfig` and `ifconfig`

- `winipcfg`

- `arp`

- network analyzers

The *ping* command

The packet Internet groper, or ping, utility tests connectivity between source and destination systems. The command syntax is as follows:

```
ping  ip_address or host_name
```

In this format, `ip_address` or `host_name` identifies the remote system. Options will vary depending on the operating system. The `ping` command uses two of the most important ICMP types — echo request and echo reply.

You can read more about ICMP types at the following location: www.iana.org/assignments/icmp-parameters.

Using Windows, you can open a command prompt and type the following:

    ping 128.143.22.122

This command yields the following result:

    Pinging 128.143.22.122 with 32 bytes of data:

    Reply from 128.143.22.122: bytes=32 time<10ms TTL=64
    Reply from 128.143.22.122: bytes=32 time<10ms TTL=64
    Reply from 128.143.22.122: bytes=32 time<10ms TTL=64
    Reply from 128.143.22.122: bytes=32 time<10ms TTL=64

Because a reply was received, a connection exists between your computer and the computer with the IP address 128.143.22.122. To stop `ping` replies at any time, simultaneously press the CTRL and C keys.

To test communication with another system by name, you can type the following:

    ping www.blakearchive.org

You would see a result similar to that in Figure 2-5.

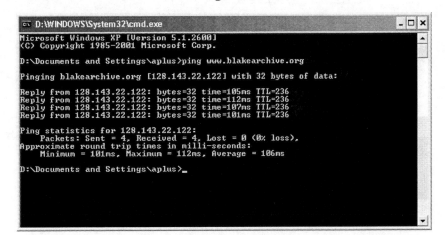

Figure 2-5: Ping results, Windows XP Professional command prompt

Generally, you should ping an IP address first to ensure that you have connectivity. You can ping a host name to ensure that DNS is working properly.

Ping gives you a way of testing DNS name resolution if you know a host's name and IP address. If you can ping the host by IP address but not by host name, a problem exists with name resolution. If you cannot ping the host by either method, a problem exists with network communication.

Ping has several options, including the following:

- **-n** – specifies the number of echo request packets to issue. The default is 4.

- **-l** — allows you to send larger packets than the default size of 32.

- **-a** — provides the host name if you know only the IP address.

NOTE:
Make sure you understand that the `ping` command accepts arguments.

You can read about additional ping options by entering `ping /?` at any command prompt.

Note: You may be unable to ping systems outside your LAN if you are behind a firewall. Many systems administrators turn off a network's ability to issue or respond to ping requests at the firewall. In addition, you will be unable to ping a particular system if that system's ability to respond to ping requests has been disabled.

The ability to test connectivity among computers on a network is extremely important if problems occur.

The *tracert* and *traceroute* commands

The `traceroute` utility can determine the path between the source and destination systems. This command also provides information on round-trip propagation time between each router and the source system.

The `tracert` command syntax for Windows is as follows:

    tracert host_name or ip_address

In this example, `ip_address` identifies the remote system.

The `traceroute` command syntax for UNIX/Linux is as follows:

    traceroute ip_address

Sometimes problems located far from your local network can compromise your network's performance. For example, if a company router or gateway fails, your Internet access may be interrupted. This disruption may cause name service failure, loss of e-mail service, or complaints from users who cannot access the Web. The traceroute program can locate such failures.

Following is an example of output returned by the `tracert` command on a Windows computer (UNIX uses the `traceroute` command and has a slightly different result format):

```
tracert www.CIW-certified.com

Tracing route to www.CIW-certified.com [64.128.206.9] over a maximum of 30
hops:

 1    2 ms    1 ms    2 ms    192.168.1.1
 2   13 ms    9 ms   12 ms    10.160.64.1
 3   10 ms   11 ms   11 ms    68.2.9.21
 4    9 ms   10 ms    8 ms    68.2.13.166
 5    9 ms   12 ms   13 ms    68.2.13.30
 6   27 ms   16 ms    9 ms    chnddsrj02-ae2.0.rd.ph.cox.net [68.2.14.5]
 7   32 ms   24 ms   20 ms    langhbr01-ae0.r2.1a.cox.net [68.1.0.232]
 8   21 ms   25 ms   25 ms    eqix.lsan.twtelecom.net [206.223.123.36]
 9   18 ms   18 ms   24 ms    66.192.251.26
10   40 ms   33 ms   35 ms    core-01-so-0-0-0-0.phnx.twtelecom.net [66.192.7.17]
11   36 ms   42 ms   39 ms    hagg-01-ge-0-3-0-510.phnx.twtelecom.net
[66.192.247.73]
12   40 ms   43 ms   45 ms    206-169-207-8.static.twtelecom.net [206.169.207.8]
13   44 ms   51 ms   42 ms    www.ciwcertified.com [64.128.206.9]

Trace complete.
```

The output from `tracert` shows the sequence of routers that the packets cross on the route from the local machine to the specified destination machine. In this case, the packets are traveling from Queen Creek, Arizona, to a machine named *www.CIW-certified.com*. In this example, the path from Queen Creek to *www.CIW-certified.com* involves 13 hops.

NOTE:
See **Optional Lab
2-2: Using the tracert
utility**.

The tracert program tries each stage of the path three times and reports the round-trip time for each stage.

The *route* command

The route command is used to display and manually configure the routes in a routing table. It is available on many operating systems, from Linux to Windows XP Professional and Windows Server 2003. Following is an example of the output from the Windows XP Professional route command:

```
c:\>route print
=====================================================================
Interface List
0x1 ......................... MS TCP Loopback interface
0x1000003 ...00 e0 98 76 80 65 . Linksys EtherFast 10/100 USB Network Adapter
=====================================================================
=====================================================================
Active Routes:
Network Destination        Netmask          Gateway       Interface  Metric
          0.0.0.0          0.0.0.0      192.168.2.1  192.168.2.101       1
        127.0.0.0        255.0.0.0        127.0.0.1      127.0.0.1       1
      192.168.2.0    255.255.255.0    192.168.2.101  192.168.2.101       1
    192.168.2.101  255.255.255.255        127.0.0.1      127.0.0.1       1
    192.168.2.255  255.255.255.255    192.168.2.101  192.168.2.101       1
  255.255.255.255  255.255.255.255    192.168.2.101  192.168.2.101       1
Default Gateway:       192.168.2.1
=====================================================================
Persistent Routes:
  None

c:\>
```

Review the preceding output. Notice the default gateway, as well as information about how packets are routed locally. The route command provides additional options that allow you to add and delete routes on your system.

The *netstat* command

The netstat command is available in all IP-enabled operating systems. It is designed to provide information about the following:

- The services that are listening on your system. All services use ports. A port can be either a TCP port or a UDP port (there are 65,536 TCP and UDP ports). For example, the Microsoft World Wide Web Publishing Service (the IIS Web server) listens for requests on TCP port 80. Whenever a Windows 9x/Me, NT/2000 or XP system shares a network folder, it will listen on TCP port 139, among others. To list all listening ports, use the netstat -a command.

- The connections made from other systems. If, for example, a remote host connects to your system's Web server, you can use the netstat command to determine the port this remote client opened to connect to your Web server. Usually, a remote client will open a random port above 1023 to access port 80 at your server. After the remote client opens a port to your server, a socket is established.

socket
The end point of a connection (either side), which usually includes the TCP or UDP port used and the IP address. Used for communication between a client and a server.

The netstat command displays the contents of various network-related data structures, such as the state of **sockets**. More specifically, this command displays information about packets processed by your system on the network. The command syntax is as follows:

    netstat options

Options will vary depending on the operating system. To learn about options for commands, open the command prompt and type the following:

    netstat -?

NOTE:
Some TCP/IP utility options are case-sensitive, unlike MS-DOS or Windows family command-line commands.

By itself, the netstat command displays only established active connections on the system. This command results in the following response:

```
Active Connections
Proto   Local Address   Foreign Address     State
TCP student13:1037 192.168.3.13:1040   ESTABLISHED
TCP student13:1041 192.168.3.13:1050   ESTABLISHED
TCP student13:1046 192.168.3.13:1040   ESTABLISHED
TCP student13:1050 192.168.3.13:1050   ESTABLISHED
TCP student13:1599 207.199.11.24:ftp   ESTABLISHED
```

In the preceding response, four TCP connections have been established between student13 and a server with IP address 192.168.3.13. Another TCP connection has been established with an FTP server at 207.199.11.24. These TCP connections use the registered TCP port numbers 1037, 1041, 1046, 1050 and 1599. The FTP connection also uses the reserved TCP port number for FTP, which is 21.

The *nbtstat* command

The nbtstat command is somewhat similar to the netstat command. It is used only in Microsoft systems that use TCP/IP, NetBEUI or IPX/SPX. Microsoft systems use special computer names called NetBIOS names, which you learned about earlier. Microsoft networking often uses these names for name resolution. The nbtstat command is used to query the server's local database of NetBIOS names. Relevant nbtstat commands include the following:

- **nbtstat –r** — reads the cache and displays names that have been registered on the Windows system.

- **nbtstat –R** — cleans the existing cache.

NOTE:
Make sure you can clearly differentiate between netstat and nbtstat.

If you make a change in regard to Microsoft networking, you should always use the nbtstat -R command. Doing so resets the cache without restarting the system. Using this command is important after altering the %systemroot%/lmhosts file in Windows 9x/Me, the %systemroot%/winnt/system32/drivers/etc/lmhosts file in Windows NT/2000, or the %systemroot%/lmhosts file in Windows XP. Using the nbtstat -R command rereads the updated file and updates the system using the new information.

For more information about nbtstat, enter /? at any command prompt.

The *ipconfig* command — Windows NT/2000/XP

The Windows NT/2000/XP ipconfig (Internet protocol configuration) command is used to display the Windows NT/2000/XP IP configuration. You have already used the ipconfig command to determine your physical address in a previous lesson. By default, this command displays only the IP address, subnet mask and default gateway.

The command syntax is as follows:

```
ipconfig    options
```

To view all the IP-related configuration information, use the /all option. This option displays additional information, such as the hardware address. Following is an example of using the ipconfig command with the /all option:

```
ipconfig   /all
```

This command yields the following results:

```
Windows IP Configuration:
    Host Name                   student13
    DNS Servers
    Node Type                   Broadcast
    NetBIOS Scope ID
    IP Routing Enabled          No
    WINS Proxy Enabled          No
    NetBIOS Resolution Uses DNS No

Ethernet adapter RTL80291:
    Description                 Novell 2000 Adapter
    Physical Address            00-00-1C-3A-62-BD
    DHCP Enabled                No
    IP Address                  192.168.3.13
    Subnet Mask                 255.255.255.0
    Default Gateway             192.168.3.1
```

The ipconfig command also renews and releases IP addresses from a DHCP server. If no adapter name is specified, all IP leases will be released.

For example:

```
ipconfig   /release adapter
ipconfig   /renew adapter
```

In the following lab, you will use the ipconfig command to analyze your computer's IP address configuration. Suppose your child must complete an after-school project in which she must post her work to a moderated online forum specially set up by her teacher. Your computer, which is using a newly installed NIC, is unable to access the Internet, and you suspect the problem may be in the TCP/IP configuration. You want to determine the MAC address of your network card. How would you use the ipconfig command to do so? What other configuration data can you view by using ipconfig?

Lab 2-1: Identifying IP configuration and MAC address information

In this lab, you will locate your computer's IP address configuration and MAC (physical) address.

1. Select **Start | Run**, type *cmd* and press **ENTER** to open a command prompt.

2. Enter the following command:

   ```
   ipconfig /all
   ```

3. Your system's configuration information will display, as shown in Figure 2-6.

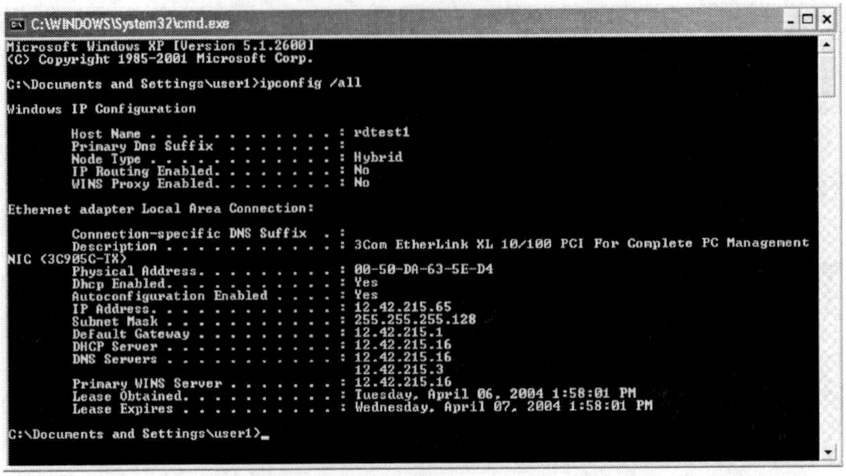

```
C:\WINDOWS\System32\cmd.exe                                              _ □ x

Microsoft Windows XP [Version 5.1.2600]
(C) Copyright 1985-2001 Microsoft Corp.

C:\Documents and Settings\user1>ipconfig /all

Windows IP Configuration

        Host Name . . . . . . . . . . . : rdtest1
        Primary Dns Suffix  . . . . . . :
        Node Type . . . . . . . . . . . : Hybrid
        IP Routing Enabled. . . . . . . : No
        WINS Proxy Enabled. . . . . . . : No

Ethernet adapter Local Area Connection:

        Connection-specific DNS Suffix  . :
        Description . . . . . . . . . . : 3Com EtherLink XL 10/100 PCI For Complete PC Management
NIC (3C905C-TX)
        Physical Address. . . . . . . . : 00-50-DA-63-5E-D4
        Dhcp Enabled. . . . . . . . . . : Yes
        Autoconfiguration Enabled . . . : Yes
        IP Address. . . . . . . . . . . : 12.42.215.65
        Subnet Mask . . . . . . . . . . : 255.255.255.128
        Default Gateway . . . . . . . . : 12.42.215.1
        DHCP Server . . . . . . . . . . : 12.42.215.16
        DNS Servers . . . . . . . . . . : 12.42.215.16
                                          12.42.215.3
        Primary WINS Server . . . . . . : 12.42.215.16
        Lease Obtained. . . . . . . . . : Tuesday, April 06, 2004 1:58:01 PM
        Lease Expires . . . . . . . . . : Wednesday, April 07, 2004 1:58:01 PM

C:\Documents and Settings\user1>_
```

Figure 2-6: TCP/IP configuration, Windows XP

4. Write your computer's adapter address (physical address), IP address, subnet mask and default gateway in the spaces provided.

Adapter address: _____

IP address: _____

Subnet mask: _____

Default gateway: _____

5. Close the command prompt window.

The *ifconfig* command — UNIX/Linux

The ifconfig (interface configuration) command is the UNIX equivalent of the ipconfig command. It displays the hardware and software configurations of the NIC.

The following is an example of using the ifconfig command:

```
ifconfig
```

The command yields the following results, depending on the NIC and network configuration:

```
eth0  Link encap:Ethernet HWaddr 00.A0.24.55.29.E8
      inet addr:192.168.3.11 Bcast:192.168.3.255 mask:255.255.255.0
      UP BROADCAST RUNNING MULTICAST MTU:1500 Metric:1
      RX packets:17 errors:0 dropped:0 overruns:0 frame:0
      TX packets:95 errors:0 dropped:0 overruns:0 carrier:0
      collisions:0 txqueuelen:100
      Interrupt:9 Base address:0x300

lo    Link encap:Local Loopback
      inet addr:127.0.0.1 Mask:255.0.0.0
      UP LOOPBACK RUNNING MTU:3924 Metric:1
      RX packets:22 errors:0 dropped:0 overruns:0 frame:0
      TX packets:22 errors:0 dropped:0 overruns:0 carrier:0
      collisions:0 txqueuelen:0
```

The *winipcfg* command — Windows 95/98/Me

The Windows 95/98/Me winipcfg command is used to determine your network card's IP configuration and Ethernet address; it is the equivalent of the ipconfig command used in Windows 2000 and XP. To use winipcfg, you would select Start | Run, and then type the following command at the run command line:

```
winipcfg
```

NOTE:
Remember that you can use the ipconfig command in Windows 98, for example. However, winipcfg is the standard command for Windows 95/98/Me.

The Windows IP configuration and Ethernet adapter information will appear. From the drop-down menu, select your computer's NIC, such as 3COM Etherlink PCI. Your screen will resemble Figure 2-7, depending on your IP configuration and NIC.

NOTE:
The drop-down list permits adapter selection on a system with multiple network adapters, which includes modems configured for dial-up access.

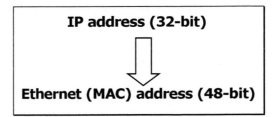

Figure 2-7: Windows Me IP configuration

You can also enter winipcfg at the MS-DOS prompt.

The *arp* command

To understand the arp command, you should review the information about ARP discussed earlier. ARP resolves software addresses to hardware addresses.

Assume that the following two hosts exist on a TCP/IP Ethernet network: node1 and node2. Node1 knows the IP address of node2. However, node1 cannot send data to node2 unless node1 knows the Ethernet (hardware) address of node2. ARP resolves IP addresses to Ethernet addresses, as shown in Figure 2-8.

IP address (32-bit)

⬇

Ethernet (MAC) address (48-bit)

Figure 2-8: Resolving IP addresses to Ethernet (MAC) addresses

The arp command displays ARP information. It will show the physical (MAC) address of computers with which you have recently communicated. The command for viewing the ARP cache is as follows:

```
arp -a
```

NOTE:
You need to recognize this command and its use, but there is seldom any need to directly execute the arp command.

This command yields the following result:

```
Interface: 192.168.3.13
    Internet Address        Physical Address        Type
    192.168.3.11            00-60-83-7c-24-a2       Dynamic
    192.168.3.15            00-60-97-24-db-df       Dynamic
    192.168.4.12            00-aa-00-38-e7-c3       Dynamic
```

To delete an entry from the ARP cache, use the following syntax:

```
arp -d IP address
```

NOTE:
Every TCP/IP host will maintain its own ARP cache.

In this example, IP address identifies the entry you want to delete.

Network analyzer

Network analyzers allow network administrators to analyze data traversing a network. The data is "captured" by the network analyzer as it is transmitted across the network. After it has been captured, the data can be closely studied. For example, you can view the Ethernet header, which indicates the physical (MAC) addresses of both the source and the destination nodes.

Network analyzers can help an administrator troubleshoot and manage a network. Most network analyzers support several network protocols, such as TCP/IP and IPX/SPX. If you are viewing the packets on your network and notice a computer sending error messages, you can identify the computer and determine the problem. A free, powerful open-source network analyzer is Ethereal (*www.ethereal.com*).

A network analyzer can help troubleshoot and manage a network by providing the following services:

- **Monitoring network traffic to identify network trends**. This practice helps establish a network baseline. For example, you may notice that network traffic is heaviest in the morning when all users start their computers.

- **Identifying network problems and sending alert messages**. Problems (such as traffic exceeding a given parameter) can be predefined by the network administrator.

- **Identifying specific problems**. Problems might include error messages generated by a network device, which can then be repaired.

- **Testing network connections, devices and cables**. Network analyzers can send test packets over the network. The packets can be traced to discover faulty components or cables.

Figure 2-9 shows the results of a packet capture using Ethereal.

NOTE:
Network Associates Sniffer Basic was previously called NetXRay. The open-source program Ethereal is another popular analyzer for both Linux and Windows systems. It is located at *www.ethereal.com*, and is primarily a packet sniffer.

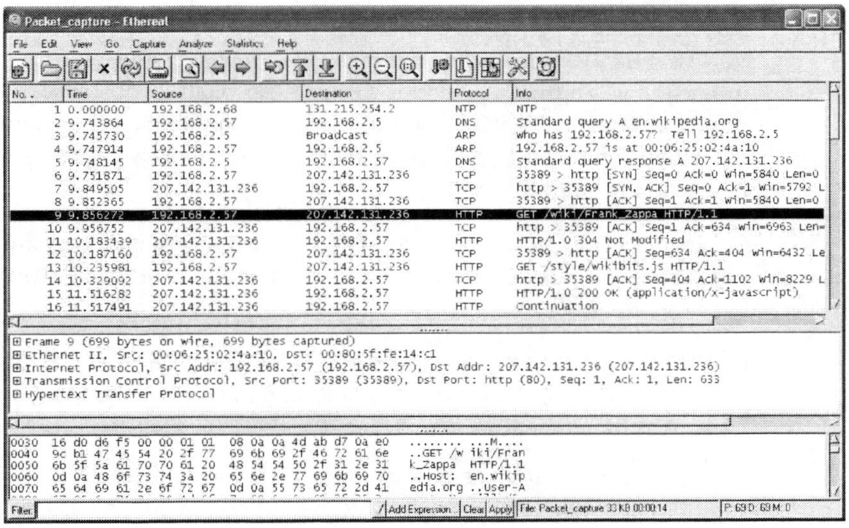

Figure 2-9: Ethereal packet capture

Troubleshooting considerations

OBJECTIVE:
3.6.1:
Troubleshooting IP-enabled systems

As you troubleshoot connectivity problems on a LAN and to the Internet, consider the following:

- **DNS name resolution** — Have you entered the correct address for a DNS server? For a WINS server? If you can ping an IP address but not a host name, there is a problem with DNS.

- **Hosts file configuration** — Is the lmhosts file accurate? Many systems check this file before going to a DNS server for name resolution.

- **Static versus dynamic IP addressing** — If you are adding a new host to a network, determine how the other hosts obtain an IP address. It is generally not wise to use both static and dynamic IP addressing on the same network because confusion can result if two nodes try to use the same address. Either configure all hosts to use DHCP or APIPA, or configure all hosts to use manually entered (static) IP addresses.

- **Default gateway and subnet mask** — Be sure that you have specified the correct IP address for the default gateway if you need to access the Internet. In addition, ensure that you have entered the correct subnet mask, because this information helps the system determine whether an address is local or remote.

OBJECTIVE:
3.6.3: Client-side vs. server-side in troubleshooting

Using the diagnostic tools and interpreting your findings will help you determine whether the problem is on the client side or on the server side. For example, if you cannot ping another system on your network, you probably have a client-side connectivity problem. If you are able to ping your default gateway by IP address but not by name, there may be a problem with DNS (server-side) or there may be an incorrect entry in the lmhosts file (client-side). If you can ping your default gateway but cannot ping an address on the other side of the router, there may be a problem with the router.

If you can access the Internet (in other words, you already know that you have no connectivity problems) and you are suddenly unable to access your e-mail, check your account and password settings. After verifying these client-side issues, contact your ISP to see whether service is available. Occasionally, SMTP and POP servers are temporarily unavailable.

OBJECTIVE:
3.6.4:
Troubleshooting
cable and ADSL
modems

**Digital Subscriber
Line (DSL)**
A high-speed direct
Internet connection
that uses all-digital
networks.

cable modem
A device that allows
computers to
communicate over
a network by
modulating and
demodulating the
cable signal into a
stream of data.

Asymmetric Digital Subscriber Line (ADSL) and cable modem

Verifying the IP address, subnet mask and default gateway settings is especially important when troubleshooting Asymmetric Digital Subscriber Line (ADSL) and cable modems. Many ISPs offer static IP addresses to their **Digital Subscriber Line (DSL)** and cable customers, and you may be required to manually enter the IP addresses for the host and the gateway.

Cable and ADSL modems are designed for use with a single system. However, an entire home network can be connected through a **cable modem** by using an additional router. This router can be:

- A Windows or Linux system with one or two NICs, using software to translate addresses. Software can include Windows Internet Connection Sharing or the Linux `iptables` command.

- A dedicated router or firewall, such as those sold by Cisco Systems®/Linksys® (*www.linksys.com*) or NETGEAR, Inc. (*www.netgear.com*).

If you are using your own router and want to connect your modem to that router, you may need to use a crossover cable to establish the connection. You learned about crossover cables earlier in the course.

Sometimes cable and ADSL modems are reconfigured automatically by your ISP. Reconfiguration may include a new DHCP address, or even a new version of the operating system used on the modem. The operating system used for the cable modem is often referred to as firmware. Sometimes, a cable or ADSL modem will use a static IP address, so it is important to obtain information concerning your IP address either from the provider or from configuration information given at the time of installation.

As you troubleshoot connections, check for basic connectivity by pinging local IP addresses rather than DNS names; you want to discover basic connectivity first, then discover any problems with DNS resolution. You can then ping the default gateway. Simplifying your network may be necessary to test one element. For example, many home offices these days use a router to enable multiple systems to communicate with the Internet through a single cable/ADSL modem. If your network experiences problems, attach one of the workstations directly to the cable/ADSL modem. You may need to configure this workstation to use either DHCP (the most common option) or a static IP address, depending on your system provider. You can then determine whether the problem exists with the cable/ADSL modem.

Often, the best way to troubleshoot connectivity issues with these devices is to power them down, detach your connections, reattach your connections, and power them on again. You may want to wait one or two minutes before powering up the devices again. These devices reinitialize themselves when they are powered on, and your connectivity problems may disappear.

If you are still unable to access the Internet or your e-mail messages, contact your ISP. Service may be down, and several ISPs have recorded messages informing you of service outages and their expected duration.

Case Study
Communication Breakdown

Paul has been asked to troubleshoot a problem with a cable modem connection for a small office. This office used seven Windows workstations and three Linux systems. One of the Linux systems acted as a router, which allowed the internal workstations to communicate with the Internet. The connection has been working for a year, but suddenly all Internet access has failed. Office workers noticed the problem as soon as they tried to access the Internet to perform essential financial transactions for the company. The workers at the office have little knowledge of Internet connectivity, and have offered Paul a contract to fix the problem. Paul took the following steps:

- He used the ping utility to ensure that all local systems (systems in the office) could communicate with one another by IP address. His tests were successful, which showed that the systems could at least communicate on a basic level.

- Because the office network used a local DNS server, he then used the ping utility to confirm that all systems could communicate with one another by host name. This test was also successful, showing that DNS resolution was not the problem.

- Next, he used the ipconfig and ifconfig utilities to discover the default gateway. He noticed that the office was using reserved IP addresses that were statically configured. He then pinged the default gateway by IP address and host name. All tests showed that the default gateway (the Linux system) was responding. However, he still could not access the Internet from any of the systems.

- Paul then took one of the workstations and connected it directly to the cable modem. He configured the system to use DHCP, which is what the cable modem required of any workstation or system attached to it. Still, no Internet access was available. These results suggested that the problem was either with the cable modem itself or with the ISP's network. He then returned the network configuration of the office back to normal.

Paul knew that he could do little or nothing to resolve a problem with the ISP. However, he knew that he could still see whether the problem existed with the cable modem. Paul powered off the cable modem, waited a few minutes, and then powered it back on again. Internet access was restored. Paul checked the cable modem and found that it now had a different IP address, as well as a different version of the operating system; apparently, a glitch had occurred after the ISP updated the software during the night. With Internet access restored to the office, Paul was able to collect his fee from a grateful customer.

Consider the following questions:

- If rebooting the cable modem had not resolved the problem, what could Paul have done in regard to the ISP?

- Why did Paul take one of the workstations and connect it directly to the cable modem?

- Why was it important for Paul to configure the workstation to use DHCP in this particular instance? Is it possible that some cable or ADSL modems would require a fixed IP address instead? If so, where would you get this information?

Lesson Summary

Application project

How do you think the term "Request for Comments" originated? Investigate by locating, downloading and reading RFC 1000. Would you like to join the Internet Society and become a part of the standardization process? If so, contact the Internet Society (*www.isoc.org*) on the Web.

Must the loopback address be 127.0.0.1? No, but this address is recommended. To check your loopback address, locate and open the hosts file using your operating system's search feature. The loopback address is listed in the file. To test the loopback address, open the command prompt and enter the command `ping 127.0.0.1`. You should receive a reply from your own computer (loopback), which means your NIC is configured properly for TCP/IP. Enter the command `ping 127.34.34.100`, which will also provide a successful reply. The entire 127 class A address has been reserved for the loopback address. Exit the hosts file and close the command prompt.

Skills review

In this lesson, you studied the four layers of the Internet architecture model: network access, Internet, transport and application. You discussed RFCs, including the different states of protocols. You also defined common Internet protocols and matched them to their corresponding Internet layers. You learned about the routing process and about the routing protocols that are used to transfer packets from source to destination. You studied the key concepts of 32-bit IP addresses, including IP address structure, address classes, addressing rules and reserved addresses. You also studied subnet masks and learned about diagnostic tools used to troubleshoot TCP/IP networks.

Now that you have completed this lesson, you should be able to:

✓ Define and describe the Internet architecture model and various Internet protocols.

✓ Describe the purpose of Requests for Comments (RFCs).

✓ Explain the routing process, including static versus dynamic routing, and interior versus exterior routing protocols.

✓ Compare and contrast Routing Information Protocol (RIP) with Open Shortest Path First (OSPF).

✓ Describe port numbers and their functions, including well-known and registered port numbers.

✓ Explain IP addressing, address classes, default subnet masks and the use of private IP addresses.

✓ Identify the usefulness of IPv6.

✓ Define the TCP/IP properties needed to configure a typical workstation.

✓ Describe various diagnostic tools for troubleshooting TCP/IP networks.

Lesson 2 Review

1. Explain how the OSI/RM layers equate to the Internet architecture model layers.

   _____

   _____

   _____

   _____

   _____

2. Name the four maturity-level states through which a protocol must pass before it becomes a standard.

   _____

3. Define demultiplexing.

   _____

   _____

4. What type of routing is being used when a router is involved in communication between two computers that are not on the same network?

   _____

5. Routing Information Protocol (RIP) and Open Shortest Path First (OSPF) are examples of what type of routing protocol?

   _____

6. What provides structure to the approximately 4 billion possible Internet addresses.

   _____

7. Name the four types of broadcast addresses.

   _____

8. Name the four basic parameters that can be configured for a workstation on a TCP/IP network.

   _____

   _____

Lesson 2
Supplemental Material

This section is a supplement containing additional tasks for you to complete in conjunction with the lesson. These elements are:

- **Activities**
  Pen-and-paper activities to review lesson concepts or terms.

- **Optional Labs**
  Computer-based labs to provide additional practice.

- **Lesson Quiz**
  Multiple-choice test to assess knowledge of lesson material.

Activity 2-1: Reviewing TCP/IP protocols

In this activity, you will review what you have learned about TCP/IP (Internet) protocols. Match the protocol name with the correct function.

1.	IP	A.	Broadcasts a request to translate an Internet (IP) address into a physical (MAC) address.
2.	FTP	B.	Proprietary Microsoft protocol used for NetBIOS name resolution.
3.	DHCP	C.	Standard protocol for transferring e-mail messages.
4.	SMTP	D.	Basic data transfer method used throughout the Internet. A connectionless protocol.
5.	WINS	E.	Protocol used for transporting HTML documents.
6.	ARP	F.	Used for transferring files between computers.
7.	HTTP	G.	Provides TCP/IP client systems (hosts) with address and configuration property information.

Understanding the protocols used by different operations can be helpful when troubleshooting communication failures.

Activity 2-2: Determining classes and valid IP addresses

In this activity, you will determine the class of each IP address and whether it is a valid IP address for a computer. If it is not a valid IP address, explain why in the spaces provided.

	IP Address	Class	Valid? Yes or No	Explanation
1.	192.23.111.8			
2.	10.1.1.256			
3.	148.108.62.95			
4.	127.0.0.1			
5.	245.255.123.49			
6.	100.54.100.90			

	IP Address	Class	Valid? Yes or No	Explanation
7.	162.34.0.0			
8.	127.65.18.191			
9.	1.1.1.1			
10.	208.152.84.255			
11.	225.37.257.34			
12.	255.255.255.255			

Activity 2-3: Determining default subnet masks

In this activity, you will determine the default subnet mask for each IP address. Write your answers in the spaces provided.

1. 17.223.13.22

_____

2. 194.10.99.2

_____

3. 211.34.126.10

_____

4. 152.4.202.69

_____

5. 128.156.88.1

_____

   **Optional Lab 2-1: Viewing port number assignments**

In this optional lab, you will visit the IANA Web page that reports port assignments made by ICANN.

Note: Your computer must have Internet access for you to complete this lab.

1. Open any Web browser.

2. Enter the following URL in the browser's Address text box.

    www.iana.org/assignments/port-numbers

3. Review the port assignments, including both well-known and registered ports.

4. Enter the following URL: ***www.iana.org/numbers.html***

5. This page is more complex because it describes various parameters and protocols that help IP-based networks function. Browse this page, making sure to notice at least the following information:

    - **Online Application for a System (Well-Known) Port Number.** This information provides a form that allows a company to have ICANN and IANA create a well-known port number for a specific service.

    - **Online Application for a User (Registered) Port Number.** This information provides a form that allows a company to have ICANN and IANA create a registered port number for a specific service.

    - **Protocol and Service Names.** This information provides official names for most known protocols.

    - **Operating System Names.** This information provides official names for most known operating systems.

6. When you are finished, close your browser.

In this lab, you learned more about port number assignments, and about how ICANN and IANA cooperate to regulate Internet communication.

NOTE:
You should not make an application for any port numbers at this time.

Optional Lab 2-2: Using the tracert utility

In this optional lab, you will experiment with the `tracert` program.

Tech Note: If you are behind a firewall, you may not be able to conduct this lab successfully because many firewalls will disable ICMP at the firewall.

Note: This lab requires Internet connectivity.

1. Open a command prompt.

2. Use the `tracert` command to determine the path from your computer to your favorite location on the Internet. For example, enter the following:

    `tracert www.icann.org`

3. How many hops does it take to reach ICANN? What is the round-trip time? Compare `tracert` command output for paths from your computer with paths from computers in the United States (*www.ansi.org*) and in Europe (*www.iso.ch*).

4. If possible, disconnect your computer from the Internet. Run the `tracert` command to an Internet location, such as *www.icann.org*. What happens? Can you determine where the breakdown occurred? Write the result in the space provided.

    _____

    _____

5. Close the command prompt window.

Lesson 2 Quiz

1. The Internet layer of the Internet architecture model:

    a. transmits datagrams over the attached network.
    b. addresses and routes packets on TCP/IP.
    c. accepts application-layer data and provides the flow of information between hosts.
    d. interacts with the transport-layer protocols to send or receive data.

2. What is Transmission Control Protocol/Internet Protocol?

    a. A suite of protocols that allow computers running the same operating system to communicate
    b. A suite of protocols that allow computers from different vendors with various operating systems to communicate
    c. A single protocol that allows computers from different vendors with various operating systems to communicate
    d. A single protocol that allows computers running the same operating system to communicate

3. Which of the following protocols in the TCP/IP protocol suite is a connectionless network-layer protocol?

    a. IP
    b. TCP
    c. UDP
    d. FTP

4. Address Resolution Protocol (ARP), used to translate Internet addresses into physical addresses, is used at which of the following Internet layers?

    a. Network access layer
    b. Application layer
    c. Transport layer
    d. Internet layer

5. Which process determines the path a packet will travel across a network?

    a. Mapping
    b. Traveling
    c. Routing
    d. Searching

6. Which routing protocol is sensitive to such criteria as available bandwidth and security?

    a. Open Shortest Path First (OSPF)
    b. Routing Information Protocol (RIP)
    c. File Transfer Protocol (FTP)
    d. Transmission Control Protocol (TCP)

7. What is the reserved port number used by SMTP to transfer e-mail messages?

    a. Port 21
    b. Port 80
    c. Port 25
    d. Port 53

8. Which of the following Internet address classes is reserved for experimental or future use?

   a. Class E
   b. Class D
   c. Class C
   d. Class B

9. Which of the following is an example of a class C address?

   a. 191.13.162.11
   b. 192.168.101.14
   c. 237.141.12.22
   d. 127.0.0.1

10. The Internet Corporation of Assigned Names and Numbers (ICANN) has reserved three blocks of IP address space for:

    a. corporate networks.
    b. private networks.
    c. educational networks.
    d. non-profit networks.

11. You are creating a company network that will support 200 hosts. What address class would conserve address space and still support that number of hosts?

    a. Class A
    b. Class B
    c. Class C
    d. Class D

12. Which of the following default subnet masks corresponds to a class A address?

    a. 255.255.255.255
    b. 255.255.255.0
    c. 255.255.0.0
    d. 255.0.0.0

13. What is the default subnet mask for a class B address?

    a. 255.255.255.255
    b. 255.255.255.0
    c. 255.255.0.0
    d. 255.0.0.0

14. Which of the following diagnostic tools helps determine connectivity between source and destination systems?

    a. The `tracert` command
    b. The `ipconfig` command
    c. The `ping` command
    d. The `netstat` command

15. On a Windows network, what do you call the computer name of a Windows computer?

    a. Domain name
    b. NetBIOS name
    c. Host name
    d. WINS name

Lesson 3: Internetworking Servers

Objectives

By the end of this lesson, you will be able to:

- Identify and describe the functions and features of various internetworking servers, including file, print, HTTP, proxy, mail, instant messaging, mailing list, media, DNS, FTP, news, certificate, directory, catalog, fax and transaction servers.

- Describe how each type of internetworking server uses TCP/IP suite protocols.

- Describe access-security features of an HTTP server, including user names, passwords and file-level access.

- Define MIME, and explain how MIME types are used by HTTP and mail servers.

- Describe the functions of DNS, including the DNS hierarchy, root domain servers, top-level domains and DNS record types.

- Define "daemon" and identify the functions of Internet-related daemons.

Pre-Assessment Questions

1. Which protocol is usually used when transferring HTML page content from a Web server to a client browser?

   a. HTTP
   b. NNTP
   c. MIME
   d. FTP

2. Which is the preferred protocol for transferring a 5-MB file between two systems over the Internet?

   a. HTTP
   b. NNTP
   c. MIME
   d. FTP

3. What is a directory server?

   _____

   _____

Version 1.2

Overview of Internetworking Servers

Traditional networks are designed to store files in central sites and databases, and then present them to users at remote workstations. These files and databases that network users share are called network services.

With the advent of the Internet, network services have become more distributed, or decentralized. This distribution and management of network services across the Internet is often called internetworking.

The advent of TCP/IP has allowed network services to become more accessible to the Internet. Common servers found on isolated networks and on the Internet include the following:

- File
- Print
- HTTP
- Proxy
- Mail

- Mailing list
- Media
- DNS
- FTP
- News

- Certificate
- Directory
- Catalog
- Fax
- Transaction

The following sections will discuss each of these server types.

File and Print Servers

Possibly the most common types of servers, file and print servers are a major factor in the increasing popularity of networks. These servers are often incorporated as one service (file and print) even if only one of the services is used on a server.

File server

File servers are network servers that store data files and programs. A file server is basically a remote disk drive that is shared by the network users. File servers are not the same as application servers: An application server runs programs and processes data; a file server stores files and programs. A file server can be any computer that shares a file, folder or entire disk drive with the network. It should be a powerful server capable of high speeds, security and data protection.

Print server

Network printers allow multiple users to send print jobs to the same physical printers. Without network printing capability, any user who wanted to print would need a printer physically attached to his or her computer, or would need to copy the document to a computer that had a printer attached. Because this arrangement would become cost-prohibitive in even small offices, most LANs use network-printing functions.

Line printer/line printer daemon (LPR/LPD)

print queue
A mechanism that stores print requests until they are passed to a printing device.

The UNIX network operating system can use the LPR/LPD printing protocol to submit print jobs to network printers. When a user submits a file for printing, the file is transmitted over the network in one direction (unidirectional). The LPR initiates commands and the LPD executes them. The commands manage the submission of print jobs to the printer, such as **print queue** management, and the transfer of print jobs from the print queue to the printer.

In the following lab, you will learn how to set up a computer as a file server. File sharing is an integral part of every network. Suppose you are the supervisor in a medical office. You may need to store patients' records in files on a single file server so that your employees can access those records. But you want to control access permissions to the files because some patient records are extremely confidential. How would you set up the file server so that your employees could access only certain files?

Lab 3-1: Creating a file server

In this lab, you will create a shared folder on your computer to act as a file service so that other users on the same LAN can access and modify files stored in the folder.

1. Open Windows Explorer and create a new folder named **Shared** on drive C.

2. Right-click the **Shared** folder and click **Sharing And Security**. This step displays the Sharing tab of the Shared Properties dialog box (Figure 3-1).

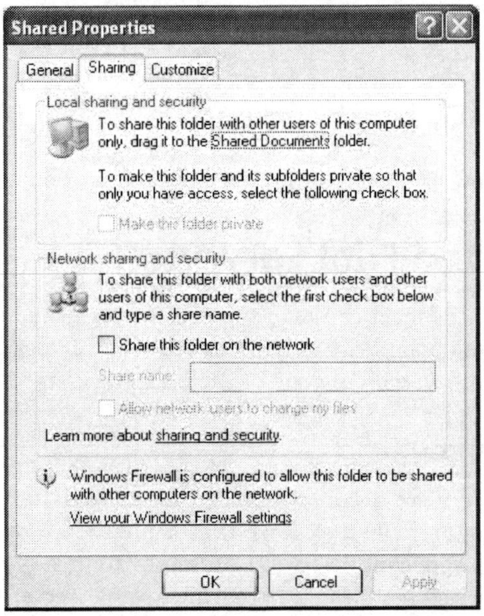

Figure 3-1: Shared Properties dialog box — Sharing tab

3. Select **Share This Folder On The Network**. Notice that the folder name *Shared* displays in the Share Name text box. The share name is the folder's network name. Anyone accessing your shared folder over the network will see it as "Shared."

   Note: This share name must be unique on your system. If another share exists with this name, enter a new name. By default, shares have read-only permission.

4. Select **Allow Network Users To Change My Files** to specify full permission for the share.

   Note: If the share is read-only, others can access your files, but they cannot modify the files or copy anything to your shared folder.

Note: Windows XP Professional defaults to a simplified file-sharing menu that allows either full control access or read-only access to a share. Share-level and NTFS file system (NTFS) permissions are not shown by default. To change this simplified menu to one that allows you to grant specific permissions to selected groups of users (granular permissions), select Start | Control Panel | Appearance and Themes | Folder Options. (If the Appearance and Themes link is not visible, click the Switch To Category View link.) When the Folder Options dialog box appears, click the View tab. Scroll down and find the Use Simple File Sharing (Recommended) check box, deselect it, then click OK. Right-click a shared folder and click Sharing And Security. You will see that the Sharing tab has changed, and that a new tab, Security, has been added. You can now exercise granular control over your shares.

5. Click **OK** to close the Shared Properties dialog box. Notice that the Shared folder icon displays with a hand under the folder (Figure 3-2). You can now "serve" files to other users over the network. Any files you put into the Shared folder are available to the network.

Figure 3-2: Shared folder named "Shared"

6. Double-click the **Shared** folder. Create a text document in the folder by right-clicking anywhere in the Shared folder window and selecting **New | Text Document**. Name the file with your name, such as *Sarah.txt*.

7. Open the text file, enter a line of text, then save and close the text file.

   At this point, other users on the same LAN can access the Shared folder on your hard disk drive as if it were a file server. For example, other users can view the contents of the folder, open the Sarah.txt file, modify it and then save it in the Shared folder. Other users can also copy and move files between the Shared folder and their own computers. Shared folders provide for a quick and efficient way to transfer files between computers on a LAN. Using shared folders is much simpler than sending documents by means of FTP or e-mail.

8. Close the Windows Explorer window.

   Using a file server is similar to accessing folders on your own computer. The only difference is that you must access the folders through the network. You can also back up documents on a file server. The simplicity and ease of use of file servers make them extremely popular on LANs.

Shared folders are commonly implemented on company LANs so that files are accessible to company employees and departments.

HTTP Server Essentials

The World Wide Web is a collection of computer systems running the HTTP service. (Remember that HTTP, on which the Web operates, is a TCP/IP application-layer protocol.) These computer systems (servers) act together as document delivery systems. Documents are delivered to systems running Web browsers (also called clients) as well as to user agents. These client systems request documents from HTTP servers, which are usually called Web servers. The documents that the server processes may be from a disk archive, or they may be created dynamically when the client requests them. The HTTP server and the Web browser are examples of client/server communications. A Web browser is a software application that interprets and displays HTML documents. Worldwide interaction between the HTTP server and the Web browser also exemplifies the hyper-distributed networking involved in Web-based networking.

A Web site is a collection of documents and applications that create documents. The site is organized around a Web server process, which runs as a daemon process on UNIX systems and as a service on Windows XP Professional systems. (You will learn more about daemons shortly.) The Web server process binds to TCP port 80 by default and listens for incoming requests from clients such as Web browsers. These requests are formed in a language called Hypertext Markup Language (HTML). The applications used by Web servers to create documents dynamically are called Common Gateway Interface (CGI) applications (or scripts).

NOTE:
Daemons will be presented later in this lesson.

Web server

The server has access to a set of documents that it may return to a client in response to an appropriate request. These documents are located in a mass storage device, such as a hard drive, in a specific location that the server can read. These documents can be in a wide range of formats. For example, the server probably has access to a large collection of HTML documents as well as the associated image files in a range of formats. In addition, the server may be able to supply many other multimedia documents, such as sound files and video clips.

HTTP servers and MIME

Multipurpose Internet Mail Extensions (MIME)
A protocol that enables operating systems to map file name extensions to corresponding applications. Also used by applications to automatically process files downloaded from the Internet.

An HTTP server can download any file type. Although a Web browser renders only certain types of images, HTTP can process a variety of file types. The **Multipurpose Internet Mail Extensions (MIME)** system allows HTTP and e-mail attachments to identify the files they must use. A version of MIME that encrypts MIME data, called **Secure MIME (S/MIME)**, is used for secure transmissions.

The different **MIME types** are classified under broad headings (text, image, application, audio and video), and then subclassified by exact type. For example, an HTML document has MIME type "text/html," whereas a plain text document has type "text/plain."

Secure MIME (S/MIME)
Secure version of MIME that adds encryption to MIME data.

Whenever data is passed between a Web server and a browser, the data is labeled with its MIME type. The recipient uses the MIME type to render the information. For example, when a Web server sends an HTML document to a browser, it labels the document with its MIME type (text/html) so the browser can display the document properly. When a Web server sends an Adobe Acrobat file (application/x-pdf) to a browser, the browser will open the correct plug-in (namely, Adobe Acrobat Reader) to view the file. A plug-in is a program installed as part of the browser to extend its basic functionality.

MIME type
Identifies the contents of a file in the MIME encoding system using a type/subtype format; examples are image/jpg and text/plain.

When a Web browser requests a server resource, the server deduces the resource's MIME type from the extension part of the document name. For example, the server understands a request for the Uniform Resource Locator (URL) http://www.machine.com/info.html as referring to a document of type text/html, and labels the document with that type when it returns the document to the browser. The correspondence between file name extensions and MIME types may be hard-wired into the server, or may be configurable.

NOTE:
A key point is the purpose of MIME and how it is used in HTTP and mail servers.

Images and MIME type

Similarly, if a Web server presents images, then it will use MIME to present it. If, for some reason, you need to present a nonstandard image format — in other words, one that was not Graphics Interchange Format (GIF), Joint Photographic Experts Group (JPEG) or

Portable Network Graphics (PNG) — you will need to define a MIME type to accommodate the proprietary format.

File storage

You should store all files away from the Web server's root unless you need to create a virtual directory. A virtual directory is a folder that resides on the same server or another server and acts as if it resided on the server's root. It hides the actual location and name of the original folder. You will learn more about virtual directories later in this lesson.

Naming the initial document

Although most servers allow you to define any name for the initial HTML document, most servers use index.html. So, when you want to create a page that will automatically render in a client's Web browser, you should discover the name that your server is configured to report. Other common initial document names include welcome.html, main.html, default.htm, default.html and default.asp.

Additional server considerations

NOTE:
This section on additional server considerations is important for you to understand. The topics covered are applicable to all servers, especially account access, permissions, logging, and monitoring server and network bandwidth use.

Following is a brief discussion of issues concerning the use of an HTTP or other type of server.

HTTP servers and the operating system

HTTP servers work closely with the computer's operating system. One way to describe their interaction is that an HTTP server resides "on top" of the other services that form the operating system. Some servers, such as Apache server and Microsoft Internet Information Services (IIS), typically work on only one type of operating system. Other HTTP servers, such as Zeus and Sun ONE (previously Netscape/iPlanet Enterprise Server), provide versions that will work with a variety of operating systems.

Server security and operating system security

permissions
Instructions given by an operating system or server (or a combination thereof) that restrict or allow access to system resources, such as files, user databases and system processes.

Most Web servers can restrict files, folders and directories by establishing **permissions**. Permissions include the ability to read a file (read permission), create or delete a file (write permission), execute programs (execute permission) or deny access (no access). Operating systems can also establish permissions.

For example, the Linux operating system can restrict access to a certain resource, such as a file or directory. Apache server (or any other server) can restrict access to a specific resource. Operating system permissions generally take precedence over those granted by an HTTP server. Sometimes, the operating system and HTTP server permissions should be combined to ensure that a folder is secure.

NOTE:
You should know the basic permissions: read, write, execute and no access.

However, permissions can also become confused. CGI scripts and programs (files), for example, require execute permission. Therefore, the folder in which a script resides must have execute permission, as well. Naturally, you must determine whether both the Web server and the operating system allow execute permission. If the operating system forbids all executable program files in that folder, the administrator must change this setting, even though the Web server has already given execute permission.

Access control

An important part of setting up and managing a Web server (or any other server type) is access control, which is similar to permissions. Most Web sites offer access to the general public; users do not need special permission to access such server resources. This type of access is often called anonymous access. However, some sites want to restrict access to some or all of their server resources. An Access Control List (ACL) defines the permissions for a resource by specifying which users and groups have access to the resource. For example, the Web site may offer certain documents only to registered or paying users. Alternatively, the site may offer access to personal information, which must be supplied only to the owner of that information. The traditional method of restricting access to server resources is based on a database of permitted users, who must supply a password to access particular server information. The database of permitted users may be:

- Users with accounts on the host system. IIS, for example, uses the system account database on the host computer as its database of permitted users.

- A special database managed by the server itself (for example, the National Center for Supercomputing Applications [NCSA] server).

The second method separates people with permission to access Web server information from those with more global permission on the host system. Because thousands of users may be allowed to access information, the second method is much better for restricting access.

 Web servers that limit access to resources need a method for users to identify themselves; usually some form of password is required. Password-based access to the server is vulnerable to password sniffing, unless the server uses a method for exchanging encrypted passwords. Password sniffing is a method of intercepting the transmission of a password during the authentication process.

Access control and the server account

The access control restrictions discussed previously are enforced in the following two stages:

1. The Web server process checks to see whether certain actions are allowed, based on its configuration information.

2. The operating system enforces restrictions on actions the Web server process can perform.

The operating system restrictions are based on the fact that the Web server process is owned by a user account on the host computer, and is subject to limitations imposed on that account. For example, if the Web server process is owned by an account called "http" and the http user does not have read permission in a certain directory, the server cannot access that directory, regardless of the server's internal configuration. In general, the restrictions imposed by the operating system are more reliable than those imposed by the Web server alone.

To take advantage of the security mechanisms provided by the operating system, the Web server process must be owned by an account with the fewest permissions needed for it to perform its task. In particular, the server should not be owned by a super-user or administrator account because a Web server process with these permissions is unconstrained by the operating system. For example, people use e-mail every day to communicate. Using an e-mail account requires a user name and password in conjunction with authentication (as you learned earlier, authentication is the ability to verify a person's identity). Remember that the Web server may demand permissions that the operating system may deny, especially when using CGI scripts.

Aliases and virtual directories

As part of their configuration options, most Web servers allow flexible mapping of URL path names to file names. This kind of mapping has various names, including virtual directories and aliases. Some of the advantages of flexible mapping of URL path names to file names include the following examples:

- The more flexible the mapping from URL path names to file names, the more freedom the administrator has to arrange files on the disk.

- If a set of documents may be reasonably accessed under several URL path names, all these URL path names can be mapped to the same file names.

For example, suppose you want a server to be able to supply a collection of documents called doc1.html, doc2.html, and so forth, located in the directory /home/sales/docs. The server root directory is /usr/local/etc/httpd, but you want browsers to access the file doc1.html under the URL http://www.ciw-certified.com/sales/doc1.html. To allow this access, you must configure the server to map the URL path /sales/doc1.html to the actual file path /home/sales/docs, instead of to /usr/local/etc/httpd/docs/sales /doc1.html.

Logging

NOTE:
Logging can be important to both management and security control, but can require significant disk space on a very active Web site.

Web servers and a majority of server types generate a log of the requests they handle. In addition to helping monitor correct server operation, these logs eventually contain information about who uses the server resources, which resources are most popular and how users initially find the site. The following three types of information are usually collected in server logs:

- **Access data** — Each time a client issues an HTTP command to the server, the command is logged.

- **Referrer data** — Part of the information transmitted by a browser to a server is the URL at which the browser is pointing when it makes the request. This information may be logged to indicate how users enter the site.

- **Error data** — Server errors (including improperly formatted HTTP requests, dropped TCP connections and access violations) are logged to help monitor server operations.

Monitoring server and network bandwidth use

Monitoring server and network bandwidth use is key to maintaining consistent performance. It allows network administrators to identify network bottlenecks in a timely manner. Bottlenecks usually occur when a server or network is flooded with traffic and cannot perform at acceptable levels.

Most network users are not tolerant of network servers that perform inconsistently — fast one day and slow the next. So the first objective is to bring about consistency in the performance. However, to detect inconsistencies, an administrator must have something to measure against, namely a baseline of normal network performance.

baseline
A recording of network activity, obtained through documentation and monitoring, that serves as an example for comparing future network activity.

A **baseline** is a recording of network activity, obtained through documentation and monitoring, that serves as an example for comparing future network activity. Baselines should be recorded when a network is running correctly. If problems are introduced to the network, the new network behavior can be compared with the baseline. Baselines can be used to determine bottlenecks, identify heavy traffic patterns, and analyze daily network use and protocol patterns.

The Windows XP Professional Performance Monitor can determine a baseline for the number of packets per second sent to a system over a network. Performance Monitor allows you to collect data for a particular variable over time. This baseline will allow you to determine the amount of network traffic sent to your system during normal traffic periods. It can also determine a baseline for processor (CPU) and memory use on the server.

During peak network traffic periods, or when performance is noticeably slower, Performance Monitor can be used to collect data and compare it with the baseline. If the new data shows a significant increase in network traffic, processor or memory use, changes may be required. For instance, a faster processor or more RAM may need to be installed on the server. You may need to increase your network bandwidth by upgrading the network from Ethernet to fast Ethernet, or replace a problem hub with a switch.

Server and network monitoring software such as Performance Monitor are essential to monitoring server and network bandwidth use.

Common Web servers

NOTE:
Additional information is provided about popular Web servers later in this lesson.

The most common Web servers include Apache server (*www.apache.org*), Microsoft IIS and Sun Java System Web Server (*www.sun.com*). Originally, Apache server operated exclusively on UNIX systems. However, in 1998 it was ported to Windows servers. As of this writing, Apache servers represent more than half of those used on the Internet.

Each of these Web servers implements the topics covered in the preceding section, which includes account access, permissions and logging. All servers can be monitored to determine their system and network bandwidth use.

Server-side languages

Web servers often run programs to help enhance a Web page or provide access to database servers. These programs are called server-side applications. Examples of server-side technologies include:

- **JavaServer Pages (JSP)** — Sun's solution. You can learn more about JSP at *www.sun.com*.

- **Active Server Pages (ASP) and .NET** — Microsoft's server-side scripting solutions. ASP is an older solution. You can learn more about ASP and .NET at *www.microsoft.com*.

- **PHP Hypertext Preprocessor (PHP)** — An open-source solution. You can learn more about PHP at *www.php.net*.

Each of these languages can be used to implement CGI.

Open Database Connectivity (ODBC)

data source name (DSN)
A text string that is used to reference the data source by application programs.

As you learned earlier, ODBC is a standard developed by Microsoft that allows databases created by various vendors to communicate with one another. ODBC is often used with server-side languages. It is also used by database servers. When creating an entry in ODBC, you need to register the database in ODBC and provide a **data source name (DSN)**, which contains all the necessary connectivity information. Specific information you need to provide includes the vendor's database driver, the name of the database, a user ID and the location of the database. Several types of DSN exist. The most common are the system DSN, which all users can employ, and a user DSN, which is designed for use only by a specific user.

Database Server

A database is a file that stores information in a series of tables and columns. Tables in a database contain fields that allow data to be read and cross-referenced. Many different types of databases exist, including flat file databases (for example, the Windows registry) and relational databases. A relational database allows you to manipulate information contained in tables and columns. All database servers present relational databases, and make it possible for remote individuals (for example, users with Web browsers) and hosts (for example, Web servers) to access the data. A database server can be installed on a dedicated system or on the same system as a Web server. In either case, a Web server is often configured to present HTML/XHTML pages that present information obtained from a relational database.

Database servers and the Structured Query Language (SQL)

Structured Query Language (SQL)
A language used to create and maintain professional, high-performance corporate databases.

All database servers use the **Structured Query Language (SQL)** to create, maintain and query databases. Commands such as "select," "from" and "join" can be used to create, maintain and manipulate tables. Often, a Web site administrator will need to use SQL to ensure that a Web page presents valid database information on a page.

Examples of database servers include:

- Oracle (*www.oracle.com*).

- IBM DB2 (*www.ibm.com*).

- Microsoft SQL Server (*www.microsoft.com*).

Proxy Server

OBJECTIVE:
3.4.2: Common Internet services/protocols

A proxy server is an intermediary between a network host and other hosts outside the network. Its main functions are to provide enhanced security, manage TCP/IP addresses and speed access to the Internet by providing caching server functions for frequently used documents.

In a network setting, a proxy server replaces the network IP address with another, contingent address. This process effectively hides the actual IP address from the rest of the Internet, thereby protecting the entire network.

Proxy servers can provide the following additional services:

NOTE:
You need to understand that a proxy server is often used to cache Web pages on larger networks.

- **Caching of Web documents** — If corporate users access information on a Web server from the Internet, that information is cached to the local proxy server. This caching allows anyone on the corporate intranet to access the same information from the local system instead of repeatedly downloading the files from the Internet. This feature reduces the amount of network traffic produced on the Internet, which leads to improved performance for the corporate intranet and the Internet.

- **Corporate firewall access** — A proxy server can provide safe passage for corporate users to the Internet through a firewall, allowing protected use of HTTP and FTP. You will learn more about firewalls later in the course.

- **Filtering client transactions** — A proxy can control access to remote Web servers and their resources by filtering client transactions. Filtering is accomplished by limiting or denying access to specific URLs, specific host IP addresses, domain names, host or computer names, Web contents and specific users. For example, you can deny access by anyone in a company to http://www.nonsense.com/ by specifying that URL in a proxy server's configuration. You can also deny access _from_ a particular computer within a company, using the computer's name or IP address to limit access. In addition, you can deny access to an individual by specifying that person's user name.

- **Transaction logging** — Generally, a proxy server supports transaction logging. Network administrators can track client activity and customize which data to record. Some of the data that can be logged includes accessed URLs, dates and times, and the byte counts of all data that has been transferred. Information on routing and success of a transaction can also be logged and used to evaluate network performance.

- **Securing internal hosts** — A proxy server can help isolate internal systems so that they cannot be as easily attacked from systems based on the Internet.

NOTE:
Open the Network And Internet Connections window of the Control Panel, click Internet Options, then click the Connections tab. Next, click the LAN Settings button to open the window in which you can enter proxy settings. Similar windows are available in Mozilla Firefox and other browsers.

Proxy server configuration

If your network uses a proxy server, you must ensure that all the clients are properly configured. For example, to browse the Web, you must enter the correct address of that proxy server into your browser. Otherwise, the proxy server will ignore any requests you make.

Furthermore, you must configure every application to work with your proxy server, including Web browsers, Telnet applications and FTP programs. Otherwise, not all applications will be able to access outside networks. Browsers from both Mozilla and Microsoft provide proxy server configuration, and you can obtain third-party programs that will allow almost any application to work properly with a proxy server.

Mail Server

OBJECTIVE:
3.4.2: Common Internet services/protocols

A mail server stores and/or forwards e-mail messages using several protocols, including SMTP, POP3 and IMAP. As you learned earlier, these three protocols all reside at the application layer of the OSI/RM.

SMTP is responsible solely for sending e-mail messages. In UNIX, the sendmail program activates in response to a command and sends the requested message.

 Do not confuse SMTP with the protocols that store and access mail. SMTP only sends the e-mail message. If you are using UNIX, the sendmail program uses SMTP to relay the message to the receiver. If you are using Windows XP, you will use a program such as Microsoft Exchange Server, or one from another vendor.

Two methods are used to store and access e-mail messages. The first is POP3. POP3 servers store and forward e-mail messages to the host. For example, if you were to send an e-mail message, the message would be stored in the appropriate mail server until the recipient downloaded it from the server. The POP3 server responds to a request, asks for a password, and then forwards the messages immediately.

IMAP, the second method, handles messages in a more sophisticated manner because it allows a user to browse and manage files remotely, whereas a POP3 server forces a user to download files before reading, deleting or otherwise managing them.

Popular mail servers include Netscape Messaging Server and Microsoft Exchange Server. The former supports Windows XP, UNIX and NetWare platforms, whereas the latter is available only for Windows XP.

Mail servers and MIME

NOTE:
Make sure you understand the function of MIME, and understand that it can be used on both HTTP and mail servers.

MIME is commonly used to transmit files with e-mail. For instance, you use MIME to attach a GIF image or a Microsoft Word document to an e-mail message. MIME identifies a file type, encodes the file and decodes it at the receiving end so it will display properly. MIME performs these steps by adding a header to each file. The MIME header contains the encoding method and the type of data contained within.

The identity of a file is determined by the MIME type. As discussed earlier, the different MIME types are classified under broad headings (text, image, application, audio and video), and then subclassified by exact type. E-mail typically uses MIME for non-text file transfers. For example, a GIF file is MIME type image/gif.

Whenever data is passed between an e-mail sender and recipient, the data is labeled with its MIME type. The recipient uses the MIME type to render the information. For example, when an e-mail client sends a QuickTime video to a recipient, it labels the file with its MIME type (video/quicktime) so the recipient can execute the file properly. The same procedure is used by a Web server to transmit files to browser clients.

Unusual documents or graphic formats may not be defined by MIME types. In this case, you must manually associate a file with the appropriate program. For example, you may receive a configuration (CFG) file type attachment that you cannot open; you may not have the program needed to run or read it, or a MIME type may not have been defined. In either case, you can save the file to your Desktop, right-click the file, and click the Open With option. Choose the proper application to run the file, and the file will execute. If you do not have the proper application, you need to install the application on your computer to run the file.

To learn more about MIME types, visit the MIME Information Page at:

www.hunnysoft.com/mime

Problems with mail servers

Mail servers can experience various problems, including the following:

- A virus or worm attack. A virus is a program that replicates itself on computer systems, usually through executable software, and causes system damage.

- The e-mail server may be running low on RAM or disk space.

Sometimes, however, problems with other network devices can slow e-mail. For example, if you experience slow e-mail, a firewall or other intermediate device may be creating a bottleneck.

Instant Messaging (IM)

OBJECTIVE:
3.4.2: Common Internet services/protocols

Instant messaging (IM) is a computer-based method of communication that typically runs as a service on a mail server. You can use IM to type and view messages sent to one or more recipients, and view the responses immediately. Unlike e-mail, which can be sent whether your recipient is online or not, instant messages can be sent only to contacts who are currently online — that is, logged on to an IM service.

To use IM, you must install a client on your system and then register for service. Instant messaging allows you to specify a list of contacts (known as a buddy list or a contact list) with whom you would like to communicate. When you log on to your IM service, the status (online or offline) of each of the contacts in your list will display. To open an IM session, you specify an online contact and open a window where you and your contact can type messages that both of you can see.

NOTE:
ICQ stands for "I Seek You." ICQ servers use the proprietary protocol ICQv5 for communication.

In June 1998, America Online (AOL) acquired Mirabilis.

Instant messaging became very popular in November 1996, when a company called Mirabilis introduced a free IM utility known as ICQ. When you logged on to your ICQ service, your client communicated with an ICQ server, sending it your IP address and the number of the port on your computer that is assigned to the ICQ client. Your client also sent the names of everyone on your contact list to the ICQ server. The ICQ server then created a temporary file with the connection information for you and the list of your contacts.

The server also reported those contacts who were logged on. The server sent a message back to your ICQ client with the connection information for your online contacts and displayed their status as "online." The server also sent a message to your online contacts, notifying them that you were online.

Today, several IM services, clients and servers are used. Yahoo!, MSN and AOL use their own proprietary protocols and clients. Instant messaging clients are available from a variety of sources, including the following:

- AOL Instant Messenger (*www.aim.com*)

- Miranda Instant Messenger (*www.miranda-im.org*).

- Yahoo! Messenger (*http://messenger.yahoo.com*)

- Windows Live Messenger (*http://get.live.com/messenger/overview*)

- Windows Messenger (comes with Windows XP and uses the same protocol as Windows Live Messenger)

- ICQ Instant Messenger (*http://web.icq.com*)

GAIM is a multiprotocol instant messaging client for Linux, BSD, MacOS X and Windows. It is compatible with AIM, ICQ, Windows Live Messenger, Yahoo!, Internet Relay Chat (IRC), Jabber, Gadu-Gadu and Zephyr networks. GAIM allows you to perform IM with users at various other networks (such as AOL, Yahoo! and MSN) simultaneously. You can download GAIM for Windows at *http://sourceforge.net*.

Mailing List Server

OBJECTIVE:
3.4.2: Common Internet services/protocols

A mailing list server is a standard SMTP server that can automatically forward an e-mail message to every member on a distribution list. Some mailing list servers, such as LISTSERV (*www.listserv.net* or *www.lsoft.com*), are designed for this purpose. Other SMTP servers, such as Microsoft Exchange Server, can be configured as mailing list servers.

Another name for a mailing list server is "reflector." An autoresponder is not a mailing list server; rather, it is a technology you can enable on a Web server. You can configure a Web server to automatically use an SMTP server to answer an inquiry or order from a user.

A mailing list server allows people to work together even though their e-mail accounts reside on different e-mail servers across the Internet.

For example, suppose James establishes a mailing list server for a company project. The account to which everyone will send e-mail messages concerning this project will be project@company.com. This account and the distribution list both reside on the mailing list server. James' e-mail address, james@fender.com, is on the mailing list server's distribution list, as are the following: patrick@gibson.com, joseph@hamer.com, jill@40.com and susan@metallica.com. If Jill were to send an e-mail message to project@company.com, then James, Patrick, Joseph and Susan would receive exact copies of this e-mail message. In fact, the server would also send Jill a copy because she is also on the list of recipients. The server will forward this message to every person on the list James has configured, as shown in Figure 3-3.

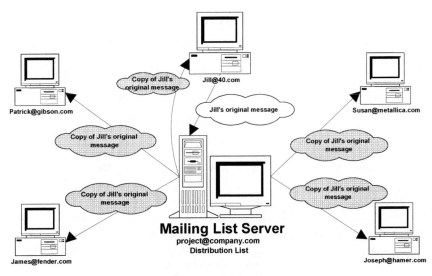

Figure 3-3: Mailing list server

In effect, a mailing list server allows you to imitate a newsgroup. The main difference is that any e-mail message you send does not remain persistent on a central server for a given time. Mailing lists have become popular because many users consider e-mail messages easier to manage than newsgroup postings.

Mailing List Manager (MLM)

The interface that allows you to configure a mailing list server is often called a Mailing List Manager (MLM). Using an MLM, you can customize the behavior of the mailing list server. For example, you can configure a moderated list, which means that a designated individual will screen all submissions before they are sent to everyone on the list.

Public and private mailing lists

You can create public or private mailing lists with a mailing list server. Examples of public mailing lists include the well-known LISTSERV and Majordomo groups. Topics covered by such lists range from aviation to zoology. You can configure a public mailing list server to allow anyone to join the list at any time.

The specific syntax and information requirements differ from one public mailing list server to another. Most servers allow users to join a mailing list automatically by having them send an e-mail message with the word "join" or "subscribe" in the body of the message or the header. Users can unsubscribe from a mailing list by sending an e-mail message with words such as "unsubscribe" or "remove" in the message or header.

Go to the LISTSERV Web site at *www.lsoft.com* to view a comprehensive list of the LISTSERV mailing groups.

In a business setting, mailing list servers are generally not configured to allow automatic subscriptions. Advanced mailing list servers also allow you to encrypt e-mail messages, giving you reasonable assurance that no one can read your messages without authorization.

Mailing list server vendors

Following are several popular mailing list server vendors:

- Sun ONE Messaging Servers (*www.sun.com/software*)

- LISTSERV (*www.listserv.net* or *www.lsoft.com*)

- Microsoft Exchange Server (*www.microsoft.com*)

- SparkLIST (*www.sparklist.com*)

Often, mailing list servers come bundled with other products.

Media Server

A media server offers **streaming audio and video** over a network. This type of server is suited for intranets as well as the Internet. More popular vendors include RealNetworks RealPlayer 10 (*www.real.com*), Microsoft Windows Media Services (*www.microsoft.com*) and Netscape Media Server (*www.netscape.com*).

streaming audio and video
Audio and video files that travel over a network in real time.

buffer
A cache of memory used by a computer to store frequently used data. Buffers allow faster access times.

These servers are useful because businesses and other organizations use the Internet to conduct long-distance conference calls as personally as possible. Generally, these servers use UDP ports and **buffers** to achieve the effect of a real-time connection.

Remember that UDP is a connectionless protocol, so media servers must find some way to simulate a continuous connection. Some of the latest developments attempt to improve transmission quality by paralleling UDP streams. These strategies help enhance the illusion of a real-time connection.

DNS Server

Invented by Paul Mockapetris in 1984, DNS is a mechanism used on the Internet to translate host computer names into IP addresses. For example, CIW Certification has a Web server that can be accessed using the FQDN of *www.CIW-certified.com*. The same Web server can also be reached by entering the IP address *http:// 64.128.206.9*. Both the name and the IP address refer to the same Web server, but the former is much easier to remember. Without DNS, users would be forced to enter long numerical strings every time they needed access to any part of the Internet.

NOTE:
You need a general understanding of what DNS servers do and when they are appropriate as part of a network. DNS was introduced in an earlier lesson.

DNS servers, also called name servers, contain the server application that supports name-to-address translation. You were introduced to DNS servers earlier in the course. Typically, the system on which the name server resides is called the name server system.

DNS is a decentralized system: It does not depend on one source for updates, and one server does not store all the data. Instead, DNS is a distributed database that exists on name servers across the Internet.

As you have already learned, the ICANN is responsible for DNS management.

Hosts file

Until DNS was implemented, a single file known as the hosts table was managed and updated by the Stanford Research Institute Network Information Center (SRI-NIC). Whenever network administrators needed the latest hosts table for their name servers, they downloaded it from the SRI-NIC FTP server. As the Internet grew, this file became very large and difficult to manage, and no longer provided an effective way to distribute name-to-address data.

The hosts file on your computer (which you were introduced to earlier in the course) is similar to the hosts table used earlier for the Internet. The hosts file is a simple text file that is referenced locally by applications and commands for name-to-address resolution. The format for entries is as follows:

```
Internet-address   official-host-name aliases
```

For the hosts file to provide local diagnostics, the loopback address (127.0.0.1) must be included. After the loopback address is entered, you can add any IP address and corresponding host name that you require (the number sign [#] is used for comments). For example:

```
# List the loopback address.

127.0.0.1      localhost

# You can list as many IP-to-host addresses as you need.
# These entries will
# override your computer's DNS settings.

192.168.3.15   student15      patrick
```

In Windows XP, the hosts file can be opened with Notepad. It is located at:

```
%systemroot\system32\drivers\etc
```

DNS hierarchy

domain name space
The three-level domain name hierarchy (root-level, top-level and second-level domains) that forms the DNS.

DNS is hierarchical and distributed. It consists of three levels — root-level, top-level and second-level domains — and is often referred to as the **domain name space**. Figure 3-4 shows the domain name space.

NOTE:
You need to understand DNS hierarchy.

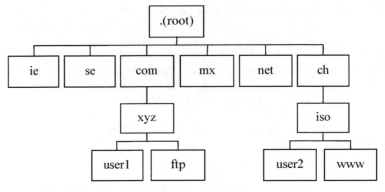

Figure 3-4: Domain name space

Following is a description of each level in the DNS hierarchy.

Root-level domain

The root-level domain is the top of the hierarchy. It contains entries for each top-level domain. The root-level domain is updated daily and replicated on root domain servers across the Internet. It is expressed by a period (.). This period is usually removed from the end of domain names (for example, *www.company.com* instead of *www.company.com.*).

Top-level domain

The top-level domain is one level below the root-level domain. It consists of categories found at the end of domain names (such as .com or .uk). It divides domains into organizations (.org), businesses (.com), countries (.uk) and other categories. Each top-level domain has a master server that contains entries for all registered second-level domains (such as company.com).

The top-level Internet domains are described in Tables 3-1 through 3-3. The first seven domains are associated with the United States and are assigned by the Internet Network Information Center (InterNIC). However, the majority of top-level domains are country codes. Each country assigns domain names using its own standards. The third type of top-level Internet domains (shown in Table 3-3) is designated by category; these domains were recently approved by the ICANN.

Table 3-1: Top-level Internet domains — original

Top-Level Domain — Original	Description
com	Commercial organizations
edu	Educational institutions
gov	Government institutions
mil	Military
net	Network support centers (ISPs)
org	Other organizations (originally nonprofit)
int	International organizations (rarely used; country codes used instead)

Table 3-2: Top-level Internet domains — ISO country codes (samples)

Top-Level Domain — Country Codes	Description
au	Australia
ca	Canada
ch	Switzerland
fr	France
ie	Ireland
mx	Mexico
se	Sweden
uk	United Kingdom
us	United States

Table 3-3: Top-level Internet domains — categories

Top-Level Domain — Categories	Description
aero	Travel industry
biz	Businesses
coop	Cooperatives
info	Content and research-related sites
museum	Museums
name	Personal Web addresses
pro	Professional

Second-level domain

The second-level domain is one level below the top-level domain. Second-level domains include the businesses and institutions that register their domain names with the top-level domains (through their respective registrars).

Second-level domains include registered names such as the following:

- iso.ch

- amazon.com

Second-level domains can also be categories of top-level domains. For example, the United States domain (us) is further categorized into a second-level domain for each state, such as California:

- ca.us

Companies and academic institutions in the United Kingdom (and most other countries) are also categorized, as shown:

- co.uk

- ac.uk

NOTE:
Subdomains are somewhat common in directory-based enterprise networks.

Finally, second-level domains can be divided into subdomains. For example, a subdomain of company.com may be as follows:

- sales.company.com

A host computer of that subdomain may be identified as follows:

- user1.sales.company.com

DNS components

DNS consists of the following two key components:

- **Name server** — a server that supports name-to-address translation and runs the DNS service.

- **Name resolver** — software that uses the services of one or more name servers to resolve an unknown request. For example, if a host requests www.novell.com, and the DNS server does not have the name information, it will use name resolver software to ask another name server on the DNS hierarchy. DNS clients and servers use name resolver software.

In UNIX, the resolver is actually a group of routines that reside in the C library */usr/lib/libc.a*. In Windows, the TCP/IP properties contain a DNS tab that must be configured with the IP addresses of the DNS servers.

DNS server types

zone file
A file containing a set of instructions for resolving a specific domain name into its numerical IP address.

DNS follows the standard client/server model: The client makes a request, and the server attempts to fulfill that request. DNS servers can fill several different roles, depending on the organization's needs. No matter what role the server takes, the client must specify the name server's domain name or IP address. The following server types are included in the DNS model:

- **Root server** — Root servers can identify all top-level domains on the Internet. If a client requests information about a host in another domain, any server (except a secondary server, which will be introduced shortly) can communicate that request to the root server. Most server administrators will never configure a root server.

- **Primary server** — A primary server is the authority for a domain and maintains the DNS databases for its domain. It is the first DNS server in a domain. Companies and ISPs that implement their own DNS and participate on the Internet require a primary server. Primary servers are also called master servers.

- **Secondary server** — A secondary server receives its authority and database from the primary server. Secondary servers are used by server administrators to provide fault tolerance, load distribution, and easier remote name resolution for the primary DNS server. Secondary servers are also called slave servers.

- **Caching-only server** — A caching-only server is one that does not contain its own **zone file**, but receives entries from other DNS servers.

- **Forwarding server** — A forwarding server is one that receives requests, and then forwards them to other servers.

UNIX name daemon (named)

The name daemon allows a UNIX computer to function as a DNS server. The most common implementation of UNIX DNS is the Berkeley Internet Name Domain (BIND). Microsoft DNS is based on the BIND implementation, but does not adhere strictly to it. UNIX BIND servers are the most widely used DNS servers on the Internet. You will learn more about daemons shortly.

DNS records

NOTE:
You need to be familiar with these basic DNS records.

Every domain consists of DNS records. A DNS record is an entry in a DNS database (on a primary server) that provides additional routing and resolution information. Many different types of records can be configured, but only a few are needed for full address resolution and routing. Table 3-4 lists the most common DNS records.

Table 3-4: Common DNS records

DNS Record	Function
Name Server (NS)	Identifies DNS servers for the DNS domain.
Start Of Authority (SOA)	Identifies the DNS server that is the best source of information for the DNS domain. Because several backup DNS servers may exist, this record identifies the primary server for the specified DNS domain.
Address (A)	The most commonly used record; associates a host to an IP address. For example, you can establish an association between an IP address and a Web server by creating an address record.
Canonical Name (CNAME)	Creates an alias for a specified host. For example, the name of a WWW server is server1.company.com (Web servers are commonly named WWW). A CNAME record creates a "WWW" alias to the server1.company.com host so it can also be accessed at *www.company.com.*
Mail Exchanger (MX)	Identifies a server used to process and deliver e-mail messages for the domain.

These records are the most widely used. Many other types of records are used with DNS for different functions.

DNS hierarchy example

NOTE:
See **Activity 3-1: Diagramming DNS server relationships.**

You work at company XYZ with the domain name xyz.com. You send an e-mail message to a person at the International Organization for Standardization (ISO), which has the domain name iso.ch. Before your computer sends the message, it needs the IP address of the iso.ch mail server. Following are the steps taken in this process:

1. Your computer sends a DNS request to your configured name server.

2. Your name server queries itself for the requested entry. If an entry does not exist in its cache, it will forward the request to the Internet's root servers.

3. A root server will send your name server the reference information for the requested domain's (iso.ch) primary and secondary name servers.

4. Your name server will query the iso.ch primary (or secondary) name server for the requested record. The request will be fulfilled with the iso.ch name server sending the requested IP address.

5. Your name server will provide your computer with your request's IP address.

The *nslookup* command

NOTE:
You need to know how this command is used and be able to recognize the command output. The nslookup utility is commonly used to test communication with and operation of DNS servers.

The `nslookup` command can be used to query Internet domain name servers to learn name-to-IP-address mappings. This command is used for any system (for example, a workstation or a server). The user has the option to request a specific name server to provide information about a given host or to get a list of all hosts in a given domain. The `nslookup` command is usually used at a command prompt or a UNIX/Linux terminal. By default, the `nslookup` command will query the default DNS server used by the system you are using.

You can use `nslookup` as a one-time command or as an interactive command. When used as a one-time command, it will return information for only one system or zone. Following is the syntax for using `nslookup` as a one-time command:

```
nslookup options address
```

Following is an example of a one-time use of `nslookup`:

```
nslookup www.ciw-certified.com
```

The output displays the following results, depending on your system's DNS configuration:

```
Server:    ns1.sprintlink.net
Name:      www.ciw-certified.com
Address:   64.128.206.9
```

You can also use `nslookup` interactively. At a command prompt or terminal, simply issue the following command:

```
nslookup
```

You will then be placed into an nslookup session, which allows you to make queries for multiple systems. You can also use an interactive session to list the contents of entire zones (if allowed), and switch from your default DNS server to another DNS server (if allowed). Your command prompt or terminal will change from a standard prompt to the > (greater than) character. You can then issue commands to determine name resolution. Following is an example of a typical nslookup session:

```
>james
    Server:    192.168.2.5
    Address:   192.168.2.5#53

    Name:      james.stangernet.com
    Address:   192.168.2.5
               www.ciw-certified.com
    Server:    192.168.2.5
    Address:   192.168.2.5#53

    Non-authoritative answer:
    Name:      www.ciw-certified.com
    Address:   64.128.206.9
    exit
C:\>
```

In the preceding session, the user searched for a system named james, which is contained in his server's DNS zone. If this name was not contained in the zone, an error message would be displayed. The second query was for the system named www.ciw-certified.com. Notice that the `exit` command allows you to end an nslookup session and return to your command prompt or terminal. In many systems, nslookup has been deprecated and replaced with commands such as `host` or `dig`.

The phrase "non-authoritative answer" can mean either of the following:

- The DNS server that returned this information is not authoritative for the system you have asked about (for example, it is a secondary DNS server). A primary DNS server that has not been appropriately configured may also return this message.

- The DNS server that has given this information has been configured as a secondary DNS server.

To obtain a list of all nodes in a given domain, such as ciw-certified.com, execute the following sequence of commands:

```
nslookup

> ls ciw-certified.com
```

You must have permission to list the domain with the DNS administrator. If not, you will receive an error that says: "***Can't list domain: Bad error value."

In some operating systems (for example, Red Hat Linux), the nslookup command has been deprecated in favor of the host and dig commands.

Movie Time!

Watch the following CIW v5 Foundations Movie to learn even more about this topic.

Using DNS (approx. playing time: 14:00)

All movie clips are © 2007 LearnKey, Inc.

In the following lab, you will use the `nslookup` command for both a one-time and an interactive session. Suppose you are on the IT staff of a company that sells hair removal products through an electronic storefront, and you have been asked to test the operation of the default DNS server. You also want to obtain a list of all nodes in a particular domain. How would you use the nslookup utility to perform these tasks?

Lab 3-2: Using the nslookup utility

In this lab, you will use the nslookup utility.

Note: Your firewall may forbid nslookup queries.

1. Using the Start menu, select **Start | Run** to display the Run dialog box, type *cmd*, then press **ENTER** to open a command prompt window.

2. Type *nslookup www.ciw-certified.com*, then press **ENTER** to issue a one-time command.

   Record the information you found in the space provided:

   _____

   _____

3. Type *nslookup* and press **ENTER** to begin an interactive session.

4. Conduct searches for the following systems:

```
ftp.microsoft.com
ftp.redhat.com
www.bbc.com
```

5. Type *exit* and press **ENTER** to end the session.

6. Close the command prompt window.

In this lab, you used the `nslookup` command. You issued a one-time command and conducted an interactive session.

FTP Server

Most of the Internet server suites include an FTP server. However, you should always check to see whether an FTP server is included, or whether you need to obtain a separate FTP daemon or service. Even though FTP is one of the oldest protocols, it remains one of the most consistently used of all the servers discussed in this lesson. FTP is different from SMTP because FTP allows you to transfer files between servers in real time, and to transfer much larger files.

In most situations, if you have a file approaching 2 megabytes (MB), you should transfer it by means of FTP, because sending such a large file through a mail server slows that server and the network. In addition, if the mail server has difficulty transferring a large file, it will no longer forward that message. However, it will not delete the message; the message will remain in the e-mail server queue until a server administrator deletes it. With FTP, on the other hand, if a problem occurs with the file, you need only resend it. Thus, little administrative intervention is needed.

Finally, sending files by means of FTP is faster than using e-mail.

Logging and access control

FTP servers log all traffic (which is usually anonymous). You can consult the FTP server logs to determine the amount of traffic.

Although you can password-protect an FTP site, many administrators choose to allow anonymous access. To strengthen security, they ensure that no sensitive information is kept on the FTP server. One reason FTP servers generally use anonymous logon access is that the protocol requires passwords to be sent unencrypted. This openness allows hackers to obtain passwords with special programs called packet sniffers, or protocol analyzers.

You will learn more about FTP server security later in the course.

News Server

News servers use the Network News Transfer Protocol (NNTP). Like the standard office bulletin board, a news server allows users to post information in an easily accessible location. Using a news server, you can secure specific newsgroups, or (as in the case of the popular **Usenet** newsgroups) you can leave them open to the public. One of the most important uses for a newsgroup is to provide a forum for groups to communicate while developing projects.

newsgroup
On Usenet, a subject or other topical interest group whose members exchange ideas and opinions. Participants post and receive messages via a news server.

A network news service consists of objects, both physical and virtual. A service can usually be configured to accept file attachments, which can allow members to exchange files as part of a public conversation. These files will remain persistent for a specified period, creating a message-based forum. The news server thus allows a company to document a project and enhance collaboration.

The newsgroup's name is also its network address, written in a hierarchy index form. For example, rec.sport.football.college is a **newsgroup** with the topic of college football, whereas rec.sport.soccer is about soccer. Both hierarchies begin with "rec" (recreation) and "sport" before subdividing into different names of sports.

NOTE:
You need a general understanding of the function of a news server.

To read a newsgroup, the user opens a news reader software program, such as that found in Microsoft Outlook Express or the Mozilla Thunderbird newsgroup news client. The news client locates the news server containing the newsgroup and requests access. After access is granted, the client can access the newsgroups on the news server.

When one newsgroup server communicates with another to gain access to the central newsgroup files, the action is called a newsfeed.

Most Internet newsgroups are generated and maintained by contributors. Generally, whoever maintains a newsgroup charges no access fees and has no formal means of enforcing standards for articles. Contributors often identify themselves only by an e-mail address.

Newsgroup policies

The news server helps organize resources with the emphasis on distributing and locating information rather than owning or controlling it. Following are the basic policies of this legacy:

- Usenet is a public collection of newsgroups originally developed in the university community, with rules and procedures based on academic freedom and peer review. For example, users can call for a vote on banning offensive material, but lack the means to enforce a ban.

- Public newsgroups have no restrictions on access. Private newsgroups are restricted to specific users. Secure newsgroups encrypt articles transmitted between users and servers. Usenet newsgroups are always nonsecure, reflecting the academic culture of open dissemination.

- Moderated newsgroups carry only articles approved by a moderator. Unmoderated newsgroups operate without restrictions on content.

- Intranet and extranet newsgroups can help a company develop and track projects. Often, these groups are password-protected so that only specified users can gain access.

Newsgroup security

Secure Sockets Layer (SSL)
A protocol that provides authentication and encryption, used by most servers for secure exchanges over the Internet. Superseded by Transport Layer Security (TLS).

Many administrators use news servers to create secure newsgroups. You can achieve security by enabling user-specific password protection, or by means of a **Secure Sockets Layer (SSL)** session. Although both of these solutions are secure, an SSL session provides greater security. To enable an SSL session, you need to obtain a certificate that enables encryption. You can obtain a certificate from a company such as VeriSign, or configure and use a certificate server.

Certificate Server

OBJECTIVE:
3.4.2: Common
Internet
services/protocols

Transmitting information over the Internet can be risky. Information you send is passed from one computer to the next until it reaches its destination. During the transmission, other users can eavesdrop on the transmission or intercept your information, and even change the contents of your message.

key
A variable value, such as a numeric code, that uses an algorithm to encrypt and decrypt data. Some applications encrypt and decrypt with the same key, whereas other applications use a pair of keys.

Certificate servers validate, or certify, **keys**. Keys are strings of text generated from a complex series of encryption algorithms that allow you to secure communication for a company or group of users. Many Web servers, such as IIS, create keys that, after having been validated, can be applied to other servers, such as news servers, mail servers or Web servers. The purpose of this process is to create a way for people to communicate and be reasonably sure that others are not eavesdropping or assuming a false identity.

NOTE:
You need a general understanding of the role of certificates in security.

The nature of e-mail and newsgroup servers and protocols makes them susceptible to identity theft. Digital certificates help minimize this security risk by authenticating users before they transmit information. A digital certificate is a password-protected, encrypted data file containing message encryption, user identification and message text. It is used to authenticate a program or a sender's public key, or to initiate SSL sessions. It must be signed by a certificate authority (CA) to be valid.

Directory Server

OBJECTIVE:
3.4.2: Common
Internet
services/protocols

A directory server is a dedicated server that identifies all resources on a network. It makes these resources available to authenticated users. For example, a directory server allows a company to provide a directory of names, network services, e-mail addresses, department personnel, company contacts and address information to all users.

The most efficient solution does not include the storage of current company or individual contact list databases. Most employees do not update their own contact lists; such outdated information can affect accuracy and performance. The most effective way to improve access to such information is to use only one database and one access protocol.

NOTE:
You should understand the function of a directory server. In particular, you must be familiar with LDAP (presented later in this section).

For example, a directory server allows users to remotely access such information quickly from a central location because it allows them to query the database without affecting network performance. An administrator need only configure employee e-mail programs to query the database.

 Many companies give their employees electronic address books that contain a centralized list of e-mail addresses and contact information. The IT department updates the address book so the latest version is always available. Thus, company employees can automatically access it using their e-mail programs.

Additional directory service uses

A directory service enables a company to reuse the information in its directory, keep management costs from increasing, and avoid re-entry of user information for every application that requires such information. A directory service can also help administrators manage applications and users, and can help users locate other users or e-mail addresses.

In addition, a directory service can help with the following procedures:

- Locating and managing all company accounts with the same directory.

- Allowing users, both inside and outside the network, to use the service. For example, an office in one city can store the directory information about all its members on one server. Users outside that office can also access the information, with permission.

- Maintaining a single database of e-mail contacts.

Directory service protocols

Two protocols serve as the basis for most directory services: X.500 and the Lightweight Directory Access Protocol (LDAP).

X.500

X.500 is used to manage user and resource directories. It is based on a hierarchical system that can classify entries by country, state, city and street, for example. The X.500 protocol was designed to offer a global directory. It has had limited success on its own because it is complex and difficult to implement, but it has been the basis for many other directory services.

X.500 directories offer the following characteristics:

- **Scalability** — can be offered as a global database, but can also be divided into smaller databases for efficient management.

- **Synchronization** — can synchronize with other directories to ensure all data is current.

- **Replication** — can replicate with other X.500 directories, thereby making all database copies identical (for reducing retrieval time) and creating backup copies.

Lightweight Directory Access Protocol (LDAP)

NOTE:
LDAP may one day become an Internet-wide directory service.

LDAP was developed from X.500 at the University of Michigan. It is easier to implement than X.500 because it is based on TCP/IP, allowing communication on both intranets and the Internet. LDAP uses a simplified X.500 directory structure and a simplified directory-access method.

Whereas the X.500 directory-access method is also called the Directory Access Protocol (DAP), the LDAP acronym incorporates "lightweight" to denote a simpler structure. Netscape Directory Server (NDS) uses the LDAP standard for its directory structure and its access method.

When Netscape adopted LDAP as its standard, the rest of the Web community followed. Eventually, the Internet may provide public "White Pages" for e-mail addresses and users with LDAP. The LDAP directory structure is hierarchical, similar to an X.500 directory.

Catalog Server

OBJECTIVE:
3.4.2: Common Internet services/protocols

A catalog server provides a single point of access that allows users to centrally search for information across a distributed network. In other words, it indexes databases, files and information across a large network and allows keyword, Boolean and other searches. If you need to provide a comprehensive searching service for your intranet, extranet or even the Internet, a catalog server is the standard solution.

A catalog server keeps an index, or catalog, of all the documents for which it is responsible. In this way, it is a meta-index rather than a single index. The catalog server prevents users from having to browse an enormous number of documents.

Robots

Catalog servers can automate the indexing process with the use of robot programs that use algorithms and search parameters to find and index files, folders and other materials. Most catalog servers are preconfigured to search for the most common file name extensions, such as .xls, .pdf, .doc, .html, .txt, and so forth.

You can customize search results to present full documents or summaries, and most catalog servers can also conduct SSL sessions to ensure that search queries remain confidential.

Fax Server

OBJECTIVE:
3.4.2: Common Internet services/protocols

A fax server is an alternative to providing individual fax machines throughout a company location. For instance, many companies purchase a fax machine for each department in the company. For larger companies, this policy can result in dozens of machines. The fax machines must also be conveniently located for the employees.

A fax server provides a centrally located fax system for all company departments, and can save costs from purchasing dozens of individual fax machines. Fax servers consist of a bank of fax modems. These modems allow outgoing and incoming faxes to be processed by the next available fax modem.

Both internal and remote company employees can use the fax server. With the acceptance of digital signatures in electronic commerce (or e-commerce), documents can be signed and faxed without ever existing in paper form.

Because fax services do not consume large amounts of network resources, a fax service is often installed on a server running another service. For instance, fax services are often installed on company file servers.

Transaction Server

OBJECTIVE:
3.4.2: Common Internet services/protocols

When a transaction takes place, such as ordering office supplies over the Internet with a company credit card, a transaction server guarantees that all required databases are updated. It verifies that all parts of a transaction have taken place successfully. In some cases, this task is complicated. For example, the online merchant's database must reflect the transaction, as well as the credit card company's, and in some cases, the manufacturer's database.

Transaction servers are intended as client/server replacements for Customer Information Control System (CICS) mainframe servers. Transaction servers are Web-based and allow a network to provide a stand-alone solution or a bridging tool to mainframe servers. Some transaction servers, such as Microsoft Transaction Server, are designed to interact with Web-specific databases through the use of ASP.

A transaction server also comes preconfigured to connect to databases, thereby enabling the spontaneous transfer of information. Specifically built to enable a three-tier solution, transaction servers allow high-volume transactions with minimal network overhead.

If a transaction is unsuccessful because one of the databases fails, the server will execute preprogrammed actions, such as canceling the transaction.

The Internet Daemon: inetd and xinetd

daemon
A UNIX program
that is usually
initiated at startup
and runs in the
background until
required.

The program inetd is a UNIX service, or **daemon**, that starts other Internet servers or services. This UNIX service is called a daemon because it waits and listens in the background until summoned by another process. Because of its ability to launch, or "spawn," other services and servers, the Internet daemon is often referred to as a super-server. The inetd service runs when the UNIX system starts up. By configuring the inetd.conf file, shown in Figure 3-5, you can use inetd to listen on specified well-known TCP and UDP ports (0 to 1023). When the inetd daemon receives a request for a recognized port, it will launch other services to support the request.

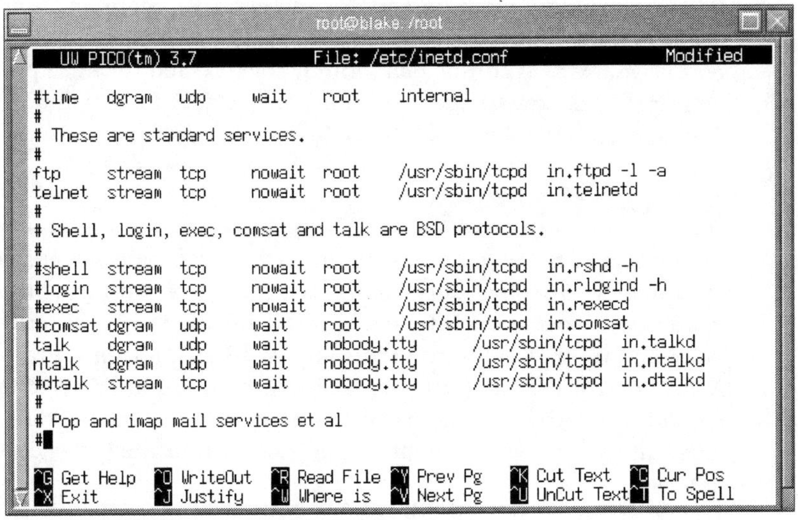

Figure 3-5: Sample inetd.conf file

You can use inetd to launch any UNIX server. These services typically include the following servers:

- **smtpd** — the SMTP daemon.

- **tftd** — the Trivial File Transport (TFT) daemon.

- **telnetd** — the Telnet daemon.

Additional servers include smbd and nmbd, which are the Samba service daemons that allow a UNIX system to participate in a Microsoft NetBIOS network. Some Web administrators use inetd to start their Web servers in response to client requests.

xinetd

More modern versions of UNIX and Linux use a modified form of inetd known as xinetd. This daemon is considered more secure because it provides more control over how daemons are run and over the remote systems that can use a particular daemon. The xinetd daemon can be found in Red Hat Linux version 7.0 and later.

Configuring xinetd

The xinetd daemon does not use one file to configure each of the daemons for which it is responsible. Rather, it uses a separate configuration file for each service instead of all services. These files are usually located in the /etc/xinetd.d/ directory, as shown in Figure 3-6.

```
root@blake: /root
[root@blake /root]# ls /etc/xinetd.d/
eklogin           imaps           krb5-telnet.rpmsave   pop3s    telnet
eklogin.rpmsave   ipop2           kshell                rexec    tftp
finger            ipop3           kshell.rpmsave        rlogin   wu-ftpd
gssftp            klogin          linuxconf-web         rsh      wu-ftpd.works
gssftp.rpmsave    klogin.rpmsave  ntalk                 swat
imap              krb5-telnet     opieftpd              talk
[root@blake /root]# █
```

Figure 3-6: xinetd configuration files

Security concerns

Because they launch other servers and services, inetd and xinetd can present a security problem if they are not configured properly. Both daemons have super-user, or "root," permission, which can be deliberately misdirected to cause problems on the server. Also, both inetd and xinetd spawn a new process each time you use them. Therefore, use these daemons carefully because they can deplete system resources.

Mirrored Server

Although a mirrored server is not an internetworking server itself, it can provide data redundancy to protect data on any type of server. Mirroring causes two sets of write operations to occur each time a write request is issued. A mirror set is established between two physical hard drives (or partitions). Mirroring can occur locally or remotely. A local mirror means that a server has a second hard drive that stores data. A remote mirror means that a remote server (either in the same building or in a completely different city or country) contains an exact duplicate of the data.

The mirrored set can exist on one computer or two separate computers, as shown in Figure 3-7.

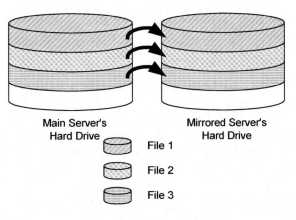

Main Server's Hard Drive   Mirrored Server's Hard Drive

File 1

File 2

File 3

Figure 3-7: Mirrored server

Data is written to the primary, or original, drive when a write request is issued. Data is then copied to the mirrored drive, providing a mirror image of the primary drive. If one of the hard drives fails, all data is protected from loss.

Most network operating systems allow any portion of a drive to be mirrored, including the operating system files, which protect the entire system. Mirroring is one level of the Redundant Array of Inexpensive Disks (RAID) standard, which is not discussed in this course.

Choosing Web Server Products

As a networking professional, you will need to make and justify decisions. Part of this decision-making process is learning what a company truly requires and then making the appropriate choices.

Following are descriptions of some industry-standard Internet servers. This list is not comprehensive and does not constitute an endorsement of any product. However, this discussion will give you a sense of the available products.

Apache Web server

Apache Web server is a tested, well-accepted solution. It is considered extremely reliable. As of this writing, more than half of all Web sites deliver their information with this server. Originally designed to support UNIX, Apache now supports Windows systems as well (for example, Windows Server 2003 and Windows XP). All versions are available free of charge.

open source
Characterized by providing free source code to the development community at large to develop a better product; includes Apache Web server, Netscape Communicator and Linux.

Apache Web server includes no formal support system (such as a customer support desk) because it has been developed by a not-for-profit, membership-based group called the Apache Software Foundation (*www.apache.org*). The Apache Web server is part of the **open-source** movement. However, you can obtain configuration and support information from many sources by entering the keyword "Apache" in your favorite search engine.

A downloadable version is available at the Apache HTTP Server Project site (*http://httpd.apache.org/*). The Apache Web server is not packaged with additional Internet services. You must obtain other server programs for news, FTP and so forth. However, many different developers have combined Apache Web server with other services. Apache2Triad, for example, provides Apache Web server, as well as PHP, MySQL (a SQL server), Perl and an FTP server. You can learn more about Apache2Triad at *http://apache2triad.sourceforge.net*.

Microsoft Internet Information Services (IIS)

IIS is now in its sixth version, and includes HTTP, FTP, NNTP, SMTP, certificate, ASP, index (catalog) and transaction services.

IIS 5 operates only with Windows NT, Windows 2000 Server or Windows NT/2000 Professional; IIS 6 operates only with Windows Server 2003 and Windows XP Professional. Both are free of charge, but you must purchase a license for the appropriate Windows operating system. You can obtain a copy from the Microsoft Web site (*www.microsoft.com*).

graphical user interface (GUI)
A program that provides visual navigation with menus and screen icons, and performs automated functions when users click command buttons.

One of the strengths of IIS is that it allows you to use a remote server to store and retrieve files. The remote server need not be a Web server itself, a fact that allows you to distribute processing load evenly.

Because IIS is a Microsoft product, you can obtain worldwide, fee-based support. You can also administer it from a **graphical user interface (GUI)** or through HTML forms. Additionally, you can issue commands from a DOS session.

Sun ONE servers

Sun Microsystems helped define the Web, and its servers are among the most tested. Additionally, its products support many platforms, including OS/2, Windows NT and 2000, Solaris, AIX, HP-UX, AS/400 and S/390.

The popular Sun ONE Web Server (previously the Netscape/iPlanet Enterprise server) continues to be widely used on the Web. The Sun ONE Messaging Server (previously the Netscape/iPlanet Messaging Server) is still used as an Internet mail server. The Sun ONE Directory Server (previously the Netscape/iPlanet Directory Server) is used to store and manage identity profiles, access privileges, and application and network resource information.

The Sun ONE servers include servers with server-side JavaScript interpreters, which allow you to use JavaScript to connect to databases; in addition, you can implement other server-side scripting applications. For more information, consult the Sun ONE site (*www.sun.com/software*).

Java software and Web servers

servlet
A small Java application that runs on a server.

Many Web servers use Java. Any time Java code is compiled and runs solely on the Web server, it is known as a servlet. A Java **servlet** is a database connection method. Servlets allow the following:

- Chaining, which allows output from one servlet to be given to another servlet, either on the local computer or on a remote computer

- Connections to databases

- Near-universal support on systems (for example, Windows, Linux, Solaris)

Java Virtual Machine (JVM)
The artificial computer that runs Java programs and allows the same code to run on different platforms.

In order for Java servlets and other applications to function, however, you must first install a **Java Virtual Machine (JVM)** on your system. You can obtain a JVM from various vendors. The standard JVM is available from Sun (*www.java.com*).

Case Study
Keeping E-Mail Addresses Current

Lars is the e-mail administrator for a medium-sized company that operates offices in Stockholm, Buenos Aires and Singapore. These offices communicate daily, and must continue to do so as efficiently as possible. Owing to the high rate of turnover as well as the distances between the offices, users cannot easily obtain current e-mail addresses for their associates.

Lars recommends to Chen, the IT administrator, that they implement a directory server using the Lightweight Directory Access Protocol (LDAP). Lars' reasons are as follows:

- LDAP enables clients to query a database quickly over long distances without affecting network performance.

- The database would provide a centralized, current listing of the associates in each of the offices, and would be managed by Lars.

- By configuring employee e-mail programs to query the database, employees will have instant access to current associate e-mail information.

*   *   *

Do you think any other server types or protocols would be as effective as the proposed solution? Can you think of any other benefits to using a directory server and LDAP?

Lesson Summary

Application project

Which particular software products are used at your company? Two popular Web servers are Apache and Microsoft IIS. Research both Web server products on the Internet to determine the best product for your company. Influencing factors include your current network operating system and the costs involved. Ask questions such as the following: Will the Web server provide interoperability within the company's existing infrastructure? If you already have a Web server, would it be difficult to migrate the current Web server to a new Web server?

Skills review

In this lesson, you learned about the major types of internetworking servers. Specifically, you studied file, print, HTTP, proxy, mail, mailing list, media, DNS, FTP, news, certificate, directory, catalog, fax and transaction servers. You learned about how each server uses different protocols from the TCP/IP suite, and how each server performs a different function to enhance business on TCP/IP networks.

Now that you have completed this lesson, you should be able to:

✓ Identify and describe the functions and features of various internetworking servers, including file, print, HTTP, proxy, mail, instant messaging, mailing list, media, DNS, FTP, news, certificate, directory, catalog, fax and transaction servers.

✓ Describe how each type of internetworking server uses TCP/IP suite protocols.

✓ Describe access-security features of an HTTP server, including user names, passwords, and file-level access.

✓ Define MIME, and explain how MIME types are used by HTTP and mail servers.

✓ Describe the functions of DNS, including the DNS hierarchy, root domain servers, top-level domains, and DNS record types.

✓ Define "daemon" and identify the functions of Internet-related daemons.

Version 1.2

Lesson 3 Review

1. What three types of information are usually contained in server logs?

   _____

2. What is a proxy server?

   _____

   _____

3. What function does a mirrored server perform?

   _____

4. Define a mailing list server.

   _____

   _____

5. What do media servers do?

   _____

6. Domain Name System servers are composed of what two key components?

   _____

7. What protocol does a news server use?

   _____

8. What is the primary benefit of using a certificate server?

   _____

9. What is a catalog server?

   _____

   _____

10. Explain the function of the inetd daemon.

    _____

Lesson 3
Supplemental Material

This section is a supplement containing additional tasks for you to complete in conjunction with the lesson. These elements are:

- **Activities**
  Pen-and-paper activities to review lesson concepts or terms.

- **Optional Labs**
  Computer-based labs to provide additional practice.

- **Lesson Quiz**
  Multiple-choice test to assess knowledge of lesson material.

Activity 3-1: Diagramming DNS server relationships

In this activity, you will diagram the relationships among DNS root servers, primary or master servers, and client systems. Use the space provided to draw the relationships.

Include the following servers from the DNS model: root, primary and secondary. Remember to include the client.

Activity 3-2: Recommending the appropriate server

For this activity, read the following scenarios, and then consider the server type you would recommend. Write and explain your answer in the space provided.

1. You are the administrator of a small company that requires extensive security. Although security is a concern, you must also consider the costs associated with obtaining certificates. Which server would you recommend?

2. After noticing that your company's access to the Internet is slowing, you determine that you need to provide a way to ease the burden on your HTTP server. What type of server would help you accomplish this goal?

_____

_____

_____

3. You require your Web site to search a large number of remote sites so you can use your site as a central access point to all this information. You also require this server to automate the indexing process. Which server would you recommend?

_____

_____

Optional Lab 3-1: Viewing installed services

In this optional lab, you will view the installed services on your system.

1. From the Desktop, open the **Control Panel** and click **Add Or Remove Programs**.

2. Click Add/Remove Windows Components to display the Windows Components Wizard, which displays installed Windows XP components.

   Installed services are identified by a check. These can include one or more of the following:

   • Certificate services

   • Internet information services

   • Networking services

   • Other file and print services

   A gray check box indicates that only part of the available selections for a service have been installed.

NOTE:
In Step 3, ensure that you click Networking Services to select it; you should not deselect the check box.

3. Click **Networking Services**, then click the **Details** button to display the Networking Services dialog box, which lists the selections available under Networking Services. Click **Cancel** after viewing the list.

4. Close the Windows Components Wizard, the Add Or Remove Programs window and the Control Panel.

5. Select **Start | Help And Support** to display the Help And Support Center.

6. In the toolbar, click the **Support** button, then click the **Advanced System Information** link in the bottom of the left pane.

7. In the Advanced System Information pane, click the **View Running Services** link to display a list of the services installed on your computer and their current status.

8. Scroll through the Services list. Services with a status of *Running* are currently running on your computer. Services can be configured to start automatically when Windows starts, manually as needed, or can be disabled.

9. Exit the Help And Support Center.

Lesson 3 Quiz

1. What two servers are often incorporated as one service?

   a. HTTP and directory servers
   b. Mail and catalog servers
   c. File and print servers
   d. News and media servers

2. How does the HTTP server interact with TCP/IP?

   a. HTTP enables multiperson text input, which allows many individuals to access and read the same message.
   b. HTTP validates keys used to decode encryption algorithms.
   c. HTTP allows many users on a network to access the same files.
   d. HTTP listens on port 80 for incoming requests from clients, such as Web browsers.

3. Instructions given by a server that restrict or allow access to system resources are called:

   a. passwords.
   b. permissions.
   c. file access protocols.
   d. rules.

4. The protocol that identifies a file type, encodes the file using the file type, and decodes it at the receiving end to display properly is called:

   a. Simple Mail Transfer Protocol (SMTP).
   b. File Transfer Protocol (FTP).
   c. Post Office Protocol (POP).
   d. Multipurpose Internet Mail Extensions (MIME).

5. The .com, .gov, .org and .edu categories can be found in which of the following DNS domain levels?

   a. Second-level domain
   b. Root-level domain
   c. Top-level domain
   d. Base-level domain

6. The name daemon:

   a. allows a UNIX computer to access Windows programs.
   b. allows a UNIX computer to function as a DNS server.
   c. allows a computer running NetWare to access Windows programs.
   d. allows a computer running NetWare to function as a DNS server.

7. You are a mail administrator and you receive complaints that users can receive mail but cannot send it. Which mail server should you troubleshoot?

   a. SMTP server
   b. IMAP server
   c. POP3 server
   d. NNTP server

Lesson 4: Hardware and Operating System Maintenance

Objectives

By the end of this lesson, you will be able to:

- Identify the characteristics of motherboards.

- Identify common IRQ, I/O address and DMA settings, and describe their functions.

- Identify the characteristics of IDE/ATA, EIDE/ATA-2, SATA and SCSI.

- Identify NICs and common peripheral ports, and describe their functions.

- Identify the characteristics of CD-ROMs and DVDs.

- Describe hard-drive partitioning and formatting.

- Describe the characteristics of file system types, including FAT, FAT32, NTFS, Ext3 and ReiserFS.

- Describe the uses of file system management tools, including Convert, Disk Defragmenter, Chkdsk, Disk Cleanup, Backup and Restore.

- Identify and suggest corrective measures for operating system boot problems and application failures.

- Identify methods to remotely manage and troubleshoot workstations.

Pre-Assessment Questions

1. The situation in which two or more devices share a configuration setting is called:

   a. a high-level format.
   b. a low-level format.
   c. a power spike.
   d. a resource conflict.

2. What is the name of the smallest storage allocation unit managed by an operating system?

   a. Cluster
   b. Cylinder
   c. Partition
   d. Root

3. What is direct memory access (DMA)?

   _____

   _____

Basic Hardware and System Maintenance

Periodically, all computer components experience (or appear to experience) failure. Before replacing components or obtaining the services of a qualified computer technician, you can often fix a problem yourself by performing one of the following simple tasks (depending on the component):

- Check that the component is plugged in.

- Check that the component is turned on.

- Check that all components are connected in order to operate properly (for example, ensure that the keyboard is connected to the computer).

You should also perform periodic preventive maintenance (PM) in order to avoid component failures. Preventive maintenance procedures typically include device cleaning, general maintenance, and testing.

Device cleaning

One of the primary reasons for cleaning a system is to remove accumulated dust. Dust acts as a heat insulator. Excessive dust can cause components to overheat and fail. Dust, dirt and other foreign matter can cause excessive wear on physical components. If a system is missing slot covers, for example, replace them. They will help reduce dust and make your system last longer.

If you need to remove dust from internal system components (such as the motherboard and adapter boards), use a soft brush and a static-free vacuum. You can also use compressed air to remove dust.

 Before conducting preventive maintenance on any device, turn off the device and unplug the power cord. Leaving power applied to the computer or peripheral can be a shock hazard and can cause component failure.

General maintenance and testing

planned maintenance
Any scheduled maintenance procedures, including preventive maintenance.

General maintenance means taking care of any minor problems that you discover during **planned maintenance**. For example, if you find a worn cable while cleaning a computer, you should replace the cable at that point, rather than waiting for it to fail. Other general maintenance procedures include checking items that you know can cause system problems, such as disk fragmentation. (Disk fragmentation will be discussed in detail later in this lesson.)

You should verify basic system operations after completing preventive maintenance procedures to make sure that your system is in good working order.

In the following sections, we will discuss common system components in detail, including installation, removal and configuration setting procedures that you may need to perform.

Motherboard

OBJECTIVE:
3.7.1: System component maintenance

The motherboard is the main circuit board in a computer, on which the microprocessor, physical memory and support circuitry are located. All system devices, such as the keyboard, the mouse, and serial, parallel and Universal Serial Bus (USB) devices, connect directly or indirectly to the motherboard. Many motherboards use a multilayer construction, which means that there are internal traces in addition to those on the top and bottom of the board. The internal **traces** are delicate and easily damaged, so care must be taken when handling motherboards.

The **motherboard** must be fastened to the system chassis. Usually, you will fasten the motherboard using small plastic or metal tabs that plug into the motherboard, and then onto holes in the chassis. When fastening the motherboard, take care not to allow any metal to improperly connect and ground the motherboard. The motherboard should not touch any metal object, except through proper connections (for example, to the power supply). In addition, make sure that all parts are fastened tightly to the motherboard, and that excess dust does not build up.

IRQs, I/O Addresses and DMA

In some cases, you need to provide configuration setting values when you install devices in your computer. Though there are a few exceptions, most devices will require unique configuration values. Some of these are set by the system and cannot be changed. For those that can be set or modified, you must avoid introducing **resource conflicts** (also known as device conflicts). When you install a network device adapter, you must determine which system resources are already in use so that you can identify available resources for the installed device.

In a personal computer, communication is controlled through interrupts. **Interrupt requests (IRQs)** are hardware lines that are used to identify when a device wants to communicate with the processor and to notify a device that the processor wants the device's attention. This arrangement ensures that only one device at a time can communicate with the processor. For example, when a printer has finished printing, it sends an interrupt signal to the computer so the computer can decide what processing task to perform next.

Modern computers contain 16 IRQs, numbered 0 through 15. If your system will not boot properly, or you cannot hear sound from your sound card, an IRQ resource conflict may have occurred.

An **I/O address** is a memory location that allows the system processor and system devices to communicate. Most devices will have at least one unique I/O address.

Direct memory access (DMA) is the process by which a device can directly address system memory, bypassing the processor. DMA is most often used by hard disk and floppy disk controllers, but can also be used by other peripherals. DMA is different from programmed input/output (PIO), which requires that all data first pass through the processor. PIO is now considered obsolete.

Electronic communication

You must understand how computers communicate, both internally and with one another. To understand computer communication, you need to understand how to convert values among three numbering systems: decimal (base 10), binary (base 2) and hexadecimal (base 16). Understanding the function of general mathematics in relation to your computer hardware is essential.

trace
Thin conductive path on a circuit board, usually made of copper.

motherboard
The main circuit board in a computer, on which the microprocessor, physical memory and support circuitry are located.

OBJECTIVE:
3.7.1: System component maintenance

resource conflict
A situation in which two or more devices share a configuration setting.

interrupt request (IRQ)
A hardware line over which devices can send interrupt signals to the processor.

I/O address
A memory location that allows resources to be allocated to a system device.

direct memory access (DMA)
A process that allows devices to bypass controllers and directly access memory.

Binary numbering

NOTE:
You must
understand how to
convert among
decimal, binary and
hexadecimal
numbering systems.
Otherwise, you will
not know the
languages that
computers use to
communicate.
Learning binary
conversion
techniques will also
help you later in
your career if you
want to administer
IP networks.

A computer understands only two values, 1 (one) and 0 (zero). All system elements, including memory locations and the subtle shades and hues displayed on your monitor, are defined as strings of 1s (ones) and 0s (zeros).

The number system recognized by computers is known as the binary system and is based on powers of 2. You designate binary positions by using either the 1 or the 0 in each value. You also read binary values from right to left, instead of left to right. Table 4-1 shows how binary values increment.

Table 4-1: Binary numbering

Power Notation	Decimal Equivalent	Binary Value
2^0	1	1
2^1	2	10
2^2	4	100
2^3	8	1000
2^4	16	10000
2^5	32	100000
2^6	64	1000000
2^7	128	10000000
2^8	256	100000000

Figure 4-1 represents the first nine binary values.

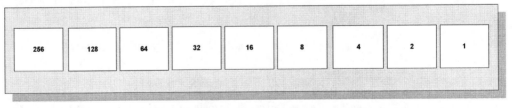

Figure 4-1: Representing numbers to ninth binary place holder

Figure 4-1 does not represent all the binary positions. It includes only the first nine binary positions. To obtain further binary positions, you would multiply 256 by 2 to obtain the decimal equivalent of the tenth binary position, which is 512. To learn further values, you can multiply 512 again by 2, and so forth.

Converting decimal values into binary

Any number, either decimal or hexadecimal, can be converted into binary. To convert decimal numbers into binary, use the preceding figure as an example and read the 1 and 0 entries. Always read binary values from right to left. Always add the positions marked with a 1. If, for example, you wanted to represent the decimal number of 2 in binary, you would write the following:

10

In the previous example, the "0" in first binary position tells you to skip the first value, which represents the decimal number of 1. You then move on to the second value, which represents the decimal number of 2. The "1" informs you that you should count that number when adding. To represent the number 5 in binary, you would enter the following:

101

In the previous example, you count the first binary position (1), skip the second (2), and count the third (4). You then add the two values (1 and 4) to get the decimal sum of 5. The numbers 10 and 33 are represented, respectively, by the following binary numbers:

1010
100001

The binary representation of the decimal number 100,000 would be:

11000011010100000

As you can see, representing 100,000 requires 17 binary values:

65536	32768	16384	8192	4096	2048	1024	512	256	128	64	32	16	8	4	2	1
1	1	0	0	0	0	1	1	0	1	0	1	0	0	0	0	0

Add all the values represented by a 1, and you will get the decimal number 100,000.

Bytes and bits

The smallest unit for binary numbers is known as a bit. A bit represents a single binary value, either 1 or 0. However, when referring to storage, you more commonly refer to data being stored in bytes. A byte is a group of 8 bits. A byte can represent any decimal value between 0 and 255.

A byte is still a very small amount of data. You will more commonly see references to kilobits (Kb), kilobytes (KB), megabits (Mb), megabytes (MB), gigabits (Gb) and gigabytes (GB). Table 4-2 lists storage values you will probably encounter.

NOTE:
Make sure that you understand the difference between bits and bytes. Computers regard 1,024 bytes as a kilobyte. A kilobyte does not equal 1,000 bytes, as you might expect.

Table 4-2: Storage values

Unit	Description
bit	A single binary digit.
nibble	4 bits, or one half of a byte.
byte	8 bits, the standard unit for measuring memory, file size and so forth.
word	The amount of data that a microprocessor can handle at one time. Usually, this is 16 bits (or two bytes).

Table 4-2: Storage values (cont'd)

Unit	Description
kilobit	1024 bits.
kilobyte (KB)	1,024 bytes. A thousand bytes. This number may seem counterintuitive, but computers consider the number 1,024 to be a thousand.
megabit	1,024 kilobits.
megabyte (MB)	1,024 KB, or 1,048,576 bytes. A million bytes.
gigabit	1,024 megabits.
gigabyte (GB)	A billion bytes. 1,024 MB, or 1,073,741,824 bytes.

Other prefixes are used to describe larger byte values, but they are beyond the scope of this course.

To give you an idea of how storage expectations have changed over the years, the original IBM PC included 64 KB of memory, and its operating system (MS-DOS 1.0) could support a maximum of 640 KB of memory. Systems now typically include 64 MB to 128 MB of memory and most current operating systems can support up to 4 GB of total system memory.

legacy adapter board
An older, non-Plug and Play adapter board.

*Sometimes, you will have to use your understanding of binary to configure **legacy adapter boards**. For example, some devices have to set the device address in binary through switch settings or jumpers.*

Hexadecimal numbering

The hexadecimal numbering system uses the digits 0 through 9, and the letters A through F. Thus, the numbers 0 through 9 are the same in both decimal and hexadecimal. However, the decimal number 10 is known as "A" in hexadecimal. The decimal number 15 is hexadecimal number F. However, the decimal number 16 is known in hexadecimal as 10, and the hexadecimal equivalent of the decimal number 17 is 11. The hexadecimal number 1A is the equivalent of 26. The pattern continues, so that the number 42 is 2A, and so forth. This scheme allows relatively small hexadecimal numbers to represent very large decimal numbers.

NOTE:
Hexadecimal is known as a "base 16" language because it repeats the same pattern every 16th digit.

Each hexadecimal digit represents the value of a 4-bit binary number. With this knowledge, you can convert hexadecimal values into binary and into decimal. Table 4-3 contains a summary of equivalent values in decimal, hexadecimal and binary.

Hexadecimal values are sometimes written with a lowercase "h" following the number to prevent users from confusing them with a decimal value. For example, you might see an address expressed as 0060h.

Table 4-3: Comparing decimal, hexadecimal and binary values

NOTE:
This table is designed to help you understand how hexadecimal works.

Decimal	Hexadecimal	Binary*
0	0	0000
1	1	0001
2	2	0010
3	3	0011
4	4	0100
5	5	0101

Table 4-3: Comparing decimal, hexadecimal and binary values (cont'd)

Decimal	Hexadecimal	Binary*
6	6	0110
7	7	0111
8	8	1000
9	9	1001
10	A	1010
11	B	1011
12	C	1100
13	D	1101
14	E	1110
15	F	1111
16	10	10000
17	11	10001
18	12	10010
19	13	10011
20	14	10100
21	15	10101
22	16	10110
23	17	10111
24	18	11000
25	19	11001
26	1A	11010
27	1B	11011
42	2A	101010
43	2B	101011
50	32	110010
100	64	1100100
1000	3E8	1111101000
1,000,000	F4240	1111010000100 1000000

* Beginning with four digits, and continuing upward.

Tech Tip *Windows 9x/Me, NT, 2000 and XP have a calculator program called calc.exe that can convert decimal values into hexadecimal and binary. However, you may sometimes need to convert these values without the aid of a calculator.*

Memory address locations and ranges are commonly expressed in decimal values. Memory and disk utilities that let you directly view content will typically use hexadecimal as a viewing option, with hexadecimal sometimes the only option available.

Converting from hexadecimal into binary and decimal

Converting from hexadecimal into binary requires that you represent each individual hexadecimal as binary. Each hexadecimal value equals four binary digits. For example, the binary equivalent of the hexadecimal number 3DC would be as follows:

3	D	C
0011	1101	1100

Thus, the binary equivalent of the hexadecimal value of 3DC is 001111011100. Properly ordering each value or group of values is important during the conversion process. To convert this value into decimal, you would place the three groups of binary numbers next to one another in the same order as each hexadecimal value, then add only the binary values marked with a 1:

2048	1024	512	256	128	64	32	16	8	4	2	1	
0	0	1	1	1	1	0	1	1	1	0	0	= 988

Thus, the decimal equivalent of the hexadecimal value 3DC is 988.

Converting from binary into hexadecimal

NOTE:
See **Activity 4-3: Converting decimal, binary and hexadecimal values** to practice converting among these numbering systems.

To convert from binary into hexadecimal, it is easiest to first group the binary numbers into groups of four, then turn each group of four into decimal numbers. Make sure you begin grouping values from right to left. If you end up with a last group containing fewer than four digits, do not worry. This happens because you need not count the very last digits to the left if they are all 0s.

Next, add each group of four binary digits and convert each group into a decimal number. Finally, convert each of these decimal numbers into a hexadecimal number.

ASCII

American Standard Code for Information Interchange (ASCII) defines a standard code for storing text (letter and number) values. The original ASCII was a 7-bit standard that defined 128 values for letters, numbers, punctuation and control characters. Most systems now support the 8-bit ASCII extended character set, which includes another 128 characters.

More recently, another encoding standard, known as Unicode, has come into common use. Unicode is an international 16-bit encoding standard that can represent the 65,536 characters that can be used in major world languages.

Communication basics

To begin understanding how computers communicate, you need to understand the terms serial and parallel and how they relate to communication. Regardless of whether a computer is communicating internally or with a remote system, all communication occurs as either serial or parallel. Figure 4-2 illustrates serial communication.

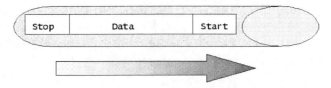

Figure 4-2: Serial communication

COM
PC serial ports are
referred to as
numbered COM
(communication)
ports. COM ports
have a maximum
transmission speed
of roughly 115 Kbps.

Serial communication occurs one bit at a time over a single line. You can move only one bit at a time because a single line can have only one value, either on or off (1 or 0). Data, in the form of bits, moves through a serial communication channel as a data stream. Serial communication is used with devices attached to a computer's serial (**COM**) port, for modem communication, and for network communication. The universal serial bus (USB), as its name implies, also uses serial communication, and allows rates of 12 Mbps (USB 1.0/1.1) or 480 Mbps (USB 2.0).

The term "bits per second" (bps) refers to how many ones or zeros a data path or data port can handle. The term "bytes per second" (Bps) describes how many 8-bit blocks a data path or data port can handle. The equivalent of 12 Mbps in megabytes is 1.5 MBps. The equivalent of 480 Mbps in megabytes is 60 MBps.

LPT
Line printer port. PC parallel ports are referred to as numbered LPT.

In parallel communication (Figure 4-3), the computer is moving several bits at a time. In a PC, this typically means moving 8 bits (a byte) or 16 bits (a word) at a time. Parallel communication requires a separate line for each data bit, as well as additional control lines to manage the data transfer. Parallel communication is used with devices connected to a computer's parallel port and the internal system buses. PC parallel (**LPT**) ports are 8-bit parallel ports. The original speed for LPT ports was 500 Kbps, though higher data rates are available.

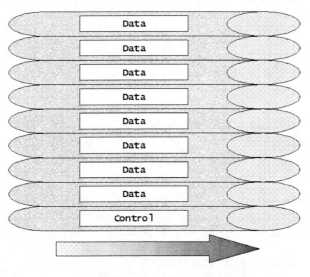

Figure 4-3: Parallel communication

IRQ, I/O address and DMA assignments

Table 4-1 lists standard IRQ, I/O address and DMA assignments. I/O address values are given in hexadecimal notation. A blank cell indicates that no standard resource assignment exists for that device.

Table 4-4: Standard resource assignments

Device	IRQ	I/O Address	DMA Channel
System timer	0	0040 - 0043	
Keyboard controller	1	0060 - 006F	
Real-time clock	8	0070h - 0071h	
COM1	4	03F8h - 03FFh	
COM2	3	02F8h - 02FFh	
COM3	4	03E8h - 03EFh	
COM4	3	02E8h - 02EFh	
LPT1	7	0378h - 037Fh	
LPT2	5	0278h - 027Fh	
PS/2 mouse port (motherboard)	12	0060h - 006F	
Floppy disk controller	6	03F0h - 0377h	2
Primary hard disk controller (primary IDE)	14	01F0h - 01F7h	Auto, if available
Secondary hard disk controller (secondary IDE)	15	0170h - 0178h	Auto, if available
Math coprocessor (if present)	13	00F0h - 00FFh	

Viewing and changing resource assignments

NOTE:
Lab 4-1: Viewing resource assignments will demonstrate the Device Manager in Windows XP that you can use to resolve resource conflicts.

You will usually not need to change a resource assignment. If you do, however, you can use Windows XP Device Manager. In Linux, you would do so by viewing files in the /proc/ directory. For example, consider the following Linux command:

```
/proc/interrupts
```

This command yields a text file you can open in any word processor to view the current IRQ settings.

Consider the following Linux command:

```
/proc/iomem
```

This command yields a text file containing I/O addresses.

In the following lab, you will view resource assignments on your system using the Windows XP Device Manager. Suppose that you have just installed a new printer on your Windows XP system in your home office, but print tests have failed. You suspect a resource conflict. How would you determine which system resources are already in use in order to identify available resources for your new printer?

Lab 4-1: Viewing resource assignments

In this lab, you will view resource assignments on your system.

1. Select **Start | Control Panel** to display the Control Panel.

   *Note: All the labs in this lesson assume that the Control Panel displays in Category view. If your Control Panel displays in Classic view, click the **Switch To Category View** link to display the Control Panel in Category view.*

2. Click **Performance And Maintenance**, then click **System** to display the System Properties dialog box. Click the **Hardware** tab, then click the **Device Manager** button to display the Device Manager window (Figure 4-4). From this window, you can view and adjust various resource settings, as necessary.

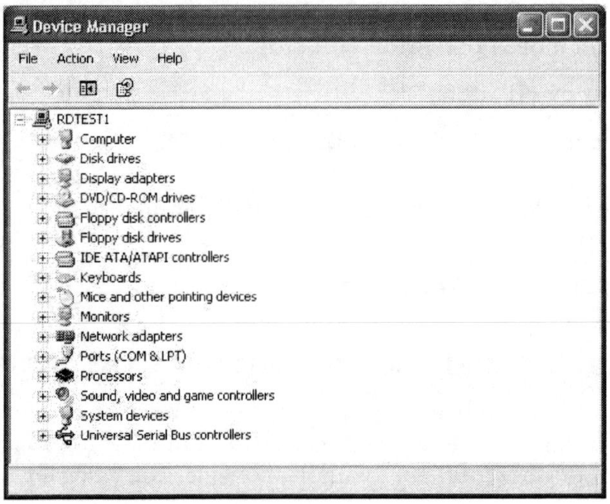

Figure 4-4: Device Manager window

<table>
<tr><td>**NOTE:**
IDE controllers will be presented later in this lesson.</td><td>3. Double-click **IDE ATA/ATAPI Controllers**, then double-click **Primary IDE Channel** to display the Properties dialog box for your primary hard drive controller. Click the **Advanced Settings** tab. Notice that *DMA If Available* displays in the Transfer Mode drop-down list for Device 0 and Device 1 (Figure 4-5).</td></tr>
</table>

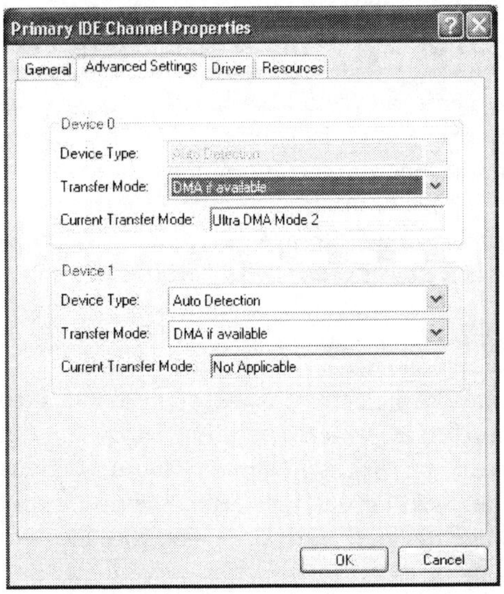

Figure 4-5: Primary IDE Channel Properties dialog box — Advanced Settings tab

4. Display the Transfer Mode drop-down list for either device. Notice that *PIO Only* is the other option you can choose. If your system has a standard IDE drive that is not working properly, you would probably need to switch the transfer mode setting to *PIO Only*. If you have a hard drive that uses DMA, a setting of *PIO Only* would cause hard drive problems.

5. Close the drop-down list without changing the device setting.

6. Click the **Resources** tab. Notice the resource settings that display for the I/O ranges and IRQ (Figure 4-6). Also notice that *No conflicts* displays in the Conflicting Device List area, indicating that your system does not have a resource conflict.

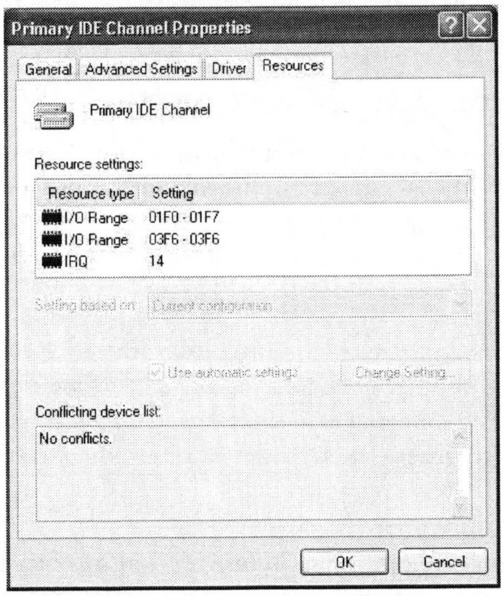

Figure 4-6: Primary IDE Channel Properties dialog box — Resources tab

7. Close all dialog boxes and windows.

Mass Storage Device Interfaces

OBJECTIVE:
3.7.1: System
component
maintenance

interface
A communication
channel between
two components.

To communicate with a motherboard, a mass storage device (for example, a hard drive or a floppy disk drive) must be connected to that motherboard through an **interface**. On current motherboards, the floppy disk drive and the integrated drive electronics (IDE) hard disk driver interface are built into the motherboard. The three most common interfaces used to connect mass storage devices in modern computers are the IDE, the enhanced integrated drive electronics (EIDE) and the small computer system interface (SCSI).

IDE/EIDE interface

IDE is a standard electronics interface used to connect mass storage devices to the motherboard. IDE, which was adopted by the American National Standards Institute (ANSI), is also known as Advanced Technology Attachment (ATA). The original IDE standard allowed for one IDE interface and support for as many as two hard disks or other storage devices. Hard disk size was limited to 504 MB and the interface supported a transfer rate of 12 megabytes per second (MBps).

An enhanced version of the interface, EIDE (or ATA-2) provides for significantly higher drive capacities. The EIDE standard is theoretically capable of supporting drive capacities of up to 137.4 gigabytes (GB). Higher data transfer rates are made possible through support for DMA. It can support two controllers (two disk channels) and up to two hard disks per controller. EIDE is the current standard for computer hard disks. Most motherboards have a built-in EIDE interface.

IDE/EIDE interface cables are long, thin and gray.

Serial ATA (SATA)

Serial ATA (SATA) provides faster speeds than standard ATA. SATA is expected to become the *de facto* standard for PC-based drives, just as EIDE has. SATA devices are connected using a cable that somewhat resembles a small Category 5 Ethernet cable.

Small computer system interface (SCSI)

bus
An electronic
pathway that
conducts signals to
connect the
functional
components of a
computer.

SCSI was originally adopted by Apple Computer as an expansion **bus** standard. Eventually, SCSI gained popularity in the personal computer marketplace, especially for applications requiring large hard disks.

NOTE:
SCSI is found in
higher-end systems,
usually on servers
meant to process
large amounts of
data.

SCSI is a parallel interface standard that allows you to connect multiple devices to a single interface adapter in a daisy chain configuration. You can attach a SCSI cable from the SCSI port on your computer to another SCSI device, then attach that SCSI device to a second SCSI device, and so on up to 127 devices. This grouping can include a mix of internal and external devices. SCSI devices include hard disk drives, floppy disk drives, printers, scanners, tape drives and a wide variety of other peripherals.

SCSI termination
A SCSI daisy chain must be terminated at both ends and only at the ends. Termination is the most common problem associated with SCSI devices. First, you must determine whether the device needs to be terminated, and second, you must select an address for the device.

Resolving device ID conflicts
Aside from termination, logical unit number (LUN) conflicts are a common cause of difficulty when installing a SCSI device. All SCSI device numbers and LUNs must be

unique. When you add a new SCSI device, it is possible for a number to conflict. If this occurs, a drive that has been in your system for some time may no longer work properly.

In addition, many adapters are preset to the SCSI ID of 7. Make sure that you do not set a SCSI hard drive with this number.

Network Interface Card

OBJECTIVE:
3.7.1: System component maintenance

You were introduced to NICs earlier in the course. Each network device must have a NIC (also known as a network adapter card). Figure 4-7 shows a typical peripheral component interconnect (PCI) network adapter that is already installed. The network adapter makes the physical connection between the device (such as a computer) and the network cabling. When selecting a network adapter, you must choose an adapter that is supported by both your computer and your network.

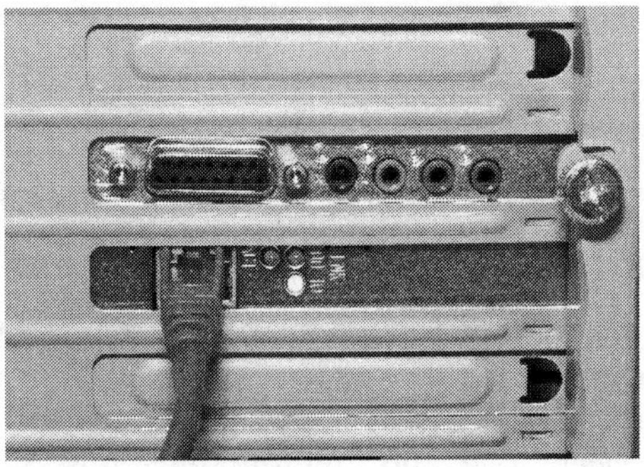

NOTE:
Usually a NIC will have lights on it. These lights indicate whether the NIC is receiving power, as well as the collisions and network traffic it is experiencing.

Figure 4-7: Installed network adapter

The network adapter is essentially a translator between the computer and the network. Networks transmit data serially, or one bit at a time. The network adapter converts the data from the computer into a format appropriate for transmission over the network.

The network adapter component that handles data transmission is called the transceiver. You were introduced to transceivers earlier in the course. All modern networking devices (for example, Ethernet cards, modems, cell phones) use a transceiver. It ensures that the appropriate data format is being used when transmitting information. Most NICs have more than one transceiver, with each attached to the different connectors available on the back of the card.

Common Peripheral Ports

OBJECTIVE:
3.7.2: Common peripherals

peripheral port
A socket on a computer in which a peripheral device is connected.

PS/2-style connector
The six-pin mini-DIN connectors introduced with the IBM PS/2.

Peripheral ports are the sockets on the back panel of the computer in which input and output devices connect to the computer. Newer computers provide many ports. If a port is unavailable for a particular device, you must install an expansion board that includes the port you need.

Newer systems have **PS/2-style connectors** for the mouse and keyboard (Figure 4-8). Most new systems also have monitor adapter circuitry built into the motherboard and a permanent monitor connector. Some systems have embedded sound card and game controller support.

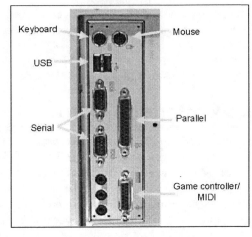

Figure 4-8: Peripheral ports

You will typically see one or two serial ports and one parallel port. In addition, modern systems have one or two USB ports on the back. Some systems have USB ports on the front of the system, as well.

Standard port use

PS/2-style keyboard and mouse ports are used as keyboard and pointing device connectors only. The mouse port should be more accurately considered a pointing device port because of the variety of pointing devices in common use. Pointing devices include mouse devices, trackballs and touch-sensitive pads, all of which connect to the PS/2 mouse port.

 Many manufacturers now color-code ports and connectors on new systems. This color-coding makes it easier for users, specifically home users, to set up their own systems.

The standard ports listed in Table 4-5 support several different types of devices. For example, a serial port can support a modem, a serial printer, a serial mouse or a digital camera interface.

Table 4-5: Standard port use

Port	Use Guidelines
First serial port (COM1)	If you are using a serial mouse, it should always be connected to COM1. If you have a PS/2 mouse, COM1 is available for use by any serial device. It is possible to print through a serial port, including COM1. Regardless of the COM channel you use, serial communications are enabled by a universal asynchronous receiver-transmitter (UART). The most common UART is 16550A.
Second serial port (COM2)	COM2 can support any serial devices, but a potential configuration concern exists: Hardware-configured internal modems typically default to using COM2 and would therefore conflict with any device connected to COM2. It is possible to print through a serial port, including COM2.
Parallel port (IEEE 1284)	The parallel port is usually used for connecting a local printer, but other devices operate through a parallel port, including network adapters and disk controllers. The IEEE 1284 standard supports five different modes: compatibility (150 KBps), nibble (50 KBps to 150 KBps), byte (up to 500 KBps), enhanced parallel port (500 KBps to 2 MBps) and extended capability (up to 2 MBps — uses DMA). You may need to enter a system's complementary metal oxide semiconductor (CMOS) to choose the most appropriate mode. Sometimes, you may need to choose a mode supported by your system and the peripheral device.

NOTE:
USB is the standard printer interface. The fastest parallel port interface is 2 MBps, which is faster than standard USB. Still, standard USB is more efficient in its data transfer.

Table 4-5: Standard port use (cont'd)

Port	Use Guidelines
USB port	The USB port can physically support any USB device. It is often used for printers, scanners, keyboards, mouse devices and external hard drives. USB hubs allow a single-system USB port to support multiple devices. However, two USB standards exist: USB 1.0/1.1 and USB 2.0, also called high-speed USB. High-speed USB is downward-compatible with USB 1.0. However, USB 1.0 does not support USB 2.0 devices. USB ports can support up to 127 peripherals. USB 2.0 supports speeds of up to 480 Mbps (60 MBps). USB 1.0 supports speeds up to 12 Mbps (1.5 MBps), although an earlier 1.0 version supported only 1.5 Mbps (less than 300 Kbps). A serial interface.
Game port	The game controller port often serves as the Musical Instrument Digital Interface (MIDI) connector. The port can connect MIDI-compliant digital music devices, such as digital keyboards.
FireWire (IEEE 1394)	FireWire is used for various devices that require high throughput, including external disk drives, digital and Web cameras, and network connections. IEEE 1394 devices support transfer rates from 100 to 400 Mbps with projected speed enhancements expected to make transfer rates much higher. As with any interface type, IEEE 1394 ports can be added using PCI adapters. IEEE 1394 ports can support up to 63 peripherals. A serial interface.

Troubleshooting port and cabling problems

Make sure that cables are properly inserted into the proper ports. Check all cables associated with a problem device and make sure they are securely plugged in. Table 4-6 lists common problems related to ports and cables, and their solutions.

Table 4-6: Port and cabling problems and solutions

Cable	Problem	Cause/Solution
Serial	Mouse fails when modem is turned on.	IRQ conflict. Change either the mouse or the modem port.
	Mouse is jittery, or modem intermittently fails.	Secure the cable into both the modem and computer.
Parallel	Slow or no printing.	Verify that the correct IEEE 1284 mode is chosen. Secure the cable on both the printer and the computer.
USB	USB 2.0 device performing slowly or not at all.	Ensure that you have a cable that supports USB 2.0 speeds. Verify that the cable is secure.
IEEE 1394 (FireWire)	The connection is intermittent.	Verify that the cable is secure.
SCSI	No communication, or communication in at least one device is intermittent after adding a new device.	Verify termination on the SCSI chain.

In the following lab, you will identify a number of the most common peripheral ports. Suppose you are a musician with an interest in digital music editing and home studio equipment. You just bought new software that enables you to use your computer to record music you compose on your synthesizer. You need to connect the synthesizer to your computer by means of a MIDI cable. Can you recognize the MIDI port on your computer?

Lab 4-2: Identifying common peripheral ports

In this lab, you will identify common peripheral ports.

1. Look at the back panel of your PC and identify each of the peripheral ports you see.

    Do you have the following ports and, if so, how many? Write your answers in the spaces provided:

    PS/2: _____   USB: _____

    Serial: _____   Game: _____

    Parallel: _____   FireWire: _____

2. Open your system and display the internal components. Point out IDE/EIDE/SATA cables, hard disk drives, CD-ROM drives, various adapter boards, and so forth.

3. Use a static-free vacuum or can of compressed air to blow dust out of the system.

Power Requirements

Electricity is measured according to different standards in North America and in Europe, and computing and networking equipment is manufactured to different standards, depending on where the equipment will be used.

If you travel to Europe and take your laptop or notebook computer that was designed for use in the United States, you will need a special plug adapter and a power inverter in order to plug into an electrical receptacle in England, for example.

CD-ROM and DVD

CD-ROMs and digital video discs (DVDs) are optical storage devices that store data on a reflective metal surface that is accessed by a laser beam. Data is written to an optical disk by burning depressions into the metal surface of the disk. These depressions are called pits; the flat areas on the metal surface are called lands. A land reflects laser light from the disk surface into a sensor and is interpreted as the binary digit 1. A pit scatters laser light from the disk surface into a sensor and is interpreted as the binary digit 0.

CD-ROM characteristics

A CD-ROM (which stands for compact disc read-only memory) is an optical storage device from which data can be read only. In other words, data cannot be written to a CD-ROM. CD-ROM drives use common mass storage interfaces. The most common type of CD-ROM device has an IDE/EIDE interface, but SCSI and USB versions are also available.

Table 4-7 lists key features of CD-ROMs, which have become a popular storage and distribution medium.

Table 4-7: CD-ROM features

Feature	Description
Storage capacity	Up to 1 GB of data.
Reliability	Not affected by magnetic fields because it is an optical medium. Does not degrade over time because the data is burned into the surface by a laser beam.
Durability	Much more durable than floppy disks. Avoid scratching the surface of a CD-ROM; data in the affected sectors may be destroyed. Can also be physically damaged by high heat.
Performance	CD-ROM drives now surpass many hard disks in performance, which has improved dramatically in the past few years.
Security	Commercially distributed CD-ROMs are a read-only medium. After the data has been written to the CD-ROM, it cannot be changed.
Mixed-media support	In addition to digital data, a CD-ROM can contain audio, image and video content, and can play audio CDs.
Cross-platform compatibility	The current ISO 9660 data format (High Sierra format) standard is supported by Windows operating systems, MS-DOS, UNIX/Linux, the Apple Macintosh operating system and others.

Writable CD-ROM

Writable CD-ROM devices allow you to create, or "burn," your own data and audio CDs. You can create your own distribution CD-ROMs, copy selected files or folders from your hard disk and duplicate existing CD-ROMs and audio CDs.

 You should always adhere to copyright regulations. It is illegal to make copies of copyrighted material, which includes both software distribution CDs and audio CDs. You are sometimes granted a limited right to make backup copies, or you may obtain copy permission from the copyright holder. Make sure that you do not violate copyright restrictions when copying any CD.

Writable CD-ROMs are available in the following two formats:

- **CD-recordable (CD-R)** — a write-once format. After the data has been written to the CD-ROM, it cannot be modified.

- **CD-rewritable (CD-RW)** — a rewritable format. You can write data to it multiple times, similar to floppy disks and hard disks. Only CD-ROM drives that support multi-read capability can read CD-RWs.

 Some early CD-RW drives were known as erasable CD-ROM drives, or CD-E drives. According to specifications, you should be able to rewrite over the same spot on a CD-RW nearly 1,000 times.

DVD characteristics

DVDs were designed and developed for use with applications in both video and data storage. They work in much the same way as CD-ROMs; data is stored in pits and lands. DVDs have a much higher storage capacity, however, because the pits are smaller and DVDs use a higher track density than CD-ROMs do.

Most DVD drives use an IDE/EIDE interface, though USB and IEEE versions are available and have become common. The physical removal and replacement procedures for internal devices are the same as for other IDE/EIDE mass storage devices. DVD drives are Plug and Play devices, but typically come with other software in addition to the required device drivers. For example, they often include **MPEG-2** decoding software and a media player so you can play DVDs on your computer.

The initial DVD standard provided 4.7 GB of storage capacity. Current DVD standards support dual-layer discs with a storage capacity of 8.5 GB. Also, a double-sided disc standard supports 9.4 GB when writing to one side of the DVD or 17 GB total when writing to both sides of the DVD. The current transfer rate is 1.3 MBps for all formats, with an access time ranging from 150 to 200 milliseconds (ms).

DVD drives are backward-compatible; those that support the newer standards can also support the initial DVD standard. DVD drives can also read CD-ROMs, including CD-RW, and play audio CDs.

Writable DVD (DVD-RW)

Though writable DVDs are not commonly seen on standard corporate desktops, specifications exist for them. Currently, four different writable DVD standards exist. Table 4-8 lists these standards and their storage capacities.

Table 4-8: Writable DVD standards

Standard	Storage Capacity	Description
DVD-R	4.7 GB per side	Write-once standard currently in use. The standard was released in 1997. Supported by most DVD drives.
DVD-RAM	4.7 GB per side	Write-once standard currently in use. The standard was released in 1997. The least expensive format, but has only limited support.
DVD-RW	4.7 GB per side	A rewritable standard. Most DVD drives are designed to read this standard. Very few DVD-RW devices are available.
DVD+RW	8.5 GB per disc	A rewritable standard. Few DVD drives are designed to read this standard. Very few DVD+RW devices are available.

CD-ROM and DVD maintenance

CD-ROM and DVD drives of all types are vulnerable to contamination. Keep the drives closed when they are not in use and check all media for foreign matter before inserting them in the drive. Commercial products are available for cleaning disc surfaces. CD-ROMs and DVDs should be handled only by the edges and care must be taken to avoid scratching the disc surface.

Commercial cleaning kits are available to clean the internal laser. Never directly touch or try to manually clean the laser.

Brush away or vacuum accumulated dust without contaminating the disc carrier area or laser. Verify that the data and power cables are securely mounted.

If a CD-ROM or DVD drive will not open because of a malfunction or power loss, it is possible to eject a disk manually from the drive. Locate the small hole on the face of the drive near the Open/Close button. Straighten a paper clip, place it (or another thin instrument) into the hole and press hard to eject the disc manually.

When a CD-ROM or DVD drive fails completely, you will generally need to replace the drive.

Client Operating System Management

As an IT professional or as an individual computer user, you may need to perform system management tasks to maintain your client operating system. In the remaining sections of this lesson, we will discuss the importance of obtaining proper operating system and software licensing, identifying common file systems, using common file system management tools, identifying ways to recover from application failures, identifying common boot problems, and identifying ways to remotely manage and troubleshoot workstations.

Software Licensing

OBJECTIVE:
3.8.1: OS and application licensing

When you purchase operating system or application software, you are actually purchasing the right to use the software under certain restrictions imposed by the copyright owner (for example, the software publisher). These restrictions are described in the license agreement that accompanies the software. Typically, these restrictions state that you have the right to load the software onto a single computer and make one backup copy. If you install, copy or distribute the software in ways that the license prohibits, such as allowing a friend or colleague to load the software on his or her computer, you are violating federal copyright law. It is imperative that you understand and adhere to the restrictions outlined in the license.

When you load operating system or application software, the license agreement typically displays during the installation process. You must indicate that you have read and understood the agreement before the installation procedure will allow you to continue.

NOTE:
Make sure that you use only properly licensed operating system and application software to avoid legal, technical and software maintenance problems.

Apart from legal consequences, using unlicensed software can also mean:

- No documentation.

- No warranties.

- No technical product support.

- Greater exposure to software viruses.

- Corrupt disks or defective software.

- Ineligibility for software upgrades.

Partitions and Logical Drives

OBJECTIVE:
3.8.4: Hard drive partitioning/ formatting

When installing an operating system on a new computer or after recovering from a hard disk failure, you will need to prepare the hard disk before it can be used. Disk preparation includes the following three fundamental steps:

1. Partition the hard disk, using applications such as Fdisk in Linux or Device Manager in Windows XP. These programs also create logical drives.

2. Create logical drives, using Fdisk or Device Manager.

3. Format the logical drives, using applications such as mkfs in Linux or Device Manager in Windows XP.

Disk partitioning

A partition is a way of dividing a hard disk's total storage space. You will typically partition a hard disk as either having a primary partition and an extended partition or having a primary partition only. A primary partition is required if you want to use a hard disk as the system's boot drive, which is the drive that will be used for system startup. You can create an extended partition if space remains after you recreate the primary partition. A hard disk can have only one extended partition. Figure 4-9 shows a drive with a primary and an extended partition.

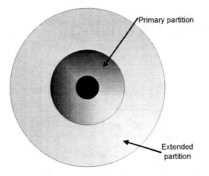

Figure 4-9: Disk partitions

active partition
A logical partition that contains the files necessary to boot an operating system. This partition is read first at boot time. If no active partition exists, or if the operating system files are corrupted or missing, the computer will report error messages.

The primary partition being used for startup must be identified as the **active partition**. This identification forces the system to read the initial load programs from that partition. A hard disk can be configured with multiple primary partitions, but only one partition can be identified as the active partition. The default, in most situations, is to partition the hard disk as a single primary partition.

Logical disk drives

A disk partition must be assigned a logical drive identifier (drive ID or drive letter) before it can be recognized by an operating system. A primary partition is treated as a single logical drive. An extended partition can be divided into multiple logical drives, as shown in Figure 4-10.

Figure 4-10: Logical disk drives

The system drive will be identified as drive C. Drive IDs D through Z are available for assignment. Drives A and B can be used as drive IDs for floppy disk drives only.

Logical disk drives are not the only devices that will need logical drive IDs. CD-ROM drives, DVD drives and other devices that are used for interactive storage must be assigned drive IDs. Drive IDs are also used to identify connections to shared file resources in a network environment.

Logical drive format

root directory
Topmost hard disk directory (folder).

After a logical disk drive is defined, it must be formatted. The format process prepares the logical drive for use by the operating system. Any attempts to write to or read from a logical drive that has not been formatted will generate an error. The format procedure creates the file system **root directory** and the files used to track disk space use.

Logical drive format is known as a high-level format. This distinguishes logical drive format from the low-level format that is sometimes required to prepare a hard disk for use. A hard disk must be prepared through low-level format before disk partitions can be defined. Low-level format is primarily the responsibility of the hard disk manufacturer, and hard disks ship already formatted.

File System Types

OBJECTIVE:
3.8.5: Common file systems

After you have created partitions and logical drives, you must format the primary partitions and the logical drives so the operating system can use them. The format process creates the drive's file system by adding information about how files should be stored on the drive to organize and manage disk storage. For example, the file allocation table (FAT) file system supported by MS-DOS and all Windows family operating systems uses a file allocation table to track **cluster** use. Because it is responsible for tracking space use, the file system also sets the maximum amount of space that can be managed as a single unit (a logical drive).

cluster
A group of sectors used as the basic unit of data storage.

The file system you choose will depend on the operating system you are running. Table 4-9 describes the most common file systems for computers and the operating systems supported by each.

Table 4-9: Computer file systems

File System	Operating System Support	Description
FAT (also known as FAT16)	MS-DOS Windows 3.x Windows 95 Windows 98 Windows NT (all versions) Windows 2000 Windows XP	The most widely supported operating system. However, it is an old file system that does not support many of the features offered by other file systems.
FAT32	Windows 95 OSR2 Windows 98 Windows 2000 Windows XP	Offers performance improvements over FAT. Also provides support for logical drives and primary partitions with greater than 2-GB capacity.
NTFS 4.0	Windows NT Windows 2000	Offers support for large hard disks. Offers a variety of important features, including the ability to assign access permissions to files and compress files "on the fly" to conserve disk space. Instead of the file allocation table, it uses the master file table (MFT), an actual file that provides information about files and folders stored on disk.
NTFS 5.0	Windows NT 4 with Service Pack 4 Windows 2000	Enhancement of NTFS 4.0, offering several new features such as the ability to encrypt files. File encryption is supported on Windows 2000 systems but not on Windows 9x or Windows NT. Also offers disk quotas, allowing disk space to be limited by partition, and enhanced logging.

Table 4-9: Computer file systems (cont'd)

File System	Operating System Support	Description
NTFS 5.1	Windows XP Professional Windows XP Home Edition Windows Server 2003	Enhancement of NTFS 5.0. Includes all the benefits of 5.0, and adds more efficient memory management, read-only NTFS partitions, and hard links. Recommended for systems that have disks larger than 32 MB. Windows XP can read earlier versions of NTFS. However, volumes formatted in earlier versions of NTFS cannot provide the same benefits as NTFS 5.1.
Ext3	Linux	Used by default in Red Hat Linux 7.2 and later. A journaling file system, which allows it to recover more quickly from system errors.
ReiserFS	Linux	The Reiser file system (ReiserFS), created by Hans Reiser, is somewhat newer than Ext3 and uses more sophisticated algorithms for storing information. A journaling file system (like Ext3). For more information, consult *www.namesys.com*.

NOTE:
Make sure you understand the FAT, FAT32 and NTFS formats.

In the following lab, you will view drive partition information. As previously mentioned, the ability to view drive partitions on a computer is very important, especially if you need to add a logical drive ID to a newly added device. Suppose you want to add a DVD drive to your Windows XP system. You will need to assign a logical drive ID to the device. How would you choose and assign the proper drive ID? What utility could you use to view your system's volume and drive partition information?

 Lab 4-3: Viewing drive partitions using Disk Management

In this lab, you will use the Windows XP Disk Management utility to view drive partition information.

1. Display the Windows XP **Control Panel**, then click **Performance And Maintenance**. Click **Administrative Tools**, then double-click **Computer Management** to display the Computer Management window.

2. In the left pane of the window, click **Disk Management** to display your system's volume and partition information (Figure 4-11).

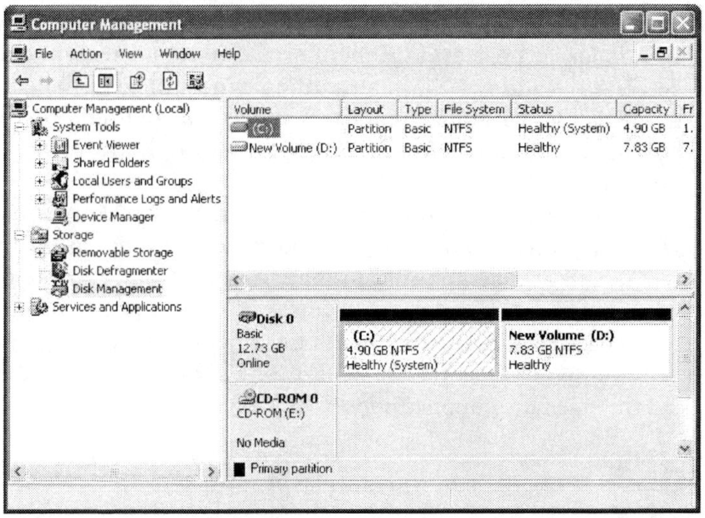

Figure 4-11: Disk Management — volume and partition information

3. Review the partition structure that exists. From this window, you can format disks and change the file system type from FAT32 to NTFS.

4. Close all windows.

File System Management Tools

You use file system management tools to maintain your hard disk and data in order to ensure that your system operates at peak efficiency. These tools also help prevent hardware problems and data loss. In the following sections, we will discuss file and directory permissions, and then discuss the purposes and uses of the Convert, Disk Defragmenter, Chkdsk, Disk Cleanup, Backup and Restore utilities.

File and directory permissions

OBJECTIVE:
3.8.6: File and directory permissions

permission bit
A file or directory attribute that determines access. Permission bits include read, write and execute permissions.

One of the primary benefits of an NTFS file system is that it allows you to secure resources. NTFS allows you to set **permission bits** on system resources (for example, files and directories). With NTFS, you can protect files so that only certain users or groups of users can read them. One group of users may be able to execute applications in a directory, whereas another group may have full access to it. The security provided by a user-based file system such as NTFS can have drawbacks, however. Consider the following potential problems:

- If permissions are applied improperly, you may take security for granted.

- Improperly set permissions can disable or damage an operating system.

Convert utility

OBJECTIVE:
3.8.7: File system management tools

Information about the files on an NTFS volume and their attributes is stored in the master file table (MFT). In Windows NT 4.0 Workstation, Windows 2000 and Windows XP, a partition or logical drive can be converted from FAT or FAT32 into NTFS by using the Convert utility. The Convert utility uses the following syntax:

```
convert drive /FS:NTFS [/v]
```

Replace `drive` with the letter of the drive you are converting into NTFS. The /v option stands for verbose and prints information about the success of the operation to the screen. In Windows XP, if a partition can be locked, the conversion will occur immediately, without a restart. Windows XP still requires you to restart the system before boot and system partitions can be converted, however.

In the following lab, you will learn how to view NTFS permissions. NTFS allows you to secure resources, such as files and directories. If, for example, you work as an IT technician at a company, you may need to divide execute permissions for files or applications among different groups of employees. Applying permissions appropriately helps ensure security as well as the smooth functioning of the various systems. Assume your company uses NTFS. What utility should you use to view NTFS permissions for various files and applications?

Lab 4-4: Viewing NTFS permissions

In this lab, you will view NTFS permissions for directories and files.

1. Open Windows Explorer and make drive C the active drive.

    Note: Drive C should be an NTFS drive. If it is not, select another drive that is NTFS, or use the Convert utility.

2. Use the appropriate commands to create a new folder and a text file on drive C.

3. Before you can view NTFS permissions for the folder and file you have just created, you may need to take a few additional steps. You are probably using a Windows XP Professional system that is not participating on a Windows domain. As a result, you will not be able to view NTFS permissions on files and directories because the Security tab in the properties for the file is not available. By default, Windows XP Professional enables simplified file sharing. You must disable simplified file sharing to see the Security tab.

    To do this, select **Tools | Folder Options** in Windows Explorer to display the Folder Options dialog box, then click the **View** tab. In the Advanced Settings list box, deselect **Use Simple File Sharing (Recommended)**, then click **OK**.

4. Right-click the folder you created, click **Properties**, then click the **Security** tab. The NTFS permissions that are assigned by default to this resource display in the Properties dialog box (Figure 4-12).

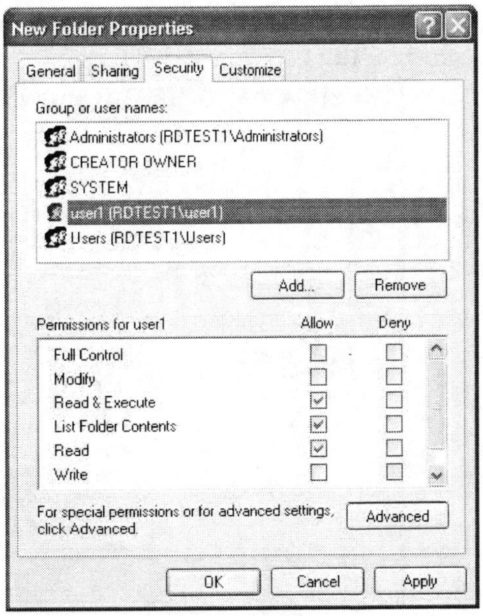

Figure 4-12: Properties dialog box — Security tab

5. Close the Properties dialog box.

6. Right-click the text file you created, click **Properties**, then click the **Security** tab to view its NTFS permissions.

7. Close the Properties dialog box and Windows Explorer.

Disk Defragmenter utility

OBJECTIVE:
3.8.7: File system management tools

Over time, as files are created and deleted, a partition can become severely fragmented. Fragmentation is one of the leading preventable causes of poor performance. Contiguous files provide good performance because the disk drive read/write heads do not have to jump from location to location. You can use the Disk Defragmenter utility to defragment hard disks and put fragmented files back together in a contiguous format.

In the following lab, you will learn how to defragment a hard disk using the Disk Defragmenter utility. Suppose your boss needs you to install a new spreadsheet application for an important new project. You install the application correctly, but find that your system now tends to start up sluggishly or exhibit other aspects of poor performance. You suspect that your hard disk may require defragmenting because you have installed and worked with many new files and programs over the past several months.

Lab 4-5: Defragmenting hard disks

In this lab, you will defragment your hard disk.

1. Display the Windows XP **Control Panel**, then click **Performance And Maintenance**. Click **Administrative Tools**, then double-click **Computer Management** to display the Computer Management window.

2. In the left pane of the window, click **Disk Defragmenter** to display the Disk Defragmenter utility (Figure 4-13).

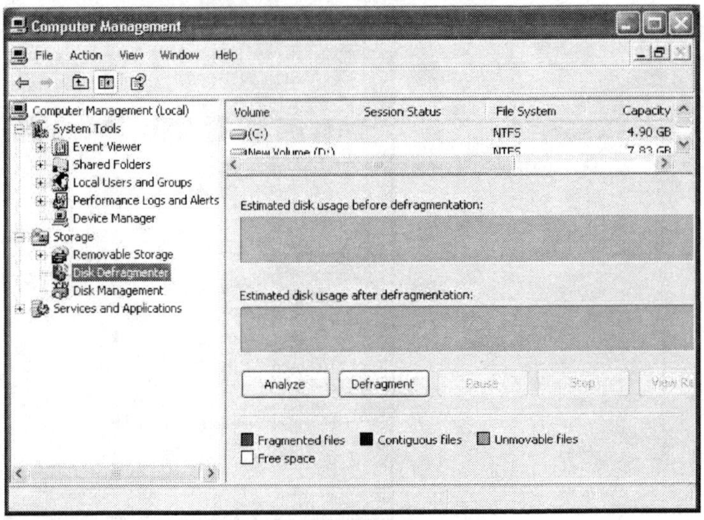

Figure 4-13: Disk Defragmenter

NOTE:
In Step 3, the defragmentation process may take several minutes to complete.

3. Select an NTFS volume in the list box, then click the **Defragment** button to start the defragmentation process.

4. When the defragmentation process is complete, click the **Close** button in the message box that displays prompting you to view the report, then close all windows.

Chkdsk utility

OBJECTIVE:
3.8.7: File system management tools

You can use the Chkdsk utility in Windows NT 4.0 Workstation, Windows 2000 and Windows XP to create and display a status report for a disk based on its file system. You can also use Chkdsk to list and correct errors on the disk, and to display the status of the disk in the current drive.

Chkdsk examples

Consider the following command:

```
chkdsk
```

This syntax will yield a status report showing any errors discovered in the current partition.

Now consider the following command:

```
chkdsk g:
```

This syntax will yield a status report showing any errors discovered in the partition you specified (in this example, G).

Next, consider the following command and option:

```
chkdsk g: /f
```

This syntax will yield a status report showing any errors discovered in the partition you specified (in this example, G), and will fix the errors.

Checking a disk in UNIX/Linux

In UNIX or Linux, you use the `fsck` command to check disk partitions. The `fsck` command performs the same function as the Chkdsk utility in Windows systems. If, for example, you wanted to check the first partition on the first hard drive, you would type:

```
fsck /dev/hda1
```

Disk Cleanup utility

Operating systems generate temporary files that you should periodically delete to conserve disk space. In some cases, deleting temporary files and directories will help you recover from application failures and from failed application installations. Common locations of temporary files include:

- C:\%systemroot%\temp (assuming a C drive).

- C:\Documents and Settings*user_name_*\Local Settings\temp.

- Directories and subdirectories created by installation programs.

You can delete temporary files manually by right-clicking them and clicking Delete, or you can use the Disk Cleanup utility.

The Disk Cleanup utility enables you to recover the disk space used by temporary files, unused applications, files in the Recycle Bin, files you downloaded as part of Web pages and files created when Chkdsk attempted to recover lost file fragments. The Disk Cleanup utility is available in Windows 98, Me, 2000 and XP.

In the following lab, you will learn how to use Disk Cleanup to delete temporary files that waste important disk space. Assume your co-workers have asked your help with minor performance problems they are having on their Windows XP systems. After questioning them, you learn that most of them have never deleted the cache of temporary files on their hard disk drives. So you decide to teach them as a group how to use the Disk Cleanup utility. After their lesson, you instruct them all to use this cleanup method at least once a week.

 Lab 4-6: Deleting temporary files

In this lab, you will delete any temporary files residing on your system.

1. Select **Start | All Programs | Accessories | System Tools | Disk Cleanup** to display the Select Drive dialog box (Figure 4-14).

Figure 4-14: Select Drive dialog box

Note: If you have only one hard disk and the disk is not partitioned, the Select Drive dialog box will not appear. Instead, when you click the Disk Cleanup command, the Disk Cleanup dialog box (Figure 4-15) will appear.

NOTE:
In Step 2, Disk Cleanup will scan the system after you click OK. The scan may take several minutes to complete.

2. Specify the drive you want to clean up, then click **OK**. This step displays the Disk Cleanup dialog box (Figure 4-15), which you use to select the types of files to remove when the utility executes. To view a list of eligible files, click the View Files button. Notice that downloaded program files, temporary Internet files and temporary offline files will be deleted, by default.

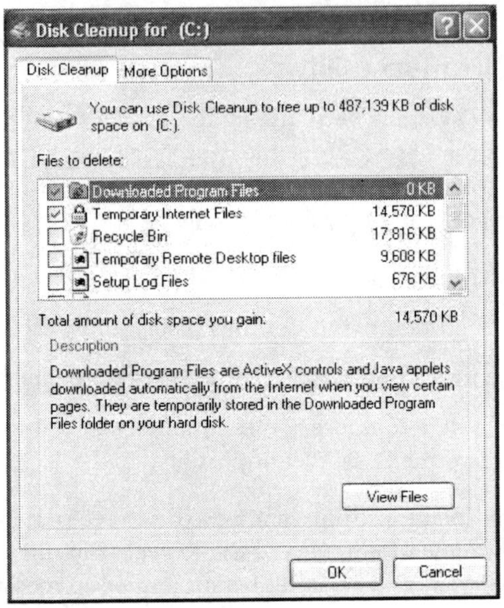

Figure 4-15: Disk Cleanup dialog box

restore point
A snapshot of a computer's settings at a particular point in time. Also known as a system checkpoint.

You can also use the More Options tab to specify to remove optional Windows components and programs that you do not use, as well as all saved system **restore points** except for the most recent one.

Note: A computer automatically creates restore points at regular intervals. If you experience problems, you can restore your computer settings to their most recent restore point (in other words, the point at which your computer was functioning with no errors or problems).

3. On the Disk Cleanup tab, click **OK**, then click **Yes** to execute the disk cleanup process. When the process is finished, all utility dialog boxes will automatically close.

OBJECTIVE:
3.8.7: File system management tools

Backup and Restore utilities

Even the best ongoing maintenance schedule cannot prevent a hard disk drive from wearing out or accidents from occurring. Keeping a current backup of all data files is essential to ensuring that data can be recovered if a hard disk drive fails. When you back up data, you store copies of folders and files to a source other than your computer's hard disk. Depending on file size and available hardware, storage sources can include floppy disks, writable CDs, network server hard disks and digital tapes.

All files and folders have archive properties that identify when the file or folder needs to be backed up. New files and existing files that have been modified have their archive attributes set to "on," indicating that they are ready for backup the next time data is backed up. Each time a file is backed up, the archive attribute is set to "off," indicating that the most recent version of the file has been backed up.

Table 4-10 describes various Windows XP data backup methods.

Table 4-10: Windows XP data backup methods

Method	Description
Full (or Normal)	All selected files are backed up and the archive attributes are reset to "off."
Copy	All selected files are backed up, but the archive attributes are not changed.
Incremental	Selected files with the archive attribute set to "on" will be backed up. The archive attributes of the backed-up files are then reset to "off." Therefore, if a file has not been modified, the next incremental backup will not back it up again.
Differential	Selected files with the archive attribute set to "on" will be backed up. However, the archive attributes are not reset and remain "on." Therefore, even if a file has not been modified, the next differential backup will back it up again.
Daily	Only files that are modified on the day the backup is run are backed up.

Backing up and restoring data in UNIX/Linux

You can use the dump command to back up files and directories on UNIX and Linux systems. The dump command allows you to conduct full, incremental and differential backups. You can then use the restore command to restore the backed up data, if needed.

Backing up data in Windows XP

In Windows XP, you can use the Backup Or Restore Wizard to back up data. The Backup Or Restore Wizard prompts you for information before starting the backup process. This information is used to complete the following four steps:

1. Select the files and folders to be backed up.

2. Select a file location or storage media for the backed-up data.

3. Specify backup options.

4. Initiate the backup.

In the following lab, you will learn how to back up data in Windows XP. If you were working on a large project at work that was scheduled to take several weeks, you would want to back up your work on a regular basis. Assume you and another co-worker were preparing copy for your company's Web site. Your tasks consisted of writing and editing large amounts of information, in both text and table format, to be posted to the company Web site as HTML documents. Which of the several backup methods — full, copy, incremental, differential or daily — would be appropriate to use in order to back up your data?

Lab 4-7: Backing up data in Windows XP

In this lab, you will use the Backup Or Restore Wizard in Windows XP to back up the new folder and text file you created in Lab 4-4.

Note: You will need a formatted floppy disk as the backup medium in order to complete this lab.

1. Insert a formatted floppy disk into the floppy disk drive.

2. Select **Start | All Programs | Accessories | System Tools | Backup** to display the Welcome screen of the Backup Or Restore Wizard.

3. Click **Next** to display the Backup Or Restore screen of the wizard, in which you specify whether to back up or restore files and settings. Notice that the Back Up Files And Settings option is selected by default.

4. Click **Next** to display the What To Back Up screen, in which you specify the items to be backed up.

5. Click **Let Me Choose What To Back Up**, then click **Next** to display the Items To Back Up screen (Figure 4-16), in which you specify specific drives, folders or files to back up.

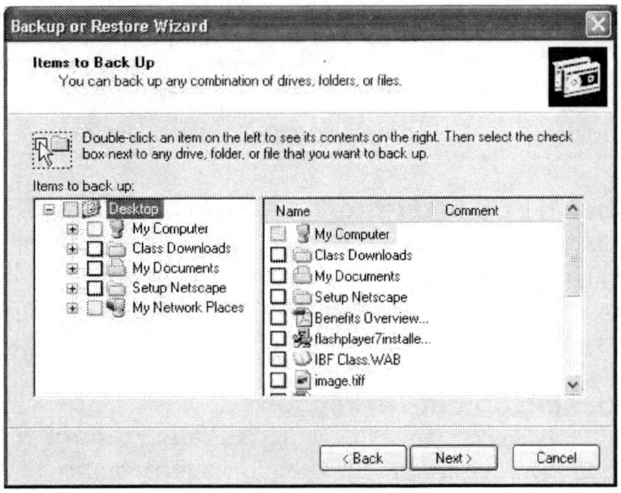

Figure 4-16: Backup Or Restore Wizard — Items To Back Up screen

6. In the Items To Back Up pane, double-click **My Computer**, then click **Local Drive (C:)** to display the contents of drive C in the right pane.

7. Select the check box to the left of the new folder you created in Lab 4-4, then click **Next** to display the Backup Type, Destination, And Name screen (Figure 4-17).

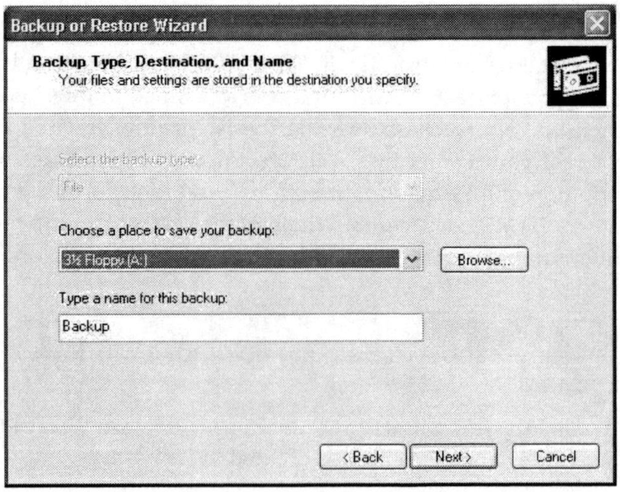

Figure 4-17: Backup Or Restore Wizard — Backup Type, Destination, And Name screen

8. If necessary, display the Choose A Place To Save Your Backup drop-down list, and click **3½ Floppy (A:)** to specify that the backup file will be saved to the disk in drive A.

NOTE:
In Step 9, when the Completing The Backup Or Restore Wizard screen displays, note that you can click the Advanced button if you want to specify a particular backup method. The default method is Normal.

9. Select the name in the Type A Name For This Backup text box, type ***Lab 4-7 Backup***, then click **Next**. This step specifies the name for the backup file and displays the Completing The Backup Or Restore Wizard screen.

10. Click **Finish** to initiate the backup. Notice that the Backup Progress dialog box displays while the backup operation is in progress.

11. When the backup is complete, close the Backup Progress dialog box.

Note: Leave the floppy disk in its drive. You will use it in Lab 4-8.

Restoring data in Windows XP

If backup data needs to be accessed, you can restore the data using the Backup Or Restore Wizard. By default, the files are restored to their original locations and existing files are not overwritten. However, using advanced options, you can specify that the files be restored in an alternative location of your choice. You can also specify whether existing files be overwritten during every backup or only if they are older than the backup files.

power spike
A short-duration high-voltage condition.

In the following lab, you will restore data that has been backed up. Suppose you had been compiling a list of potential customers for your opt-in online marketing business, backing up the list each night after you finished the day's work. Your most recent day's work, however, was lost, owing to a **power spike** caused by an electrical malfunction. You would need to recover the data from the most recent backup, which was the previous night. Restoring data allows you the option of overwriting existing files, and enables you to place restored files in a specific location on your system.

Lab 4-8: Restoring data in Windows XP

OBJECTIVE:
3.8.9: Backup and restore procedures

In this lab, you will use the Backup Or Restore Wizard in Windows XP to restore data.

Note: You must have completed Lab 4-7 before you can complete this lab.

1. Select **Start | All Programs | Accessories | System Tools | Backup** to display the Welcome screen of the Backup Or Restore Wizard.

2. Click **Next**, click **Restore Files And Settings**, then click **Next** again. This step specifies to restore data and displays the What To Restore screen (Figure 4-18).

Figure 4-18: Backup Or Restore Wizard — What To Restore screen

3. In the Items To Restore pane, double-click **File**, then click **Lab 4-7 Backup.bkf**. This step displays information for the Lab 4-7 Backup file in the right pane.

4. Select the check box to the left of **C:**, then click **Next**. This step selects the backup location and displays the Completing The Backup Or Restore Wizard screen, which summarizes the currently specified options.

5. Click the **Advanced** button to display the Where To Restore screen, in which you can specify another location.

6. Click **Next** to specify the original location and display the How To Restore screen, in which you can specify the replacement of existing files.

7. Click **Replace Existing Files**, then click **Next**. This step specifies that the backed up data will replace the existing files and displays the Advanced Restore Options screen, in which you can specify security or special system files to be restored.

8. Click **Next** and then click **Finish** to initiate the restore. Notice that the Restore Progress dialog box displays while the restore operation is in progress.

9. When the restore is complete, close the Restore Progress dialog box. Remove the floppy disk from its drive.

Troubleshooting Software

NOTE:
You should troubleshoot software settings first, then move to hardware. If a hardware component does not seem to be functioning, use the appropriate tool to determine whether the correct driver is installed (for example, Device Manager in Windows 2000 or Windows XP).

Software troubleshooting refers to any problems other than those caused by system hardware. Software problems can have a number of causes, including bugs, corrupted files, incompatibilities and virus infections.

Differentiating between hardware and software problems can sometimes be difficult. Hardware failures often initially appear to be software-related; they can be a symptom of a software problem, such as a corrupted device driver.

Tech Tip

One of the best ways to avoid software problems is to keep your software up to date. Operating system manufacturers often issue regular updates to correct known problems. Microsoft refers to these updates as service packs. Application program manufacturers will also sometimes release updates that fix known problems. Often, the main justification for the release of a new software version is to fix known bugs.

In the following sections, we will discuss software problems as they are exhibited during the operating system boot process and when applications fail.

Operating system boot problems

OBJECTIVE:
3.8.3: Boot problems and restarting

Following is a brief discussion of boot problems that can occur in workstations.

Error: No operating system

You will sometimes receive an error indicating that no operating system is present. First, make sure a floppy disk is not inserted in the floppy disk drive. Second, perform a cold boot of the system (in other words, turn your computer off and back on again) to ensure that an operating system is present. Sometimes, completely powering down the system and restarting it can solve a temporary problem that appears to be a disk failure.

Following are some common error messages, and their solutions:

- **Operating system files missing (for example, "missing ntldr" or "bad or missing command interpreter")** — Operating system files can be lost through disk corruption, file corruption or file deletion. In Windows NT and 2000, you will see a message such as "missing ntldr." In Linux systems, you will see a message that the kernel is not available. Use a boot disk, if available. Refer the problem to a help desk technician if a boot disk is not available. System reinstallation may be necessary. You may also be able to restore the system using system recovery features found in many operating systems.

- **Hard disk or controller failure** — This message indicates a hardware failure, but the problem can initially look like a software failure. Boot from a floppy disk and try to access the hard disk and controller. You will need to get the failing component replaced by a trained technician.

Occasionally you will not be able to find a cause for the system failure. In such cases, repair the system and monitor its performance. If the failure does not occur again, it could have been caused by a transient event such as a power spike.

Startup failure

Another possible startup failure condition is one in which the operating system is present, but the system cannot successfully complete startup. One possible cause is missing or corrupted operating system files. The solution is to recover (or replace) the files or reinstall the operating system. If you reinstall the operating system, you may need to restore data from backups, depending on how you run the installation.

You can also cause a system startup failure through your actions — for example, by making changes to the system registry, which is a database in which Windows stores configuration information. Depending on the changes that were made, you may be able to start up in Safe mode, which is a basic configuration that is primarily used for system troubleshooting and repair, and correct the registry. Otherwise, you may need to reinstall the operating system and restore data from backups.

Tech Tip

Depending on the nature of the edits to the registry, Windows XP may be able to correct the error. Press F8 to interrupt startup, as you would to start up in Safe mode, and select the Last Known Good Configuration option. This action will revert to the previous configuration and may allow you to start the operating system.

Blue screen of death (BSOD)

The term "blue screen of death" refers to a blue screen that displays during startup in Windows NT/2000/XP, which indicates that a critical operating system failure has occurred during startup. This failure may be caused by a transient condition, so one of the first solutions to try is to restart the system. Also, try starting up using the Last Known Good Configuration option.

If a system has been working properly and starts experiencing BSOD failures during startup, you need to determine whether the system can start up at all. Try starting up in Safe mode rather than Normal mode. If you can start in Safe mode, the problem may be one or more corrupted files or configuration settings. Restore from backups and test. If you still cannot start the system in Normal mode, reinstall the operating system.

If the problem occurs during a new installation, a component (for example, a NIC or a video driver) is probably not compatible with Windows NT/2000/XP. You will probably not be able to install Windows NT/2000/XP to run properly on the system.

NOTE:
Be cautious about editing the registry. Incorrectly editing the registry could severely damage your system.

To access Safe mode, you would restart your system and press the F8 key. Safe mode gives you access to only basic files and drivers and can be used to diagnose problems. If symptoms do not reappear when you start in Safe mode, the default settings and minimum device drivers can be eliminated as possible causes.

NOTE:
The technical name for the BSOD is the stop screen.

Windows 95/98/Me also display errors on a blue screen, but the information provided is not as complete as on the BSOD for Windows NT/2000/XP.

If a BSOD appears during startup, the system will store the information on the screen in a dump file. You can read the dump file in the /winnt/memory.dmp file. You can read more about how to parse (in other words, read) Windows NT/2000/XP blue screens at *www.microsoft.com/TechNet/prodtechnol/winntas/tips/techrep/bsod.mspx.*

System lockup

NOTE:
Sometimes, computers will freeze and screens will black out completely, rather than display the BSOD. In such cases, you will need to reboot your system.

If a system locks up often, consider the following solutions:

- Find out what application was running at the time of the lockup. The application may be incompatible with the operating system, or with a hardware component.

- Look for IRQ conflicts.

- Check log files for indications of a related problem.

When recovering from a lockup, you may need to power down your system manually by pressing the power key continually for five seconds. Otherwise, Windows may not surrender control of the system to the actual computer.

Application failures

OBJECTIVE:
3.8.2: Application failures

Application failures can take several forms in an operating system. An application may not load, or it may crash under certain conditions. After most application errors, you should try to quit the application (if it did not quit automatically) and attempt to duplicate the error. If you can consistently duplicate the error, the problem probably lies with the application. If the error does not occur at the same point or in the same fashion, the problem is probably in the operating system or a device driver.

Tech Tip

Some manufacturers list known problems on their Web sites. Others do not publish the problems, but may provide bug and other problem information through technical support. Some manufacturers charge for telephone support. Many manufacturers that charge for telephone support still provide free support by e-mail.

Next, try restarting the operating system to initialize the system and clear errors caused by transient conditions. Attempt to duplicate the error after system restart; if you cannot, the error was probably caused by a transient condition.

In the following sections, we will discuss some of the more common application failures.

Application will not start

When an application will not start, consider the following causes and solutions:

- System random access memory (RAM) may get too low and you will need to free system memory. Shut down applications running on the system.

- The current logon environment may have crashed, even though it may appear to be running properly. In all Windows systems, the logon environment is made possible by explorer.exe and other applications. Sometimes, this application will fail to execute properly. First, try logging off the system and logging back on. If doing so does not solve the problem, restart the system. To determine whether the problem is specific to your account, log on as another user and try to launch the application. If it launches in the other logon environment, review the settings for the problem account. If the problem continues, reinstall the application.

- Some applications will not load properly unless you have additional privileges. Verify your permissions.

- System RAM may get too low because application crashes will not surrender the RAM they have been using to the operating system. Restart the system.

- Some applications will not run unless your system is using a certain resolution or color level. Verify or change system resolution to solve the problem.

System log

NOTE:
See **Optional Lab 4-2: Using the Windows XP Event Viewer.**

Viewing the system log is an effective way to determine the reason or reasons for an application's failure to launch. In Windows systems, use Event Viewer to see log entries generated by the application.

In UNIX/Linux systems, the log file is called messages, and resides off the /var/log/ directory. You can also open the /var/log/messages file using various applications, including text editors such as vi. You can also use the cat command to view the entire file, as shown in the following syntax:

```
cat /var/log/messages
```

However, you may not want to read the entire log file. To read only the last 10 lines of the log file, use the `tail` command instead of the `cat` command.

Windows protection errors

Windows protection errors may sometimes occur on a system. Such an occurrence also indicates a problem with internal (operating system) management and security. Windows protection faults are often caused by device drivers that were not written specifically for your operating system. They can also be caused by applications or utilities that attempt to bypass the operating system and directly access local system hardware. Make sure you are using the most recent driver version for your operating system. Some errors can be corrected by reinstalling the operating system, but this solution means that the computer cannot be used while the operating system is being installed and configured.

Dr. Watson

NOTE:
Dr. Watson was first introduced to provide more descriptive error messages, as well as to suggest solutions.

Dr. Watson is an application debug program for Windows 9x, Windows NT 4.0, Windows 2000 and Windows XP. You can launch Dr. Watson and leave it running in the background. When a system error occurs, Dr. Watson will create an error report that contains detailed information about the system.

In the following lab, you will learn how to use Dr. Watson to view information about application errors. Dr. Watson can be especially helpful when you are trying to troubleshoot intermittent application problems. Suppose you work for the IT help desk at an insurance company. Several employees in the accounting department have been using a new bookkeeping program, but have experienced several intermittent problems since installing the new software. You may be asked to collect Dr. Watson logs as you work with the software manufacturer's technical support staff to troubleshoot these problems. How do you view Dr. Watson logs in the affected computers, which are running Windows XP Professional? What type of information is available from Dr. Watson?

 Lab 4-9: Viewing Dr. Watson

In this lab, you will view Dr. Watson settings.

1. Select **Start | Run** to display the Run dialog box.

2. Type **drwtsn32** in the Open text box, then click **OK**. This step displays the Dr. Watson For Windows dialog box (Figure 4-19).

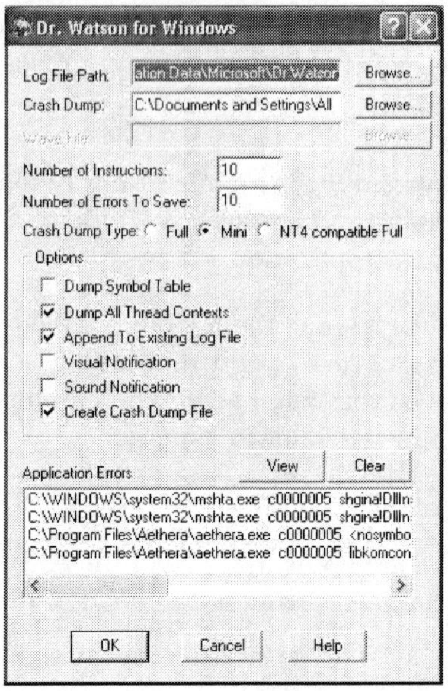

Figure 4-19: Dr. Watson For Windows dialog box

Note: You can select all check boxes in the Options section if you want to obtain more explicit information from Dr. Watson.

3. If any application errors are listed in the Application Errors list box, click one of them, then click the **View** button. This step displays the Log File Viewer for the selected error (Figure 4-20).

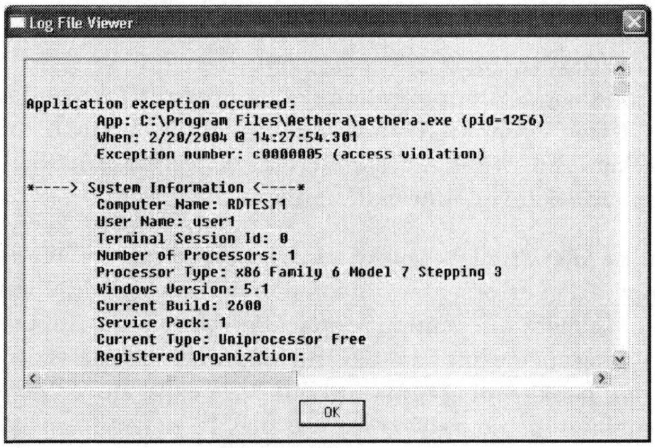

Figure 4-20: Log File Viewer

4. Close the Log File Viewer and quit Dr. Watson.

Application installation and loading failures

Application installation and loading failures can include the following situations:

- An application will not load into memory.

- An application causes an illegal operation, resulting in the BSOD.

- An application will not install at all.

Table 4-11 provides information about the most common application installation and loading failures, as well as proposed solutions.

Table 4-11: Application installation and loading errors

Failure	Solution
Incompatible application	Make sure that the application or application version is compatible with the operating system. Otherwise, find a compatible version of the application.
Lack of administrative privileges	Linux and Windows systems often require a user with full administrative privileges to install some applications. Log off and log back on as the administrator to the system. If the system belongs to a Microsoft domain, and the local administrator has been limited, log on as the domain administrator.
Registry busy or corrupt	The area of the Windows registry pertinent to the application may be locked or busy. Use Task Manager to ensure that no other applications are currently running (Task Manager provides information about programs and processes running on your computer. Press CTRL+ALT+DEL, then click the Task Manager button to open Task Manager). If the registry is corrupt, you may need to restore it from a backup.
Media failure	The local or remote drive containing the installation medium may not be available or may be unrecognized. Ensure that the drive and/or network connection is working properly.
Failed service	Start or restart the service (or daemon in UNIX/Linux). You may need to restart the entire system or log off and log back on.
Application dependency	Some applications require certain services and additional applications and libraries before installation can occur. Install all dependencies, and then install the application. In Linux, for example, an application may not run because of a problem with the X Window environment. You may need to edit the X Window configuration files (for example, the files and subdirectories in the /etc/X11 directory).
Hardware failure	The application depends on a device, such as a NIC, that is somehow unavailable. Check the device.
Leftover files from a previous (failed) installation	Regardless of your operating system, temporary files exist in a directory with permissions that forbid the current user from deleting them. Delete the files and/or directories. You may need to consult system documentation to learn where temporary files are stored for the application and specific operating system.
Insufficient drive space	An application may fail to run or install if your hard drive is full. Many applications generate log files and other files in temporary folders. If no space is available, the application will crash. Clear some space and try again.

Remote Management and Troubleshooting

OBJECTIVE:
3.8.10: Remote workstation management

As an IT Professional, you may need to manage and troubleshoot workstation problems from a remote location periodically. The following sections will review several tools you can use to access workstations from a remote location.

The tools discussed in the following sections were explained in detail in the Internet Business Foundations coursebook of the Foundations series. The following discussion will summarize the information presented in the other coursebook.

Telnet

Telnet is a TCP/IP protocol that allows you to establish a remote connection with a server and then use that computer to gather the information you need. Essentially, you are logging on to the server and accessing information as if you were sitting at it.

To use Telnet, you need an account and a password on the host computer. You can use Telnet to access some public servers, such as public libraries and government resources, using a generic password.

A Telnet command request looks similar to the following:

```
telnet rock.lib.asu.edu
```

The result of this request is an invitation to log on to the Arizona State University library system, in which you could search for a book, for example.

NOTE:
In UNIX/Linux systems, remember that all commands are case-specific. For example, typing "Telnet" will yield an error message.

Secure Shell (SSH)

Secure Shell (SSH), sometimes known as Secure Socket Shell, is a protocol that you can use to gain secure access to a remote computer and then execute commands to administer a system. Many different clients use the SSH protocol, which features a Telnet-like interface. In the past, SSH was used only on UNIX-based systems. However, an SSH server can be installed on any Windows platform using Cygwin (*www.cygwin.com*), a program that simulates the Linux environment for Windows systems.

SSH clients exist for almost any operating system (for example, Macintosh, Windows or UNIX). All SSH sessions are encrypted. However, sending encrypted authentication information across unsecured channels is potentially harmful. Configuring SSH to authenticate users with public keys rather than passwords is recommended, but does not occur by default with SSH. The latest version of the SSH protocol is SSH2. Many users now prefer SSH over Telnet. Figure 4-21 shows a sample SSH session.

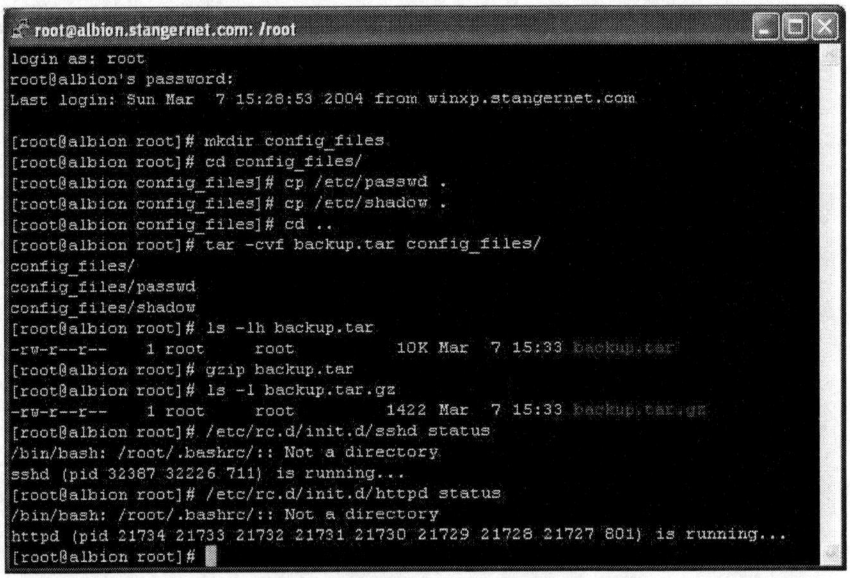

Figure 4-21: Sample SSH session

NOTE:
The "Not a directory" error is caused by a mistaken entry in a file named bashrc. The entry is referring to a nonexistent directory.

The preceding figure shows a session in which a user has logged on to a remote system named *albion.stangernet.com*. The user logged on as root (the administrative account in most systems), then backed up important configuration files (including the /etc/passwd and /etc/shadow files, which contain user authentication information). The user then archived these files and compressed them using the gzip program. Finally, the user checked the status of the SSH and HTTPD daemons.

Virtual Network Computing (VNC)

Virtual Network Computing (VNC) is a program that allows you to control a computer at a remote location. VNC consists of two components: the server and the viewer. The server listens on a specific port (for example, TCP 5800 on Windows systems) and allows clients to connect to it. Authenticated users can log on and see the server display on their remote computers. Unlike Telnet or SSH, VNC provides a full GUI display. The second component, the viewer, allows users to see the remote system's logon environment. The server and the viewer do not need to be running the same operating system.

VNC can be used in a variety of ways. In an office, for example, a systems administrator can use VNC to diagnose and fix problems on a co-worker's computer, or can access and administer server computers without having to work from the server room. Help desk staff might also use VNC to troubleshoot a computer problem for remote employees, or to install software on remote systems.

Remote Desktop

Remote Desktop is a Windows XP service you can use to gain access from your computer to a Windows session that is running on another computer. You can, for example, connect to your work computer from home and gain access to all your applications, files and network resources, as if you were using your computer at work. If you leave programs running at work, when you get home you can display your work Desktop on your home computer, with the same programs running.

When you connect to your computer at work, Remote Desktop automatically locks it to prevent others from accessing your applications and files. When you return to your computer at work, you can unlock it by pressing CTRL+ALT+DEL.

Remote Desktop also allows multiple users to participate in active sessions on a single computer. Users can leave their applications running while other users log on to the computer. Remote Desktop will preserve the state of each user's Windows session.

In addition, Remote Desktop enables you to switch from one user to another on the same computer. For example, suppose you are working at home and have logged on to your computer at work to access a file. While you are working, a family member asks to use your home computer. You can disconnect Remote Desktop, allow the other user to log on to complete his or her task, and then reconnect to your computer at work, continuing where you left off.

Remote Assistance

Remote Assistance is a Windows XP feature that allows a user to seek assistance from another person in a remote location. This feature involves allowing a trusted person at the remote location to connect to your computer and view your screen. Remote Assistance is used in conjunction with Windows Messenger (or e-mail), enabling the remote person to offer real-time assistance via instant messaging. When you accept a connection from a remote assistant, your Desktop displays on the remote computer. The remote person can send you directions for performing a task, then you can perform the task and the results will display on both your computer and the remote computer. This capability allows for instant feedback. Your remote partner can also take control of your computer. However, you have the option to decline any assistance. You retain control of your computer unless you specifically relinquish that control to the person assisting you. Remote Assistance requires both computers to be running Windows XP.

Network Maintenance in Adverse Conditions

Nevine is an archeologist who is spending six months at an archeological site in southern Egypt. She has become the *de facto* IT administrator after setting up a small computer network (using the Windows XP Professional operating system) in the main tent. Due to the frequent desert winds that blow across the Sahara and deposit dust practically everywhere, Nevine realizes she needs to set up a preventive maintenance program to keep the small network working properly.

Nevine decides to immediately perform the following tasks:

- She asks her colleagues to help seal the tent as much as possible to prevent dust from infiltrating the chamber containing the network devices.

- She checks all computers to ensure that slot covers completely cover all slot openings.

Next, Nevine decides to implement the following preventive maintenance program:

- Back up user data to high-capacity storage disks on a daily basis.

- Run the Chkdsk utility on a weekly basis to check for and correct physical disk errors.

- Run the Disk Cleanup utility on a weekly basis to delete temporary files and conserve disk space.

- Run the Disk Defragmenter utility on a quarterly basis to defragment the hard disk drives.

- Clean all adapter boards and input devices with a static-free vacuum and compressed air on a quarterly basis to remove accumulated dust.

*   *   *

What additional maintenance activities can Nevine implement to ensure the small network continues to work properly? How often should she perform these tasks?

Lesson Summary

Application project

When you have time, attempt to restart your computer in Safe mode (press the F8 key during the reboot process).

When your Desktop displays, note the differences in the Desktop between Normal mode and Safe mode. What are the differences?

Display the Settings tab of the Display Properties dialog box (right-click the Desktop and click Properties). What is your screen resolution? Open Windows Explorer and attempt to access a network drive. What happens? Restart your computer in Normal mode.

Skills review

In this lesson, you learned about the basic hardware and system maintenance procedures you should perform to minimize component failure and system problems. You learned about the maintenance issues associated with motherboards, IRQs, I/O addresses, DMA, IDE/ATA and EIDE disk drives, SATA disk drives and SCSI devices. You were introduced to peripheral ports, and you learned about CD-ROMs and DVDs.

You also learned the basics of managing a client operating system. You learned about the importance of software licensing and preparing a hard disk for use. You reviewed the characteristics of several file system types, and learned how to use file system management tools and troubleshooting software. Finally, you learned how to remotely manage and troubleshoot workstations.

Now that you have completed this lesson, you should be able to:

✓ Identify the characteristics of motherboards.

✓ Identify common IRQ, I/O address and DMA settings, and describe their functions.

✓ Identify the characteristics of IDE/ATA, EIDE/ATA-2, SATA and SCSI.

✓ Identify NICs and common peripheral ports, and describe their functions.

✓ Identify the characteristics of CD-ROMs and DVDs.

✓ Describe hard-drive partitioning and formatting.

✓ Describe the characteristics of file system types, including FAT, FAT32, NTFS, Ext3 and ReiserFS.

✓ Describe the uses of file system management tools, including Convert, Disk Defragmenter, Chkdsk, Disk Cleanup, Backup and Restore.

✓ Identify and suggest corrective measures for operating system boot problems and application failures.

✓ Identify methods to remotely manage and troubleshoot workstations.

Lesson 4 Review

1.   What are the two formats supported for writable CD-ROMs?

     _____

2.   What steps must you perform to prepare a hard disk for use?

     _____

     _____

3.   Why is it important to periodically defragment a partition on which files are
     frequently created, modified and deleted?

     _____

     _____

4.   What is the purpose of the Disk Cleanup utility?

     _____

     _____

5.   What are some of the problems associated with using unlicensed software?

     _____

     _____

     _____

                Version 1.2

Lesson 4
Supplemental Material

This section is a supplement containing additional tasks for you to complete in conjunction with the lesson. These elements are:

- **Activities**
  Pen-and-paper activities to review lesson concepts or terms.

- **Optional Labs**
  Computer-based labs to provide additional practice.

- **Lesson Quiz**
  Multiple-choice test to assess knowledge of lesson material.

Activity 4-1: Identifying backup methods

In this activity, you will review methods you can use to create backups.

1. Discuss the following methods used when backing up files. Write your answers in the space provided.

    Full:

    _____

    _____

    _____

    Differential:

    _____

    _____

    _____

    Incremental:

    _____

    _____

    _____

    _____

Activity 4-2: Reviewing CD-ROM and DVD maintenance issues

In this activity, you will review CD-ROM and DVD maintenance issues.

1. Discuss corrective and preventive measures you can undertake to resolve the following CD-ROM and DVD maintenance issues.

    Issue: CD-ROM and DVD drive contamination

    _____

    _____

    _____

    Issue: CD-ROM and DVD defects

    _____

    _____

Issue: Internal laser contamination

_____

_____

_____

Issue: CD-ROM or DVD drive door will not open because of a malfunction or lost power

_____

_____

_____

 Activity 4-3: Converting decimal, binary and hexadecimal values

In this activity, you will convert values among the decimal, binary and hexadecimal numbering systems.

Note: Do not use a calculator at first.

1. What is the hexadecimal value of 100011010? Make sure to focus on the process of determining this value, rather than just obtaining the value.

_____

_____

_____

_____

_____

2. Convert the hexadecimal value found in Step 1 into decimal.

_____

_____

_____

_____

_____

3. How would you represent the hexadecimal value of 2DF in binary?

_____

_____

_____

4. Convert the following number into both binary and hexadecimal: 91364

_____

_____

_____

5. Check your work. If you have access to a Windows 9x/Me, NT, 2000 or XP machine, you can check your work by using the calculator program. In the program, go to View | Scientific, as shown in Figure A4-1. Doing so will allow you to easily convert among decimal, binary and hexadecimal.

Figure A4-1: Scientific mode in Windows calculator program

Optional Lab 4-1: Removing dust from a PC

In this lab, you will remove dust from a PC.

1. Turn off your system, if necessary.

2. Remove the power cable from the unit.

3. Obtain either a can of compressed air or a static-free vacuum cleaner. Also, obtain a small brush. Do not use a standard vacuum cleaner because it produces large amounts of electrostatic discharge (ESD) that can damage your system.

4. Remove the case cover.

5. If possible, take the opened case outside to remove dust. However, make sure that you do not expose the system to any dangerous conditions (for example, rain). Also, make sure that you put the system in a secure place so that it cannot fall, get hit by falling objects, or otherwise become damaged.

6. As you remove dust, pay special attention to the following components:

   • Floppy disk and CD-ROM/DVD drives

- The area surrounding the CPU

- Power connectors

7. Make sure that all components (for example, adapter cards) are still properly attached to the system and that no component is out of place. Sometimes, moving the PC can loosen components.

8. Replace the case cover.

9. Turn on the system to make sure that it works properly.

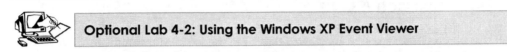
Optional Lab 4-2: Using the Windows XP Event Viewer

In this optional lab, you will use the Windows XP Event Viewer to view information about hardware or software problems your system may have encountered.

1. Display the Windows XP **Control Panel**, then click **Performance And Maintenance**. Click **Administrative Tools**, then double-click **Event Viewer** to display the Event Viewer window (Figure OL4-1).

Figure OL4-1: Event Viewer window

2. In the left pane, click **Application**, then scroll through the log in the right pane. The Application log contains events logged by applications, including application errors. Notice that some entries in the Type column are marked *Error* and *Warning*, indicating potential application errors.

3. In the left pane, click **Security**, then scroll through the log in the right pane. The Security log records events such as resource use, and valid and invalid logon attempts.

Note: The Security log may not contain any items if no events took place that would be considered a security problem. If you have enabled logon auditing, attempts to log on to your system are recorded in the Security log. Invalid logon attempts will display as security failures.

4. In the left pane, click **System**, then scroll through the log in the right pane. The System log contains events recorded by Windows XP system components, such as device drivers. The System log will contain a record of any driver or system component that fails to load during startup.

5. Close all windows.

The Event Viewer may be very helpful in resolving any application failures you encounter by providing possible reasons for the failure.

Lesson 4 Quiz

1. Which of the following describes the location through which a processor transfers data and commands to a device?

   a. DMA channel
   b. I/O address
   c. IRQ assignment
   d. PIO channel

2. You have two internal SCSI devices and two external SCSI devices connected to a single SCSI adapter. How many of the devices should be terminated?

   a. One
   b. Two
   c. Three
   d. Four

3. What type of problem may be caused by accumulated dust?

   a. Electrostatic discharge
   b. Heat
   c. Power spike
   d. Resource conflict

4. Which file system must you use to support encryption on a Windows XP computer?

   a. NTFS 5.1
   b. NTFS 5.0
   c. FAT32
   d. FAT16

5. Which of the following Windows XP utilities would you use to rearrange files into contiguous structures to improve system performance?

   a. Chkdsk
   b. Convert
   c. Disk Cleanup
   d. Disk Defragmenter

Lesson 5:
Network Security and IT Career Opportunities

Objectives

By the end of this lesson, you will be able to:

🖝 Define security.

🖝 Identify various kinds of network attacks.

🖝 Describe computer viruses and explain how to protect your network from virus attacks.

🖝 Describe authentication principles.

🖝 Explain the three major types of encryption.

🖝 Describe network security protocols and technologies, including Virtual Private Networks (VPNs), remote access server (RAS), digital certificates and Public Key Infrastructure (PKI).

🖝 Describe firewalls, security zones and common firewall topologies.

🖝 Describe security audit principles.

🖝 Describe the function of an uninterruptible power supply (UPS).

🖝 Review career opportunities in the IT industry.

🖝 Describe the importance of successfully explaining technical issues to non-technical audiences.

Pre-Assessment Questions

1. What type of attack occurs when a host or system cannot perform properly because another system on the network is using all its resources?

   a. Back-door attack
   b. Denial-of-service attack
   c. Man-in-the-middle attack
   d. Trojan-horse attack

2. Which of the following encryption methods uses a public key and private key pair?

   a. Hash encryption
   b. PGP
   c. Asymmetric-key encryption
   d. Symmetric-key encryption

3. What is the name for a mini-network that resides between a company's internal network and an external network (for example, the Internet)?

   _____

Importance of Network Security

hacker
An unauthorized user who penetrates a host or network to access and manipulate data.

Although the primary motivation for connecting systems is to share information and resources, this connectivity also makes systems and data vulnerable to unwanted activity. Connectivity always implies risk. A **hacker** can conduct many different attacks using many different methods. However, you can protect a network against unwanted entry by recognizing and implementing security techniques, including threat identification, risk and threat analysis, authentication, encryption and firewalls.

The last two sections of this lesson will explore career opportunities in the IT industry and effective ways of communicating technical information to non-technical audiences.

Defining Security

In relation to networking, security is best defined as a set of procedures designed to protect transmitted and stored information, as well as network resources. Security involves defending and protecting assets.

As an end user, you should understand how to recognize a security incident, then understand whom to contact in case of a suspected problem. This lesson will explain these steps. You should also understand essential security concepts, including common threats and attacks, encryption, firewalls, security zones and authentication.

Overview of Network Attack Types

OBJECTIVE:
3.5.1: Security attack types

Table 5-1 lists common types of attacks waged against network resources. You will learn more about these attacks throughout this lesson. This list is provided now to familiarize you with the terms.

Table 5-1: Network attack types

packet sniffing
The use of protocol analyzer software to obtain sensitive information, such as user names and passwords.

replay attack
An attack in which packets are obtained from the network or a network host, then reused.

account lockout
A legitimate practice in which a user account is automatically disabled after a certain number of failed authentication attempts.

Attack	Description
Spoofing	Spoofing (also known as a masquerade attack) involves altering or generating falsified or malformed network packets. A host (or a program or application) pretends it is another entity on a network. The entity under attack is convinced it is dealing with a trusted host, and any transactions that occur can lead to further compromise.
Man in the middle	An attack that must take place by being physically in the middle of a connection for an attacker to obtain information. Includes **packet sniffing** and **replay attacks**.
Denial of service (DOS)	DOS is a type of attack waged by a single system on one or more systems. DOS attacks involve crashing a system completely or occupying system resources (for example, CPU cycles and RAM), which renders the system nonfunctional. DOS can also involve causing legitimate system features and tools to backfire. For example, many operating systems provide for **account lockout**. If account lockout is enabled, a malicious user can purposely and repeatedly disable logon capability for user accounts. As a result, users will be unable to access any network services.
Distributed denial of service (DDOS)	DDOS involves the use of multiple applications found on several network resources to crash one or more systems, denying service to a host. DDOS is often used to consume a server's data connection.
Brute force	A brute-force attack involves repeated guessing of passwords or other encrypted data, one character at a time, usually at random. It can also involve physical attacks, such as forcing open a server room door or opening false ceilings.

Table 5-1: Network attack types (cont'd)

Attack	Description
Dictionary	Dictionary attacks involve repeated attempts to guess a password. They are similar to brute force attacks, but use a file containing a long list of words to repeatedly guess user names and passwords, instead of random values.
Back door	A back-door attack involves code inserted secretly in an application or operating system by developers; the code opens a networking port that allows illicit access into the system. Usually, only the developers know the password, but in many cases these passwords become publicly known.
Buffer overflow	A buffer overflow is a condition that occurs when a legitimate application (or part of one) exceeds the memory buffer allocated to it by the operating system. Buffer overflows can occur due to inadvertent flaws written into program code. All applications must use a memory buffer. Sometimes, however, applications can place too much information into a buffer, resulting in a buffer overflow. Applications that do not carefully check the size of information before processing it are especially vulnerable to overflows.
Trojan horse	A Trojan horse attack involves malicious code that is disguised to appear as a legitimate application. For example, a seemingly harmless game might, in fact, also contain code that allows a hacker to defeat a system's security.
Social engineering	Social engineering involves attempts to trick legitimate employees into revealing information or changing system settings in order to gain access to a network.

OBJECTIVE:
3.5.2: Social engineering attacks

 Never use any techniques or software described in this course to attack systems you do not own. Furthermore, if you ever simulate any attacks for your own research purposes, use a completely isolated network.

Avoiding attacks

You can avoid attacks by taking the following steps:

digital signature
An electronic stamp added to a message that uniquely identifies its source and verifies its contents at the time of the signature.

- **Install stable updates** — Make sure that your applications and operating systems use the latest, stable versions. All updates should originate from trusted sources (for example, the vendor that sold you the product). Verify that updates are, in fact, updates and not Trojans. For example, check for a file's **digital signature**. These solutions help avoid buffer overflow and Trojan-based attacks. Updates can also help eliminate back-door attacks, providing that the company has found all existing back doors and has not introduced new ones.

- **Use encryption** — As you learned earlier, encryption is a security technique to prevent access to information by converting it into a scrambled (unreadable) form of text. If you encrypt network transmissions, you can avoid man-in-the-middle attacks.

- **Be suspicious of information requests** — Social engineering experts rely on naive users and confusion. If you receive a request by telephone or e-mail, verify the nature of the request before divulging information. For example, reveal sensitive information only to a trusted IT worker in the presence of your manager or other appropriate individual.

- **Remain informed** — The most secure organizations take the time to inform their employees regularly about the latest attacks.

Viruses and Worms

OBJECTIVE:
3.5.1: Security
attack types

Computer viruses are perhaps the most well-known attack type. A **virus** is a malicious program designed to damage network equipment, including stand-alone computers. A virus requires an explicit action on the part of an individual or a workstation in order to spread. Viruses can spread in many ways, including the following:

virus
A malicious program that replicates itself on computer systems, usually through executable software, and causes irreparable system damage.

- **E-mail** — Unsuspecting users may attach infected documents and programs, and then send the programs to other users. Often, an unsuspecting e-mail recipient may open an infected attachment; an attachment that contains a virus is sometimes disguised as a legitimate application or image. If the e-mail recipient double-clicks this file, the virus will infect the recipient's system, and may also spread to other users.

- **Disks** — In the past, floppy disks were the primary means of spreading viruses. Increasingly, however, removable USB drives have become common methods of spreading viruses.

NOTE:
Viruses attack individual systems and are only considered a network concern because they can use the network's communication path to spread.

New viruses appear daily. You can learn about the latest virus attacks from many sources, including the following:

- Symantec (*www.symantec.com*)

- CERT® (*www.cert.org*)

- McAfee (*www.mcafee.com*)

Virus types

Many types of viruses exist, including the following:

NOTE:
Macro viruses are often passed as documents attached to e-mail messages.

- **Macro/script** — a small program written in macro code for word processing or spreadsheet applications such as Microsoft Word or Excel. When the infected file is opened, the macro is executed.

- **File infecting** — attaches itself to executable programs (or is itself executable) and is activated when the user launches the program. If you receive an executable program from an unknown source, scan the program using antivirus software before running it.

- **Boot sector** — copies itself to the boot sector of hard drives, allowing itself to be loaded into memory each time a system is started. After being loaded into memory, a boot sector virus may replicate itself on other drives (hard disk drives and floppy disks) and may completely erase the drives it accesses.

- **Stealth** — attempts to avoid detection by redirecting hard-disk-drive read requests from the virus-scanning software or by manipulating directory structure information. This manipulation causes the virus-scanning program to miss the stealth virus in its scanning process, leaving the virus on the system.

- **Polymorphic** — contains programming code enabling it to execute differently each time it is run. Because it appears as a different process each time, this virus avoids being detected by virus-scanning software.

- **Retro** — specifically attacks antivirus software. Often included with other virus types. The virus code contains a retro virus portion that disables the virus detection software, allowing another portion of the virus code to attack the operating system, applications or stored files.

Virus protection software

NOTE:
Most systems provide some level of virus protection through the BIOS.

The best defense against a virus is to regularly run an industry-recognized, currently updated antivirus program. Antivirus software identifies and removes viruses from your computer. Updates are important — even the best antivirus programs cannot protect systems if their antivirus files are outdated.

Antivirus programs are sold by companies such as McAfee (*www.mcafee.com*) and Symantec (*www.symantec.com*). Programs are also available as freeware and shareware at the TUCOWS Web site (*www.tucows.com*).

User education

Perhaps the most effective action an administrator can take to prevent viruses from infecting his or her systems is to teach network users about the potential consequences. Informing them of the potential for damage and lost productivity can motivate users to implement the following recommended practices.

- Floppy disks are the primary means of infection. Scan floppy disks every time they are used.

- If you receive an executable program from someone you do not know, do not execute it.

- If you receive an executable program from someone you know, scan it before running it.

- If you suspect a virus or detect unusual activity on your system, inform the IT department immediately.

Worms

A worm is a malicious program that can spread from system to system without direct human intervention. It is similar to a virus except that it automatically replicates.

Defeating Attacks

Table 5-2 summarizes key security concepts that can be used to defeat attempts to gain illegitimate access. These services are also described in the OSI/RM.

Table 5-2: OSI/RM security services

digital certificate
A password-protected, encrypted data file containing message encryption, user identification and message text. Used to authenticate a program or a sender's public key, or to initiate SSL sessions. Must be signed by a certificate authority (CA) to be valid.

Service	Description
Authentication	Proves identity upon presentation; for example, a user account logon name and password.
Access control	Grants various levels of file or directory permissions to users.
Data confidentiality	Provides protection of data on a system or host from unauthorized access. For example, remote users logged on to a system may be unaware that their transactions are being monitored. To ensure confidentiality, they may use some form of encryption to prevent others from understanding their communication.
Data integrity	Provides protection against active threats, such as man-in-the-middle attacks, that attempt to alter messages before they are sent or received. The integrity service prevents or recognizes such an attempt, giving the system time to recover or stop it.
Non-repudiation	Provides proof that a transaction has occurred. Repudiation occurs when one party in a transaction denies that the transaction took place. The other party may use a means of non-repudiation to prove that the transaction actually did occur. For example, a sales receipt provides a means of non-repudiation. Another example: A Web server is able to prove that a transaction has occurred by showing a log file or a cached copy of a client's **digital certificate**.

Updates

Make sure that you update your system and all applications with the latest, stable updates. Do not make the mistake of updating only the operating system (for example, simply using Windows Update or Red Hat Up2date). You must also update individual applications (for example, Netscape, Mozilla and SSH applications).

Movie Time!

Watch the following CIW v5 Foundations Movie to learn even more about this topic.

Protection from Viruses (approx. playing time: 06:30)

All movie clips are © 2007 LearnKey, Inc.

Authentication

OBJECTIVE:
3.5.4:
Authentication principles

As you learned earlier, authentication is the ability to determine a user's true identity. To communicate effectively, users in enterprise networks must ensure that they are actually communicating with the person they want to address. However, IP spoofing, falsified e-mail messages, social engineering and other techniques all intervene to defeat the authentication process.

NOTE:
Kerberos (Windows 2000/XP and UNIX) enables mutual authentication, in which the client is authenticated by the server and the server is authenticated by the client.

Networks can employ the following three methods to prove a user's identity and achieve authentication:

- **What you know** — the most common form of authentication; involves the use of passwords. When you log on to a computer network, you are often asked for a password. A password is something you know.

- **What you have** — requires you to use a physical item, such as a key, for authentication. An example is a building entry card. If you have a card (which you pass over a scanner), you will be granted access to the building. In this case, the authentication is based on possessing the card. The most powerful example of this technology type is a **smart card**.

smart card
A credit card that replaces the magnetic strip with an embedded chip for storing or processing data.

- **Who you are** — involves biometrics, which is the science of connecting authentication schemes to unique physical attributes. Examples of this method include the use of fingerprints, visual and photographic identification, and physical signatures. More sophisticated methods include retinal scans, facial maps, voice analysis and digital signatures. Each method attempts to validate an individual's claim concerning his or her identity.

Tech Note — *The term "strong authentication" describes extensive steps, including the use of encryption, to ensure authentication. Strong authentication is a combination of what you know, what you have and who you are.*

Passwords

Passwords are one of the core strengths of computer and network security, and are part of the "what you know" authentication method. If the password is compromised, the basic security scheme or model is affected. To enforce good password practice, you need to require passwords and to help users choose strong passwords (you will learn about strong passwords shortly).

Because so many different operating systems exist, no universal standard can be adopted for the ideal password. However, strong passwords generally include at least three of the following four types of content:

- Uppercase letters
- Lowercase letters
- Numbers
- Non-alphanumeric characters, such as punctuation

Strong passwords should also adhere to the following guidelines:

- Do not use common names or nicknames.
- Do not use common personal information (for example, date of birth).
- Repeat letters or digits in the password.

Essentially, you must think like a hacker: Avoid measures that may allow others to discover your password (for example, using your date of birth as your password, or writing your password on paper and leaving it in plain view).

Password aging

Password aging relates to the frequency with which users must change their passwords. Following are password-aging concepts used in most operating systems:

NOTE:
Setting password-aging parameters is not the same as setting account lockout parameters, which are discussed in the next section.

- **Maximum password age** — the amount of time a user can keep an existing password.
- **Minimum password age** — the amount of time a user must keep a password before changing it.
- **Password history** — determines the number of passwords the operating system will remember. If a user chooses a password that resides in the password history database, the operating system will force the user to choose another password.
- **Minimum password length** — the lowest acceptable number of characters for a password.
- **Password complexity** — requires the use of non-alphanumeric characters and/or uppercase letters in a password. The resulting security gain is often small because many users will resort to practices such as using password01, password02 and password03 to avoid this restriction. Although this technique does not offer optimal security, it is more secure than using the same password continually.
- **Encryption options** — for example, Red Hat Linux allows the use of md5 (theoretically non-recoverable) or 3DES passwords. Windows 2000, XP and 2003 offer similar options for encrypting passwords.

Password aging is an important concept to implement because it can make password cracking with dictionary and brute-force attacks more difficult. For setting the maximum password age, most organizations assign a value of between 30 and 90 days. Requiring more frequent changes can complicate the system or create problems: If users are asked to change their passwords more than once every 30 days, they may write down their passwords in order to remember them. As you learned earlier, others can discover a written password.

When deciding password-aging elements, compare the estimated security gain with the increase in difficulty for users. If the burden on users exceeds the value of the additional security, consider very carefully whether the measure is worthwhile.

Account lockout

Account lockout is the primary tool used to thwart password guessing. It works by disabling accounts after a specified number of invalid passwords have been entered. This technique is especially useful for preventing remote brute-force or dictionary-based password attacks. Generally, account lockout should be set up to occur after three to five invalid logon attempts.

Account reset

Account reset provides the option of automatically resetting the account after a specified interval. This option is valuable because valid users can forget their passwords, especially when password changes are required. Large organizations, especially, must often allow accounts to reset automatically after a given interval. Even an interval as short as 15 minutes will generally prevent the effective use of a brute-force password attack. One drawback to requiring manual account reset is that it allows for a possible denial-of-service attack. An attacker can disable users accounts by launching a password-guessing program.

Linux and strong passwords

By default, Linux systems use six-character passwords and also reject any password that resembles a dictionary password (in other words, any text string that looks too much like a word found in a standard dictionary). As a result, you need to use a password such as *8igMo$ne!* instead of *bigmoney*. You can, however, enforce more stringent password requirements. For example, many Linux systems administrators prefer a password of eight characters, and require two non-alphanumeric characters.

Encryption

You were introduced to the concept of encryption earlier. Encryption is the primary means to ensure privacy across the enterprise. This technique is often used to assist authentication efforts, as well. Currently, you can choose from three encryption models: symmetric-key, asymmetric-key and hash. Symmetric-key encryption is the most familiar form of encryption, but for enterprise-wide communication, asymmetric-key and hash encryption are also used.

Encryption always implies the use of algorithms. At the networking level, algorithms often create keys, or text strings that scramble and unscramble information. The following sections will introduce the three types of encryption and their algorithms.

Symmetric-key (single-key) encryption

In symmetric-key, or single-key, encryption, one key is used to encrypt and decrypt messages. Even though single-key encryption is a simple process, all parties must know and trust one another completely, and have confidential copies of the key. The first transmission of the key is crucial. If it is intercepted, the interceptor knows the key, and confidential material is no longer protected. Figure 5-1 illustrates single-key encryption.

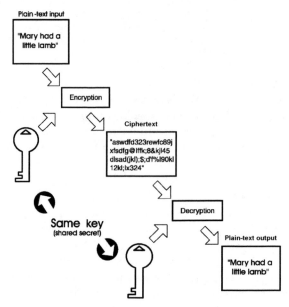

Figure 5-1: Symmetric-key encryption

An example of a symmetric key is a simple password you use to access your automated teller machine, or to log on to your ISP.

Symmetric algorithms

You can create a symmetric key with many different algorithms. This section will introduce the three most common symmetric algorithms: Data Encryption Standard (DES), Triple DES and Advanced Encryption Standard (AES).

- **Data Encryption Standard (DES)** — DES is an encryption standard that encrypts data using a 56-bit key. The same key is used to encrypt and decrypt the data. The advantages of DES are that it is fast and simple to implement. However, key distribution and management are difficult because DES relies on a single-key model.

  DES has been in production use for more than 25 years, so many hardware and software implementations use the DES algorithm. The U.S. National Institute of Standards and Technology (NIST) formally adopted DES in 1977. DES and its cousin, Triple DES, remain the standard form of encryption for many companies and organizations. Another name for the Data Encryption Standard is the Data Encryption Algorithm (DEA).

- **Triple DES** — Standard DES is considered sufficient for normal information. For sensitive information, some users employ a technique called Triple DES. In this case, the message is first encrypted using a 56-bit DES key, then decrypted with another 56-bit key, and finally encrypted again with the original 56-bit key. The Triple DES thus effectively has a 168-bit key.

  Because of the several levels of encryption, Triple DES also thwarts man-in-the-middle attacks. Normal DES is fast, and Triple DES is faster than other symmetric algorithms. The biggest advantage of Triple DES is its ability to use existing DES software and hardware. Companies with large investments in the DES encryption algorithm can easily implement Triple DES.

Encrypting and decrypting data require nothing more than passing the data through an algorithm. The process for encryption is essentially identical to the process for decryption.

NOTE:
The FineCrypt application, profiled in Lab 5-1, uses AES by default.

- **Advanced Encryption Standard (AES)** — Most security experts believe that DES and Triple DES no longer meet security requirements. The NIST began the process of determining a successor to DES. Among other requirements, the symmetric algorithm chosen for AES had to allow the creation of 128-bit, 192-bit and 256-bit keys, provide support for various platforms (smart cards; 8-bit, 32-bit and 64-bit processors) and be as fast as possible.

  The NIST chose the Rijndael algorithm out of several finalists. It allows the creation of 128-bit, 192-bit or 256-bit keys. It is a block cipher, which means it encrypts messages in blocks, 64 bits at a time. The developers were especially interested in making an algorithm that could perform quickly on various platforms, including asynchronous transfer mode (ATM) networks, Integrated Services Digital Network (ISDN) lines and even high-definition television (HDTV).

 Any of the previously mentioned algorithms can be used for symmetric encryption. Remember that both parties involved in the encryption (the sender and the receiver) must agree ahead of time on the symmetric algorithm to be used.

Symmetric encryption: Benefits and drawbacks

The benefits of symmetric encryption are its speed and strength. These features allow you to encrypt a large amount of information in less than a second.

The drawback of a symmetric-key encryption is that all recipients and viewers must have the same key, and all users must have a secure way to retrieve the key. To pass information across a public medium such as the Internet, users need a way to transfer this password key among themselves. In some cases, the users can meet and transfer the key physically. However, network users cannot always meet with one another in person.

dictionary program
A program specifically written to break into a password-protected system. It has a relatively large list of common password names it repeatedly uses to gain access.

password sniffing
A method of intercepting the transmission of a password during the authentication process. A sniffer is a program used to intercept passwords.

Another drawback is that hackers can compromise symmetric keys by using a **dictionary program**, engaging in **password sniffing**, or simply snooping through a desk, purse or briefcase.

In the following lab, you will learn how to apply symmetric-key encryption. Assume your boss sends you overseas to implement the new expansion phase of your company's sales operations. You communicate with your boss by means of e-mail, primarily because it affords greater security and confidentiality and it allows both of you to create and retain written records of your communication. Both of you will need to ensure that competitors and other outsiders cannot understand the documents you send across the Internet, so you decide to use symmetric-key encryption technology to prevent electronic snooping and unauthorized access.

 Lab 5-1: Applying symmetric-key encryption

In this lab, you will use a symmetric-key algorithm to encrypt a file.

1. Copy the FineCrypt installation binary (fcinst.exe) from the C:\CIW\Network\LabFiles\Lesson05 folder to your Desktop. If necessary, download FineCrypt from *www.tucows.com* or from *www.finecrypt.net*.

2. On your Desktop, double-click **fcinst.exe**, click the **Run** button if necessary, then click the **Continue** button to display the FineCrypt installation wizard's Welcome screen.

3. Click **Next** to display the License Agreement, then click **Yes** to accept it.

4. Click **Next** twice to install FineCrypt in the default location, then click **Finish** to exit the FineCrypt installation wizard.

5. Minimize all open windows on your Desktop, if necessary.

6. Create a text file named *aes.txt*, write a message, then save and close the file.

NOTE:
The FineCrypt wizard appears only when you run the FineCrypt application for the first time.

7. Right-click **aes.txt**, then select **FineCrypt | Encrypt With Password**.

If you have just installed FineCrypt, a wizard will appear. This wizard is designed to inform you about features that FineCrypt provides. Click **Next** as many times as necessary to finish the presentation, then click **Finish**.

Right-click **aes.txt** and select **FineCrypt | Encrypt With Password** again. The FineCrypt: Enter Passphrase dialog box will appear (Figure 5-2).

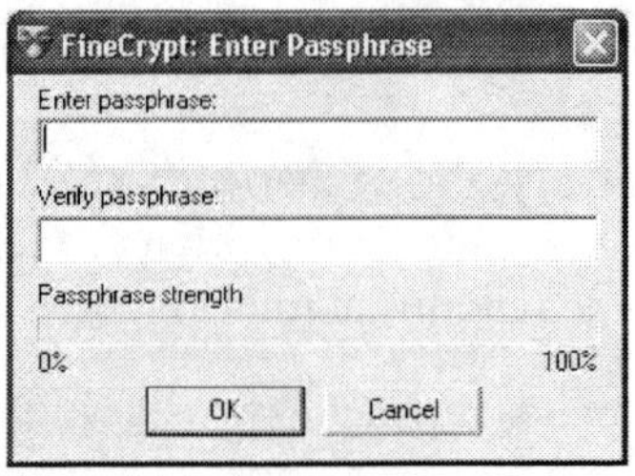

Figure 5-2: FineCrypt: Enter Passphrase dialog box

NOTE:
FineCrypt reports the strength of the password you have chosen. Choosing longer passwords results in a higher score. Additionally, using nonstandard characters will also help decrease the likelihood of someone guessing the password.

8. Enter a passphrase of your choice in the Enter Passphrase and Verify Passphrase text boxes. Make sure that this passphrase uses between eight and 16 characters. To ensure that you do not forget the passphrase, write it in the following space:

_____

9. Click **OK** to close the dialog box.

NOTE:
If you conduct this lab more than once and use the same name for the text file (aes.txt), you may be prompted to overwrite the temporary file name created by FineCrypt.

10. In the Encrypt dialog box, click **aes.txt**, then click the **Encrypt** button at the top of the dialog box. This step creates a new file named *aes.fca* on your Desktop. The file icon shows a lock with a key (Figure 5-3).

aes.fca

Figure 5-3: Encrypted file

At this point, you could transfer your encrypted file to another user. However, the other user must know your encryption password to be able to open the file. Determining how to securely communicate the password across a network is an inherent limitation of symmetric-key encryption.

In this lab, you used the FineCrypt application's AES encryption algorithm to encrypt a text file.

Asymmetric-key (public-key) encryption

Asymmetric-key encryption uses a key pair in the encryption process rather than the single key used in symmetric-key encryption. A key pair is a mathematically matched key set in which one key encrypts and the other key decrypts. Key A encrypts that which Key B decrypts; and Key B encrypts that which Key A decrypts. Because it uses two keys, asymmetric encryption is also called public-key encryption.

An important aspect to this concept is that one of these keys is made public, whereas the other is kept private, as shown in Figure 5-4. The key that you publish is called a public key, and the key you keep secret is the private key. Initially, you can distribute either key. However, after one key of the pair has been distributed, it must always remain public, and vice versa. Consistency is critical.

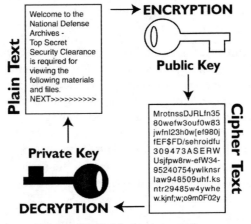

Figure 5-4: Public-key encryption

An example of asymmetric-key encryption is as follows: To send a secret message to David, you encrypt the message with David's public key, and then send the encrypted text. When David receives the encrypted text, he will decrypt it with his private key. Anyone who intercepts the message cannot decrypt it without David's private key.

Although private and public keys are mathematically related to one another, determining the value of the private key from the public key is extremely difficult and time consuming.

Asymmetric-key encryption and digital signatures

You can also use public-key encryption to create a digital signature. As you learned earlier, a digital signature helps prove that a document, file or network transmission is authentic. It also helps ensure that a file has not been improperly altered. A digital signature does not, however, ensure data privacy. It simply allows you to authoritatively prove the origin of a document, file or network transmission.

A digital signature is not a digital certificate. Rather, a digital signature is created when you use a private key and hash encryption together. Following is an example of the steps for creating a digital signature:

1. Create a message.

2. Create a hash of the message.

3. Encrypt the hash with your private key.

You now have a digital signature for your message. The recipient of your message would then use your public key to decrypt the hash. If the public key does not work, the recipient knows that this message has not come from you. Assuming that you have, in fact, sent the message, the recipient would then calculate his or her own hash and compare this new hash with the one you sent. If the hash values are the same, the document has not been altered. If the hash values are not identical, you know that the message has been altered.

Asymmetric-key algorithms

The two most common asymmetric-key algorithms are Rivest, Shamir, Adleman (RSA) and Digital Signature Algorithm (DSA).

NOTE:
RSA Security (www.rsa.com) is one of the best known companies in the field of cryptography. The RSA Security Web site contains an extensive amount of information about cryptography and security. This coursebook can discuss only a few of RSA's contributions.

- **RSA** — RSA (named for developers Ron Rivest, Adi Shamir and Leonard Adleman) is a public-key encryption system created in 1977. The RSA algorithm is used in several commercial operating systems and programs, including Windows family operating systems and Netscape browsers. It is also included in existing and proposed standards for the Internet and the World Wide Web.

- **Digital Signature Algorithm (DSA)** — DSA was introduced by the NIST, and is available openly. It is used to sign documents. Although it functions differently from RSA, it is not proprietary and has been adopted as the standard signing method in Gnu Privacy Guard (GnuPG), the open-source alternative to Pretty Good Privacy (PGP), which you will learn about shortly.

Asymmetric encryption: Benefits and drawbacks

For communication over the Internet, the asymmetric-key system makes key management easier because the public key can be distributed while the private key stays secure with the user.

The primary drawback of asymmetric-key encryption is that it is quite slow, owing to the intensive mathematical calculations the program requires. Even a rudimentary level of asymmetric encryption can require a great deal of time. Consequently, many applications use asymmetric-key encryption to encrypt only the symmetric key that encrypts the body of the message.

Hash (one-way) encryption

Hash encryption typically uses a hash table that contains a hash function. This table determines the values used for encryption. A table of hexadecimal numbers is used to calculate the encryption.

NOTE:
A common use of hash encryption is in remote logon authentication. Some authentication methods pass a hash of the user's password rather than the password itself for logon validation.

Hash encryption is used for information that will not be decrypted or read. (Hash decryption is theoretically and mathematically impossible.) For example, two different entities may need to compare values without revealing the information. Hash encryption allows someone to verify but not copy information, and is commonly used by e-mail programs and SSL sessions.

Though permanent encryption may seem illogical, there are many uses for encryption that cannot be decrypted. For example, an automated teller machine does not actually decrypt the personal identification number (PIN) entered by a customer. The magnetic stripe has the customer's code encrypted one-way. This one-way encryption is the hash code. The automated teller machine calculates the hash on the PIN that the customer enters, which yields a result. This result is then compared with the hash code on the card. With this method, the PIN is secure, even from the automated teller machine and the individuals who maintain it.

Hash algorithms

Hash encryption uses complicated mathematical algorithms to achieve effective encryption. The Message Digest (MD) and the Secure Hash Algorithm (SHA) are standard algorithms in current use. Following are the two most common hash algorithm families:

- **MD2, MD4 and MD5** — The MD algorithms are a group of hash functions that take any length of data and generate a unique fingerprint of certain length (for example, 128 bits). The process is one-way because you cannot generate the message back from the signature, and the fingerprints are unique because no two messages will have the same hash.

  These functions are to be used as message-digest algorithms to generate unique one-way fingerprints of e-mail messages, certificates and other items to ensure content integrity. The normal message digest is 128 bits long.

  MD4 and MD5 are faster than MD2. MD4 produces a 128-bit hash. However, it was susceptible to attacks that could reverse-engineer the hash codes. Therefore, it is now considered broken and is no longer used. MD5 is stronger than MD4, produces a 128-bit hash and is the most commonly used algorithm. You can learn more about MD5 in RFC 1321.

- **Secure Hash Algorithm (SHA)** — SHA is also known as Secure Hash Standard (SHS). SHA was developed by the NIST and the U.S. National Security Agency (NSA) and is used in U.S. government processing. It can produce a 160-bit hash value from an arbitrary-length string. SHA is structurally similar to MD4 and MD5. Although it is about 25 percent slower than MD5, it is much more secure. It produces message digests that are 25 percent longer than those produced by the MD functions, making it more secure against attacks.

Pretty Good Privacy (PGP)

When individuals want to communicate securely over long distances, they generally use combinations of the encryption schemes described previously. For example, a program such as Pretty Good Privacy (PGP) uses symmetric-key encryption to scramble the original message you want to send. Next, it uses asymmetric-key encryption to encrypt only the symmetric key you just used. Finally, PGP uses hash encryption to "sign" the message and ensure that no one can tamper with it. Visit *www.pgp.com* for more information about PGP.

This combination employs the strengths of each encryption method. Asymmetric encryption is quite slow, but PGP and methods such as SSL use it only to encrypt the symmetric key, not the actual message. Because symmetric-key encryption is so fast, it encrypts the message itself. Hash encryption then signs the message efficiently.

NOTE:
The availability of secure, encrypted communication is typically the key factor in determining whether to implement a VPN.

You can obtain an internationalized version of PGP at *www.pgpi.org*. GnuPG, the open-source version of PGP, is available at *www.gnupg.org*. To use an application such as PGP, you must first generate a key pair. You must then publish your public key, which you can give to anyone. You would, however, keep your private key completely secret. If you back up your private key, you must be sure to store it in a secret locked location. If anyone was to obtain this key, that individual would be able to read all your secret information.

Kerberos
A proprietary key management scheme between unknown principals who want to communicate securely. Uses symmetric algorithms and acts as a trusted third party that knows the identities of the organizations asking to communicate, but does not reveal them.

OBJECTIVE:
3.5.5: VPNs and remote access

extranet
A network that connects enterprise intranets to the global Internet. Designed to provide access to selected external users.

tunneling protocol
A protocol that encapsulates data packets into another packet.

Network-Level Protocols and Encryption

Network-level protocols and algorithms establish a secure channel at the network layer, providing privacy, integrity and authentication. For example, VPN protocols usually operate independently of the packet contents. The protocols handle the packets, and the data portion (payload) of each packet is encrypted. The function of the protocols is to deliver the packets to a destination. The protocols handle authentication just enough to identify the recipient when identification is required. SSL sessions and **Kerberos** are also vital network-level encryption methods.

Virtual Private Network (VPN)

A VPN is a configuration that allows secure communication across long distances, usually for a company **extranet**. It can extend the corporate LAN to the Internet, providing secure worldwide connectivity. In a VPN, the Internet is often the corporate network backbone, thereby eliminating the dichotomy of inside network and outside network, as well as the need to maintain many networks. VPNs are appropriate for any organization requiring secure external access to internal resources. For example, a VPN is appropriate for companies whose facilities are spread over long distances but need to communicate as if they were located together. VPNs are also important because they allow companies to embed non-Internet protocols within TCP/IP.

VPNs and tunneling

All VPNs are **tunneling protocols** in the sense that their data packets or payloads are encapsulated or tunneled into the network packets. Encryption occurs at the source and decryption occurs at the destination. For example, suppose that you administer the network of a company with two offices, one in Washington, D.C., and the other in Sydney, Australia. If your company network runs IPX/SPX or NetBEUI, and you need to create a connection between offices using the Internet, you can use a VPN and "tunnel," or encapsulate, IPX/SPX within TCP/IP. You can encapsulate other protocols, as well.

Security fundamentals (for example, authentication, message integrity and encryption) are very important to VPN implementation. Without such authentication procedures, a hacker can impersonate anyone and then gain access to the network. Message integrity is required because the packets can be altered as they travel through the public network. Without encryption, the information may become truly public.

NOTE:
PPTP provides encryption from VPN tunnel endpoint to endpoint, but not all the way back to hosts or servers.

Point-to-Point Tunneling Protocol (PPTP)
A protocol that allows users and corporations to securely extend their networks over the Internet using remote access servers. Used to create VPNs.

VPN protocols and standards

Following are descriptions of the protocols that a VPN is most likely to use.

Point-to-Point Tunneling Protocol (PPTP)

Point-to-Point Tunneling Protocol (PPTP) is a popular VPN tunneling protocol. PPTP is designed to establish a private channel between communicating systems (usually a client and a server computer) on a public network like the Internet. The protocol encapsulates data and information/control packets using the Internet Generic Record Encapsulation protocol version 2 (GREv2). PPTP works only on IP.

Layer 2 Tunneling Protocol (L2TP)

NOTE:
L2TP is used for tunneling but does not provide encryption.

Layer 2 Tunneling Protocol (L2TP) is an Internet Engineering Task Force (IETF) standard tunneling protocol. It is primarily used to support VPNs over the Internet for non-TCP/IP protocols. For instance, both Apple networks and Novell networks can create VPNs over the network using L2TP. It is a combination of PPTP and Cisco's Layer 2 Forwarding (L2F) protocol. The primary advantage of L2TP is that it is supported by more vendors than PPTP.

IP Security (IPsec)

IP Security (IPsec)
An authentication and encryption standard that provides security over the Internet. It functions at Layer 3 of the OSI/RM and can secure all packets transmitted over the network.

IP Security (IPsec) is another IETF standard that provides packet-level encryption, authentication and integrity for VPNs. IPsec is not a protocol; rather, it is a standard. IPsec is more flexible than L2TP and PPTP because you can specify different authentication methods. Using IPsec, you can:

- Use digital certificates to authenticate the sender of data.

- Use asymmetric-key (public-key) encryption to encrypt the data. This encryption is accomplished by means of the Internet Security Association Key Management Protocol (ISAKMP), which allows the receiving device to obtain a public key and authenticate the sending device using a digital certificate.

NOTE:
You can use a digital certificate or a shared public key in IPsec.

Remote Access Server (RAS)

callback
A process in which a remote access server returns a call to a remote client that has logged on in order to authenticate that client.

Do not confuse VPNs with another remote protocol technology known as remote access server (RAS). With RAS, users employ dial-up modems from their laptop or home computer to connect and log on to a RAS. The RAS host is usually located on a company network; after the user logs on to the remote access server, he or she gains access to the company network, e-mail and Internet. The main difference between a VPN and RAS is that with the latter, users connect to the private network using traditional dial-up modems instead of connecting over the Internet. RAS offers security through a **callback** feature. Callback requires a user to log on to a RAS. After logging on, the user is disconnected. The RAS calls the user back to ensure the call was made from an authorized computer.

Digital Certificate

As you learned earlier, a digital certificate is a small file that provides authoritative identification. Digital certificates verify the sender's identity. A trusted third party, known as the certificate authority (CA), is responsible for verifying the legitimacy of the digital certificate. After you receive a legitimate digital certificate from a person or host (for example, a Web or e-mail server), you can be reasonably sure that you are communicating with the proper party. Effectively, a digital certificate is the equivalent of an identification card (for example, a passport or a driver's license), because it proves the identity of an individual or company over the Web.

X.509
The standard used by certificate authorities (CAs) for creating digital certificates.

Digital certificates use the **X.509** standard. This standard ensures that certificates contain the following data about the certificate owner:

- Name, company and address

- Public key

- Certificate serial number

- Dates that the certificate is valid

- Identification of the certifying company

- Digital signature of the certifying company

Digital certificates contain digital signatures to ensure that a message has not been altered during transmission from the sender. The typical implementation of a digital signature is as follows:

1. Tina reduces her message using a hash algorithm, then encrypts the message with her private key. She has created an encrypted file that contains a distinct signature. This digital signature is an encrypted digest of the text that is sent with the text message.

2. Sarah receives the message and decrypts the digital signature with Tina's public key. This decryption allows Sarah to verify the digital signature by recomputing the signature's hash value and comparing it with the received signature's hash value. If the values match, the message has not been altered, and is authenticated.

non-repudiation
The security principle of providing proof that a transaction occurred between identified parties. Repudiation occurs when one party in a transaction denies that the transaction took place.

Authentication requires a digital certificate verified by a CA. Digital certificates are used for **non-repudiation**, which is the ability to prove that a transmission has been sent by the sender and received by the recipient. (You were introduced to non-repudiation earlier.) Sending a message with a digital certificate guarantees that the sender cannot later deny having sent the transmission, and the recipient cannot deny having received the transmission.

Public Key Infrastructure (PKI)

OBJECTIVE:
3.5.7: PKI concepts

Public Key Infrastructure (PKI) refers to a series of CAs that enable users to manage public encryption. PKI CA servers are repositories for managing digital certificates. The primary goal of PKI is to enable the secure creation and management of digital certificates. In addition to authenticating the identity of the entity owning a key pair, PKI also provides the ability to revoke a key if it is no longer valid. A key becomes invalid if, for example, a private key is cracked or made public. If you need a certificate for a server (for example, a Web or e-mail server), you will use PKI.

Table 5-3 describes essential terms that relate to certificates generated through PKI.

Table 5-3: Certificate terms

Term	Description
Certificate policy	A set of rules and procedures that describe the ways in which employees in an organization should use digital certificates.
Certificate Practice Statement (CPS)	A formal explanation of how a CA verifies and manages certificates.
Certificate expiration	The end of a certificate's expected life cycle. All certificates have valid beginning and end dates coded inside them (for example, October 31, 2009). Expiration occurs when the certificate end date has arrived. All certificates created by PKI have a specific life cycle.
Certificate revocation	The practice of invalidating a certificate before the end of its expected life cycle. Reasons for revocation may include: • Employee termination. • Employee reassignment. • Changing the company name. • Changing the DNS name of a server. • A compromised CA.

NOTE:
All certificates created by PKI have a specific life cycle.

Table 5-3: Certificate terms (cont'd)

Term	Description
Suspension	The practice of temporarily invalidating, or deactivating, a key for a specific length of time. The key can be reactivated. However, if the certificate expires during a period of suspension, a new key will need to be generated.
Renewal	The practice of renewing a key before it expires. Keys that have been revoked or that have already expired cannot be renewed.
Destruction	The practice of eliminating all public and private keys; effectively eliminates an identity from PKI.
Certificate Revocation List (CRL)	A list of certificates that are no longer considered valid. Users must manually download and then check this list.
Online Certificate Status Protocol (OCSP)	A real-time protocol that allows users to check for revoked certificates.

Firewall

A firewall is a secure computer system placed between a trusted network and an untrusted one, such as the Internet. On one side of a firewall is your company's production network, which you supervise, control and protect. The other side contains a public network (such as the Internet) over which you have no control.

The term "firewall" comes from a safety technique used in building construction. Whenever a wall separates sections of a building, such as different businesses or apartments, it is made as fireproof as possible. This measure protects the occupants and property throughout the building if one unit catches fire.

In computer networking, a network firewall acts as a barrier against potential malicious activity, while still allowing a "door" for people to communicate between a secured network and the open, unsecured network. The most common location for a firewall is between a corporate LAN and the Internet. This site is vital to the enforcement of your security policy.

Essential firewall functions

A firewall controls access to your private network (for example, your Ethernet or intranet). It can also create secure intranet domains. Furthermore, it is the primary means of enforcing your security policy, greatly simplifying the tasks of determining threats and using countermeasures. Without such a point for monitoring and controlling information, a systems or security administrator would have an excessive number of places to monitor.

A firewall can further enhance privacy by "hiding" your internal systems and information from the public. A firewall also enforces logging and provides alarm capacities. Finally, a firewall simplifies the authentication process.

Firewalls allow users from a protected network to access a public network while simultaneously making the protected company's products and services available to the public. Before you implement your firewall, you should know which services your company requires, and which services will be available to both internal and external users. The availability of services on both sides of the firewall largely determines which firewall functions you will use.

Potential firewall functions include:

- Filtering packets.

- Serving as a circuit-level or application-level gateway.

- Detecting intrusions.

- Providing enhanced password authentication.

- Logging and reporting.

- Taking evasive actions.

- Permitting encrypted access (with a VPN).

You can use these functions in a variety of combinations. Sometimes they will be used on individual computers, but most often they will be combined. Logging and reporting, for example, occur at various levels. Together, these functions form your firewall's building blocks.

Internal firewall

NOTE:
Internal firewalls are also known as enclave firewalls.

Internal firewalls are standard firewalls, but reside inside your company's internal network. Internal firewalls are meant to protect sensitive departments and divisions. They can be used in the following ways:

- To protect sensitive systems, such as those in human resources or accounting departments

- To isolate networks that still need Internet connectivity, but which use software whose behavior might cause problems with other resources in the company

Personal firewall

Personal firewalls are available for personal computers. They offer protection for an individual system instead of protecting an entire network. Tools such as ZoneAlarm (*www.zonealarm.com*) and BlackICE (*www.iss.net/products/index.html*) can detect and respond to attacks on Windows systems. To create a personal firewall in Linux, you can use the ipchains command (for kernels 2.2 and lower) and the iptables command (for kernels 2.3 and higher).

Personal firewalls offer many of the firewall features listed in this lesson, such as packet filtering, intrusion detection, and logging. When used in conjunction with antivirus software, a personal computer is very secure, provided that you update the antivirus and personal firewall software frequently.

Packet filtering

Packet filtering is the use of a router or firewall to inspect each packet for predefined content. Although packet filtering does not provide error-proof protection, it is almost always the first line of defense. Engineers usually filter packets at the external router, which discards certain types of activity entirely.

Packet filtering is also inexpensive, mainly because most routers can perform this task. A router is necessary to connect your network to the Internet, so by using your router to perform packet filtering as well, you can gain functionality with little additional cost.

Packet filtering works at the data link, network and transport layers of the OSI/RM. Implementation requires instructing the router to filter the contents of IP packets based on the following fields in the packet:

- Source IP address

- Destination IP address

- TCP/UDP source port

- TCP/UDP destination port

NOTE:
A packet filter is an excellent first line of defense, and packet filters are included on routers and firewalls.

If, for example, you want to protect your network from a group of attackers, configuring a packet filter to block all connections from that group might be the best solution. Such a configuration is recommended because packet filters are generally included on routers and firewalls.

Proxy server

proxy server
A server that mediates traffic between a protected network and the Internet. Translates IP addresses and filters traffic.

Proxy servers are very important to firewall applications because a proxy replaces the network IP address with a single IP address. Multiple systems can use this single IP address. A **proxy server** provides the following services:

- **Hiding network resources** — Hackers will see only one IP address instead of all exposed systems.

- **Logging** — A proxy server can log incoming and outgoing access, allowing you to see the details of successful and failed connections.

- **Caching** — A proxy server can save information obtained from the Internet (for example, Web pages). This cache contains copies of information found on the Internet. Internal Web clients, for example, that access the Internet through the proxy will see these copied (or cached) pages, and will thus not need to access the Internet to view them. A proxy server will regularly check these copies to see whether sites or pages have been updated. It will also automatically purge old information after a certain length of time. A common proxy server problem occurs when the server returns old information. In such cases, the administrator must purge the existing cache, or set the proxy server to update its cache more often.

Proxies are available in two basic forms: the circuit-level gateway and the application-level gateway.

Circuit-level gateway

circuit-level gateway
A firewall component that monitors and transmits information at the transport layer of the OSI model. It hides information about the network; a packet passing through this type of gateway appears to have originated from the firewall.

A **circuit-level gateway** acts as a proxy between the Internet and your internal systems. A circuit-level gateway firewall receives an outbound network packet and transmits it for the internal system. Inbound traffic works in a similar way.

As shown in Figure 5-5, the circuit-level gateway shields the internal system.

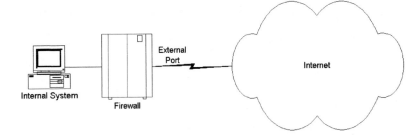

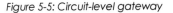

Figure 5-5: Circuit-level gateway

The transmission process begins when the internal system sends a series of packets destined for the Internet. These packets then go to the firewall, which checks them against its predetermined set of rules. If the packets do not violate any rules, the firewall sends the same packets on behalf of the internal system. The packets that appear on the Internet originate at the router's external port, which is also the device that receives any replies. This process effectively shields all internal information, such as IP addresses, from the Internet.

The circuit-level gateway has the same weakness as a packet filter: It filters packets based only on source and destination IP addresses, and source and destination ports. It does not examine the bytes of the information sent, so it cannot tell whether the data contained in the packets is legitimate or malicious.

Application-level gateway

application-level gateway
A firewall component that inspects all packets addressed to a user-level application; uses proxies to control and filter traffic on a connection-by-connection basis. Also provides authentication.

Application-level gateways perform a similar function to circuit-level gateways, but at the application level. An application gateway can serve as an SMTP firewall. In that case, external inbound e-mail messages would be received from the Internet at the firewall's external port. The firewall can then verify the source of the e-mail messages and scan all attachments for viruses before transmitting the mail to the internal network.

Although this process is rather complex, it is often necessary; neither source verification nor virus-scanning capabilities are built into SMTP specifications. Still, an application-level gateway provides the appropriate technology to implement this type of security.

 When you or your organization uses an application-level gateway, you must configure each of the clients to function with this gateway.

Most firewall systems today are combinations of packet filtering, circuit-level gateways and application-level gateways. They examine packets individually, and they use predetermined rules. Only packets that engage in acceptable activities (as defined by your security policy) are allowed into and out of the network.

Both circuit and application gateways create a complete break between your internal and external systems. This break gives your firewall system an opportunity to examine all transmissions before passing them into or out of your internal networks.

Network Address Translation (NAT)

Network Address Translation (NAT)
The practice of hiding internal IP addresses from the external network.

NOTE:
Another name for NAT is IP address hiding.

Circuit-level gateways often provide **Network Address Translation (NAT)**, in which a network host alters the packets of internal network hosts so they can be sent out across the Internet.

You were introduced to NAT earlier in the course. NAT is the practice of hiding internal IP addresses from the external network. The internal IP addresses are usually the reserved IP addresses that the ICANN recommends using for internal address schemes.

 You learned about reserved IP addressing earlier in the course. RFC 1918 outlines the reserved addresses. These addresses are ideal because Internet routers are configured not to forward them. These packets cannot traverse the Internet unless they are translated using NAT.

Following are three ways to provide true NAT:

*   Configure "masquerading" on a packet-filtering firewall.

*   Configure a circuit-level gateway.

- Use a proxy server to conduct requests from internal hosts.

When a firewall or router is configured to provide NAT, all internal addresses are translated to public IP addresses when connecting to an external host. When packets return from an external host, they are translated back so the internal network host can receive them.

Accessing Internet services

If Internet access is required and a network is located behind a proxy server or firewall, you may have problems accessing Internet services that use less-common ports. For example, most proxy servers and firewalls already allow HTTP. Difficulties may occur when you require additional services, such as e-mail, FTP and program downloads.

To avoid these common problems, perform the following tasks:

- Make sure the network has access to all Internet-related protocols used by the company. Examples include HTTP (TCP port 80), SSL (TCP port 443), FTP (TCP port 20, 21), Telnet (TCP port 23), POP3 (TCP port 110), SMTP (TCP port 25) and NNTP (TCP port 119). For certain services, such as FTP, you will need all ports above 1023 (in other words, the registered, dynamic or ephemeral ports). Each of these ports must be "opened" at the firewall or proxy server to allow traffic using that port.

- Make sure that the IP addresses assigned to the computers in your network have permission to access the Internet.

After the required ports are opened at the firewall, further rules can be applied to block ports by IP address. This capability allows administrators to regulate the services that can be accessed over the Internet by individuals or by departments.

Troubleshooting additional problems

If you experience additional access problems behind a firewall, consider the following issues:

- Verify that you are using the correct IP address and subnet mask.

- Check your default gateway and verify that the computer can communicate with systems on the same subnet.

- Verify DNS resolution.

- After you have confirmed IP information and DNS resolution, try to use multiple protocols on the Internet. Check e-mail, Web, Telnet and FTP services to determine those services that are available and those that are unavailable.

- The corporate firewall may not allow home-based account access to the corporate e-mail server. Suppose, for example, that a user can access his or her e-mail account from work but cannot access this same e-mail account from home. If you can confirm the user's basic connectivity (in other words, that the user can communicate on the Internet), you may suspect that the corporate firewall is blocking the e-mail connection. The only resolution is for the employee to use a separate e-mail account, and check e-mail from work. Ask the IT department to reconfigure the firewall to allow outside connections to the remote employee.

- Many times, a firewall can cause a bottleneck. For example, suppose that delivery time has increased for messages that are sent to people outside work. In this case, the company's firewall is serving as a bottleneck, slowing e-mail delivery to outside addresses.

Security Zones

OBJECTIVE:
3.5.6: Security zones

Security zones refer to specially designated groupings of services and computers. Security zones can be created by a firewall, a router or a switch. In this section, you will learn about four security zones: the demilitarized zone (DMZ), intranets, extranets and virtual LANs (VLANs).

Demilitarized zone (DMZ)

NOTE:
Another name for a demilitarized zone is a demarcation zone.

A DMZ is a mini-network that resides between a company's internal network and the external network (for example, the Internet). The DMZ is not part of the company's internal network, nor is it fully part of the untrusted network. The DMZ can be created by using a firewall with three NICs: One NIC connects to the trusted network, one acts as the gateway to the DMZ, and one is addressable by the Internet. A DMZ can also be created by using two routers and a firewall. One router, called a screening router, receives traffic from the Internet. The firewall then filters traffic. A second router, often called the choke router, filters traffic before it passes to the trusted network.

A DMZ is used as an additional buffer to further separate the public network from your internal private network. Many systems administrators place Web, DNS and e-mail servers in a DMZ for convenience. The benefit of this practice is that the firewall provides some protection but allows traffic to enter the network. However, a DMZ is not a completely secure zone; any server in a DMZ is less protected than it would be if it resided in the internal network. DMZs are an integral component of triple-homed bastion hosts and screened subnets, both of which will be presented later in this lesson.

Intranet

As you learned earlier, an intranet is a security zone available only to authorized organization employees. It is a private network; only company employees can have access to it. An intranet is, in many ways, a miniature private version of the Internet. It is a network that uses the same protocols as the Internet (HTTP, NNTP, FTP and so forth). However, it is completely isolated from Internet traffic. Intranets are often essential networks that allow companies to:

- Enable employees to share information with one another.

- Bridge older equipment (for example, mainframes and legacy call centers) to newer technologies (for example, database-driven Web sites and VoIP connectivity).

- Obtain human resources information.

- Connect to remote systems by means of a secure gateway.

Extranet

An extranet is a private network that allows selected access to outsiders only after they provide authentication information. These outsiders might be a specific group of users from a partner company, or a group of individuals from various locations who are allowed access to certain resources for a specific business purpose. Network and security professionals often limit extranet access according to the following parameters:

- **User name and password (or other authentication credentials)** — Access is given only after authenticating with a particular host (for example, a firewall or Web server).

- **Time** — The given authentication information will be valid only for a specific time.

- **Specific locations** — In some cases, extranet administrators will allow access only from specific IP addresses or host names.

 Extranet connections should be encrypted to avoid man-in-the-middle attacks.

Virtual LAN (VLAN)

You were briefly introduced to VLANs earlier in the course. A VLAN is a logical grouping of hosts, made possible by a network switch and most newer routers. Generally, a VLAN is not implemented by a firewall. In a VLAN, a group of hosts can be created regardless of where they are physically connected to a LAN. Members of this group will then compete with one another for network access, regardless of their physical location.

VLANs are useful in the following ways:

- **Security** — If you place hosts that receive or transmit sensitive traffic inside a VLAN, malicious users will have more difficulty sniffing network traffic. Because a VLAN can help you create a group of computers, you can also use a VLAN to apply an access policy that, for example, prohibits all traffic other than HTTP, POP3 and SMTP from entering or leaving that group.

- **Performance** — A VLAN can help reduce traffic in parts of your network. For example, if several systems are causing too much traffic for a particular segment, a VLAN can be created to isolate these systems. A VLAN can also be used to balance network load between segments.

- **Ease of administration** — The ability to separate a logical grouping of systems from their physical location makes it possible to keep a user's workstation in the same physical location, but have the workstation participate in a new group of workstations pertinent to the user's tasks. In short, a user can belong to a new department, but remain in the same physical location.

 A VLAN is not a complete security solution. It supplements firewalls and other measures.

Firewall Topologies

OBJECTIVE:
3.5.6: Security zones

Most enterprise security professionals consider the firewall to be the "choke point" through which all traffic must pass. Enterprise networks use various models to implement that choke point, depending on their needs and available resources. Each model is designed to create a matrix of filters and points that can process and secure information. The four common firewall implementations are:

- Packet filter.

- Dual-homed bastion host.

- Triple-homed bastion host.

- Screened subnet (back-to-back firewalls).

bastion host
A computer that houses various firewall components and services and is connected to a public network, such as the Internet.

The packet-filtering firewall option is the most simple, and consequently the most popular of the common topologies. Both the dual-homed bastion and the triple-homed bastion host configurations require all traffic to pass through a **bastion host**, which acts as both a circuit-level gateway and an application-level gateway. The final commonly used method is the screened-subnet firewall, which uses an additional packet-filtering router to achieve another level of security.

Packet filter topology

A packet filter firewall topology inspects only Internet addresses and port numbers after analyzing network header fields. This strategy can filter much unwanted traffic. It is inexpensive, but still provides a significant degree of protection. Figure 5-6 shows a diagram of a packet-filtering router.

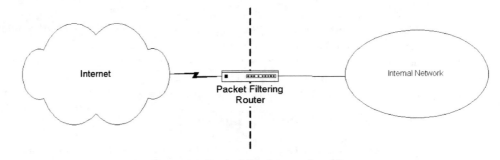

Figure 5-6: Packet-filtering configuration

A potential drawback to packet filtering is that the degree of safety it offers depends greatly on the expertise of the people who implement the filters. Another drawback is that the security of your entire network depends primarily on a single device; if a hacker defeats the packet filter, your network will no longer have a firewall in place. An additional drawback is that a packet filter cannot implement effective logging and alarms.

Dual-homed bastion host

The second commonly used firewall topology is the dual-homed bastion host. A dual-homed bastion host is a firewall with two NICs. The first NIC faces the public network, and the second NIC faces the private network. The firewall software processes all requests and filters all traffic. The benefit of a dual-homed NIC is that it is inexpensive to implement. This type of firewall has two drawbacks. First, only a single system separates your network from the public network. Second, you are not able to create a DMZ. A dual-homed bastion host is illustrated in Figure 5-7.

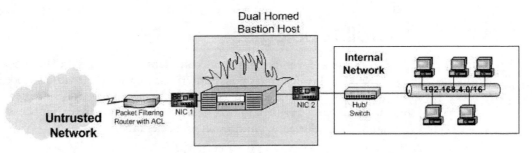

Figure 5-7: Dual-homed bastion host

Triple-homed bastion host

The third commonly used implementation of a firewall is the triple-homed bastion host, also called a three-homed firewall. The triple-homed bastion host often separates the Internet, the internal network and the DMZ.

The advantage of a triple-homed bastion host is that Internet traffic avoids the company's internal network, which keeps the internal computers safe from the public. A three-homed firewall is illustrated in Figure 5-8.

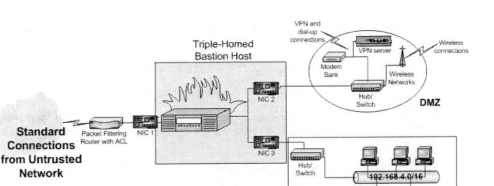

Figure 5-8: Triple-homed bastion host

Screened subnet (back-to-back firewalls)

NOTE:
The screened
subnet is a common
configuration. It is
often seen on sites
supporting
e-commerce.

The fourth commonly used firewall topology is the screened subnet, also called back-to-back firewalls. It is the most secure of the four general implementations, mainly because all publicly accessible devices, including modem pools and other resources, are placed in a secure isolated network. In this configuration, the DMZ functions as a secure isolated network positioned between the Internet and the internal network (Figure 5-9).

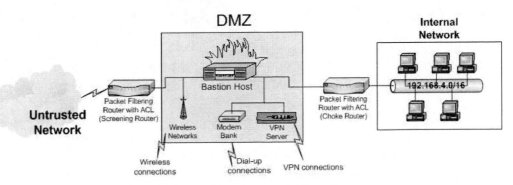

Figure 5-9: Screened-subnet firewall

This configuration uses external and internal routers. Each is configured so that its traffic flows only to or from the bastion host. This arrangement prevents any traffic from directly traversing the subnetwork, or DMZ. The external router uses standard filtering to restrict external access to the bastion host, and rejects any traffic that does not come from the bastion host.

Security Audit

An audit is a review of the state of the network. Ideally, an audit should be conducted by a party that is not responsible for maintaining the network on a daily basis; a disinterested party might be more likely to discover overlooked security problems. Also, if the systems administrator is responsible for an audit, he or she may be more interested in covering up errors or ignoring them rather than fixing them. The auditor should report findings not only to the systems administrator but also to upper management so that they can ensure that problems will be resolved. During the auditing process, an auditor should perform the following tasks:

- Conduct a "status quo" analysis, in which the auditor identifies common patterns for the network being audited.

- Conduct a risk analysis, which examines potential network problems.

- Make recommendations concerning the results of the audit.

As a novice networking professional, you will probably not be asked to conduct an audit. However, you should know about audits, and why they are necessary.

Uninterruptible Power Supply (UPS)

OBJECTIVE:
3.5.8: Uninterruptible power supply (UPS)

uninterruptible power supply (UPS)
A power supply that uses a battery to maintain power during a power outage.

An **uninterruptible power supply (UPS)** is a device that allows your computer to keep running for at least a short time when the primary power source is lost. It also provides protection from power surges. With a UPS, AC line voltage feeds into a charger that keeps the battery backup charged at all times. The computer is powered from the battery, not from the AC line, so there is no need to switch over if power is lost. Generally, if a power outage occurs, the UPS will keep the computer running long enough for you to save data and shut down the computer properly. If power is out for an extended length of time, the UPS can initiate a system shutdown before battery power is lost, thereby eliminating (or at least minimizing) data loss. A UPS will also smooth power irregularities and provide clean, stable power. Figure 5-10 illustrates a UPS.

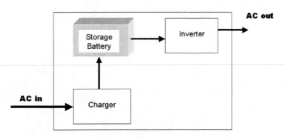

Figure 5-10: Uninterruptible power supply (UPS)

One major concern when selecting a UPS is its power rating in watts. Be sure that the UPS provides enough power to support the devices that you plan to connect. Connecting more than one computer to a UPS is usually not recommended except on UPS systems designed for that purpose. Connecting multiple systems increases the UPS power requirement. Also, only one of the systems will be able to monitor the UPS status signals.

You need to decide which computers to protect with UPS systems. Protecting all computers may not always be practical. However, you should protect mission-critical systems, including network servers and any other systems that provide data or services to a network. If a computer system must be kept running or if you must guarantee that a computer will be shut down correctly if power is lost, you should provide UPS support for that computer.

You can configure a UPS to specify the number of minutes it will provide power to the system. However, be careful not to specify to shut down a system in a time frame longer than the UPS itself can remain operational. For example, if you specify a system shutdown 45 minutes after a power loss, but the UPS can only remain operational for 30 minutes, you may lose data and services.

UPSs can also be configured to shut down entire systems automatically, shut down only certain components automatically (for example, monitors) or place components into minimal power-use mode until you manually shut down the system.

IT Industry Career Opportunities

OBJECTIVE:
3.10.1: IT career
goals

As you learned earlier in the course, IT refers to all aspects of managing and processing information using computers and computer networks. IT departments generally deal with computer, telecommunication, network and other related technologies and services to provide employees with the resources necessary to reach their organizations' goals.

IT is one of the fastest-growing career fields in the world today. IT skills are essential in all industries and are necessary in many different job roles.

Depending on your interests, training and skills, many IT career opportunities are available that relate directly to your personal goals. Various IT job roles include:

NOTE:
All these IT job roles are explained in detail in the first coursebook of this series, *Internet Business Foundations*.

- Web site designer.
- Web application developer.
- Web architect.
- Web site analyst.
- Web site manager.
- Database administrator.

- Server administrator.
- Network engineer.
- Security manager.
- Security analyst/consultant.
- PC repair technician.
- Help desk technician.

The following sections will explore methods you can employ to conduct effective job searches, create résumés, and take advantage of educational degree programs and certifications to provide you with the skills training and competitive advantage you need when searching for the IT job of your choice.

Conducting job searches

OBJECTIVE:
3.10.2: Job searches

You can employ many methods to explore career opportunities in the IT (or any) industry, such as:

- Participating in on-campus interviews (if you are a college/university student).
- Searching the newspaper classified ads for jobs.
- Visiting employment agencies and employment placement services.
- Attending job or career fairs.
- Volunteering for positions related to your career interests.
- Seeking part-time work through temporary employment agencies or internships.
- Networking (socially) and gathering employment information from friends, acquaintances, business associates and association members.
- Working with an executive search firm.
- Mailing cover letters and résumés to targeted organizations.
- Applying in person directly to targeted employers.
- Entering résumés electronically in database placement services or posting them on appropriate Web sites.
- Using Internet technology to conduct job searches.

The traditional methods of seeking employment (for example, classified ads, job and career fairs, and so forth) are perhaps the most common but least effective means of gaining employment, especially when these methods are not combined with other methods. A combination of some or all of these methods would be the most effective way to conduct a job search. However, using Internet technology may be the most effective means of gathering information about different job roles and responsibilities, and conducting a job search.

Using the Internet to conduct job searches

You can browse Usenet newsgroups using Google Groups (*http://groups.google.com*), and use search engines, such as *hotjobs.yahoo.com, careers.excite.com* and *www.monster.com*, to search the Internet for information about career opportunities in the IT industry. These sites (and many others) provide information about careers and contain thousands of job listings. By entering keywords to narrow your search to specific job types, you can retrieve available job listings that relate to your personal career goals.

In the following lab, you will search a major Web site devoted to job listings in numerous fields. Assume you are a recent college graduate with a bachelor's degree in computer science. After a summer of working as a computer repair technician in your uncle's computer service and repair shop, you decide that you want to pursue a career as a network engineer or systems administrator. How can you use Internet technology to search for entry-level jobs that suitable to your career goals?

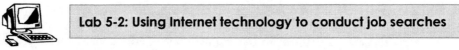

Lab 5-2: Using Internet technology to conduct job searches

In this lab, you will use Monster.com to search for information about IT careers.

1. Open **Internet Explorer**. Click anywhere in the Address text box, type *monster.com*, then press **ENTER**. The Monster.com home page and search engine will appear (Figure 5-11).

Figure 5-11: Monster.com home page

2. Click in the **Job Search** text box, type *network engineer*, then press **ENTER**. If a special offer appears, scroll to the bottom of the screen and click **No Thank You** to

access the Monster job search page and retrieve all job listings containing the specified keywords in the job descriptions.

3. Click several hyperlinks and view the job descriptions and requirements. Click the **Back** button in the toolbar to return to the search results page after viewing each hyperlink.

4. Under the Related Job Titles heading near the top of the page, click **Network Administrator**. This step retrieves all job listings containing the new keywords in the job descriptions.

5. Click several hyperlinks and view the job descriptions and requirements. Do you notice any major differences between the job roles and responsibilities of a network engineer versus those of a network administrator?

6. Enter keywords that describe a career in which you are interested, then click several hyperlinked results to obtain information about each position.

7. Close the browser.

As you can see, Internet search engines provide a wealth of information about every career path imaginable. Make sure you use appropriate keyword search techniques to help narrow your job search to specific locations and companies, if desired. You should always conduct your job searches using multiple search engines. Different search engines may yield different results for the same search string.

Creating a résumé

OBJECTIVE:
3.10.4: Résumé file formats

You can use several different file formats when you create résumés. Your choice will depend on the way in which you want to deliver your résumé. You can create résumés for delivery in hard copy (print) or electronically.

Formatting a résumé

Formatted résumés are typically created using a word-processing program such as Microsoft Word, Corel WordPerfect or Lotus Word Pro. You can create and print visually impressive résumés using a word-processing program; the full range of the software's formatting features are available to you. You would normally create formatted résumés if you intend to send printed copies to prospective employers by way of postal mail, fax, hand delivery or e-mail attachment. However, potential problems can occur when sending formatted résumés as e-mail attachments, as follows:

- Unless the recipient has the same program you used to create the résumé, he or she may not be able to view it electronically.

- The résumé's formatting may render inconsistently on different computers.

- Résumés sent as e-mail attachments are vulnerable to viruses, which may infect the recipient's computer.

Text format

Text résumés (also known as plain-text or ASCII résumés) are intended to be entered into keyword-searchable résumé databases and applicant tracking systems used by most large employers. Text résumés contain little formatting and are not necessarily designed to be visually impressive. However, they are not vulnerable to viruses and can be read by many different programs on many different platforms. Text résumés can be used to post directly to job boards, or to paste into the body of an e-mail message.

To create a text résumé, you can use Windows Notepad or any word-processing program as long as you save the document as a plain-text file with the .txt file name extension.

Rich Text Format (RTF)

NOTE:
Most basic formatting attributes are available for RTF documents. However, more complex formatting, such as tables or columns, is generally unavailable.

Rich Text Format (RTF) résumés combine the best qualities of formatted and text résumés. RTF résumés allow you to incorporate most formatting techniques to make your résumé visually appealing, but can also be read by numerous programs on many different platforms. RTF résumés are also far less vulnerable to viruses than formatted documents you create with a word-processing program.

An RTF résumé is the best choice if you intend to send your résumé as an e-mail attachment and you do not know the file type that your recipient prefers. However, you should also paste a plain-text version of your résumé in the body of the e-mail message as a precautionary measure in case the recipient cannot read the RTF version.

You can use Windows WordPad to create an RTF résumé, or you can use any word-processing program to create it as long as you save the document as an RTF file with the .rtf file name extension.

Portable Document Format (PDF)

Portable Document Format (PDF) résumés are compatible with all computer platforms and are not vulnerable to viruses. However, you need PDF software (for example, Adobe Acrobat) to create a PDF document. Visit PDF Store (*www.pdfstore.com*) for information about PDF software. PDF conversion freeware or shareware programs are also available. For example, Macintosh OS X includes a built-in program, Preview, which can convert files into PDF documents. PDF files use the .pdf file name extension.

NOTE:
Adobe Acrobat Reader software is available to download for free.

A PDF résumé (or a résumé converted into PDF) looks identical to and retains all the formatting of the original document. PDF documents retain their visual appeal and will render consistently on different computers. However, the recipient must have Adobe Acrobat Reader software to open and read a PDF document.

HTML

HTML résumés are generally created to post as Web pages. HTML, or "Web-ready," résumés are useful if you have your own Web site or have access to Web space. Some Web sites offer free Web-space hosting and your ISP may include a Web-space hosting service. HTML documents use the .htm or .html file name extension.

HTML résumés retain all the formatting characteristics of a word-processing document, although the attributes may render inconsistently in different browsers. However, HTML résumés posted on the Web have several unique advantages over other résumé formats, as follows:

- Employers can access your résumé at any time.

- Employers may discover your résumé when they perform keyword searches.

- You can add links to your résumé that point employers to other documents, graphics and photographs that further illustrate your background and skills.

In the following lab, you will learn how to create a résumé and save it in plain-text format. Assume you have conducted an online job search and have found a job listing that interests you. To apply for this job, you must submit a résumé and a cover letter by e-mail. The employer enters all résumés into an applicant tracking system. In this case, what are the advantages of submitting a plain-text résumé?

Lab 5-3: Creating a plain-text résumé

In this lab, you will create a résumé and save it as a plain-text document.

1. Open Windows XP Notepad.

2. Enter several lines of text to create the start of a résumé.

3. Select a line of text and select **Format | Font** to display the Font dialog box. Notice that the only formatting options available are font typeface, style, size and script.

4. Use the options in the Font dialog box to apply different text-formatting attributes to the lines of text. When you are finished, click **OK** to close the Font dialog box.

5. Select **File | Save As** to display the Save As dialog box.

6. Display the Save In drop-down list and click **Desktop** to specify to save the file on your Desktop.

7. Display the Save As Type drop-down list. Notice that the only option is to save the document as a text file with the .txt file name extension.

8. Specify a name in the File Name text box and click the **Save** button to save the document to your Desktop.

9. Close the Notepad window and delete the file from your Desktop.

In the following lab, you will learn how to create a résumé and save it as an RTF file. Assume you have conducted a new online job search and have found several job listings that interest you. To apply for these jobs, you must submit a résumé and a cover letter by e-mail. Several companies have requested a formatted résumé, but you do not know the type of word-processing software these companies use. In this situation, what are the advantages of submitted résumés as RTF files?

Lab 5-4: Creating an RTF résumé

In this lab, you will create a résumé and save it as an RTF document.

1. Open Windows XP WordPad.

2. Enter several lines of text to create the start of a résumé.

3. Use the tools in the Format Bar to apply font, bold, italic, color and alignment attributes to selected text.

4. Select **File | Save As** to display the Save As dialog box.

5. Display the Save In drop-down list and click **Desktop** to specify to save the file on your Desktop.

6. Display the Save As Type drop-down list. Notice that you have the option to save the document as a Rich Text Format (RTF) file, which will retain the formatting attributes you applied, or as a text document, which will remove all formatting.

7. Click **Rich Text Format (RTF)**, specify a name in the File Name text box, then click the **Save** button to save the document to your Desktop. Close the WordPad window.

8. On your Desktop, open the RTF file you just created. Notice that all the formatting attributes you applied appear in the document.

9. Select **File | Save As**, display the **Save As Type** drop-down list, click **Text Only**, then click the **Save** button. Notice that a message box appears informing you that all formatting will be removed.

10. Click **Yes** to save the file as a text document, then close the WordPad window.

11. On your Desktop, open the text document you just created. Notice that most of the formatting attributes you applied have been removed.

12. Delete the two files you just created from your Desktop.

Education and IT careers

OBJECTIVE:
3.10.5: Education and technology job roles

As technology becomes more sophisticated and complex, employers will demand a high level of technical expertise. If you have a bachelor's or advanced degree in computer science, computer engineering, management information systems or an equivalent field, your prospects for employment in the IT industry should be favorable. However, employers are seeking professionals who can also demonstrate competence in interpersonal, business and project management skills because these skills are becoming more important in the workplace.

Because IT technologies change so rapidly, continual study is necessary to keep your skills current. Colleges, universities, employers, hardware and software vendors, and private training institutions offer continuing education so that you can remain up-to-date with current technological advances.

You can demonstrate a level of competence or expertise in specific IT fields by obtaining a technical or professional certification (for example, CIW, A+, Network+ or Security+). Certified individuals, particularly in the IT field, are widely sought, and professional certifications provide you with a competitive advantage when pursuing numerous jobs.

Technical Concepts and Training

As an IT professional, you will often be required to translate highly technical concepts into information that a non-technical audience can readily understand. This task will test your communication skills, which are very important. Your ability to enable a non-technical audience to understand complex concepts will apply particularly if you find yourself working with end users or management personal, many of whom have only a basic knowledge of computers and computer networks.

Communicating technical issues to an end user

OBJECTIVE:
3.11.1:
Communicating
with end users

If you are a help desk technician, or are performing a similar job role, you must be able to understand the problems and concerns of end users as they work with computer systems they may not understand. Typically, when end users experience a technical problem, they may not know enough about what they are experiencing to be able to explain the problem accurately. You should be able to understand the information that end users provide and to understand the technical aspects of the problem. Your understanding of these aspects will allow you to provide an appropriate solution.

NOTE:
Think of people you
know who have
very few or no skills
with computers.
How would you
guide these people
through a technical
process?

You must also be able to communicate a technical response or concept in terms that end users can understand so that they can implement your solution. For example, a remote end user may call you to report that he cannot access the Internet on his computer. If the domain, IP address or subnet mask has changed, you may need to instruct the user how to make the appropriate changes on his system.

Justifying IT-related expenses

OBJECTIVE:
3.11.2:
Communicating
with management

As an IT professional, you must always keep in mind the return-on-investment (ROI) impact of IT decisions on an organization's bottom line. One of the critical questions to address before implementing a plan is to determine the benefit of purchasing hardware or software, or creating a particular product or service. Upper management will probably require you to justify the decision's benefits relative to its costs. You must be able to determine the risk and business value of each decision in order to justify purchases or plans. Frequently, you must balance these purchases or plans against other purchases and plans that you may need to abandon.

In most cases, the upper-level managers you may need to convince will not have the same level of technical expertise in computers and computer networks as you do. When presenting technically complex information to a non-technical audience, you must be able to put the information in terms that your managers can understand so that they can make informed decisions.

For example, suppose the IT department determines that system hardware upgrades are required to implement a company intranet. You will need to provide data that shows that the expected hardware costs, system down time and the employee learning curve will yield measurable increases in productivity and sales, based on the increased ability to communicate and secure information from outside attacks. Your understanding of networking technologies will help you communicate these concerns, and may help your company profit in the future.

Case Study

Sending a Résumé

Maria has learned about a job position that fits her talents. She is a CIW Associate, and has also gained experience as a project manager. The position in which she is interested is at a company that creates security software. After making initial contact with the hiring manager, she has been asked to exchange public keys, and then send her résumé as an RTF file. Maria knows about PGP, but has never used it. She decides to install PGP on her system, and then uses it to generate a key pair.

After generating her key pair, she sends her public key to the hiring manager, along with her résumé. Her hiring manager imports her public key, and is then able to decrypt and read Maria's e-mail message and attached RTF document. The hiring manager is able to read this information with confidence, knowing that Maria in fact did send it, and that it has not been improperly altered in transit.

                            *   *   *

What other methods could Maria have used to send a secure transmission to the hiring manager? In addition to saving her résumé as an RTF document, what other file format should Maria have sent as a backup, and what medium should she have used to send it?

Lesson Summary

Application project

You can apply a digital certificate to your e-mail for encryption between co-workers and various contacts. To encrypt your e-mail, you can retrieve a digital certificate from an Internet certificate authority, such as VeriSign. Access the VeriSign Web site and read the instructions for obtaining digital certificates, called digital IDs.

As a network administrator, you can purchase multiple digital IDs for your network users to ensure e-mail confidentiality. What is the cost of one VeriSign digital ID? How much would it cost to buy 500 digital IDs? If you decide to register and download digital IDs for all your network users (each user would have his or her own private key), you must be sure that all users have the public keys for all co-workers and contacts to whom they will send encrypted messages. Public keys can be downloaded from VeriSign (a database contains the public keys of all registered certificates) or sent by e-mail to each user.

After a user has loaded the public key for the destination e-mail account user, he or she can send encrypted e-mail messages that can be decrypted only by the destination e-mail account (because only the destination user has the private key). Does your company need secure e-mail? Would this security policy be beneficial? Is secure e-mail a cost-effective means of security for your company?

Skills review

In this lesson, you learned about network security threats, the common attacks waged against network resources and the most familiar attack, computer viruses. You also learned about authentication principles and the three major types of encryption.

You learned about network-level protocols that provide privacy, integrity and authentication at the network layer. You also learned about firewalls and security zones, and how they enable a business to protect itself from outside parties.

Finally, you learned about the most effective methods of conducting IT job searches and presenting résumés to hiring managers. You also learned the importance of communication skills when discussing technical issues with non-technical audiences.

Now that you have completed this lesson, you should be able to:

✓ Define security.

✓ Identify various kinds of network attacks.

✓ Describe computer viruses and explain how to protect your network from virus attacks.

✓ Describe authentication principles.

✓ Explain the three major types of encryption.

✓ Describe network security protocols and technologies, including Virtual Private Networks (VPNs), remote access server (RAS), digital certificates and Public Key Infrastructure (PKI).

✓ Describe firewalls, security zones and common firewall topologies.

✓ Describe security audit principles.

✓ Describe the function of an uninterruptible power supply (UPS).

✓ Review career opportunities in the IT industry.

✓ Describe the importance of successfully explaining technical issues to non-technical audiences.

Lesson 5 Review

1. Name the virus type that executes differently each time it is run.

_____

2. What is authentication and what is its primary purpose?

_____

_____

_____

3. What is the primary technique of ensuring privacy across the enterprise?

_____

4. Which encryption technique is designed to be used for information that will not be decrypted or read?

_____

5. What is the purpose of a firewall?

_____

_____

6. What is a bottleneck?

_____

_____

7. Why is the screened subnet the most secure of the four general firewall topologies?

_____

_____

_____

8. In which file format would you save a résumé that is intended to be entered into keyword-searchable résumé databases and applicant tracking systems?

_____

Lesson 5
Supplemental Material

This section is a supplement containing additional tasks for you to complete in conjunction with the lesson. These elements are:

- **Activities**
  Pen-and-paper activities to review lesson concepts or terms.

- **Optional Labs**
  Computer-based labs to provide additional practice.

- **Lesson Quiz**
  Multiple-choice test to assess knowledge of lesson material.

Activity 5-1: Reviewing passwords

In this activity, you will discuss the elements of strong passwords and resolve a scenario in which passwords have become compromised.

1. Discuss the elements of strong passwords and the guidelines they should follow.

    _____

    _____

    _____

    _____

    _____

    _____

    _____

2. You suspect that one or more passwords have become compromised and believe that the problem includes several passwords. Currently, users are required to change passwords every six months. What steps should you take?

    _____

    _____

Passwords are one of the core strengths of computer and network security. If the password is compromised, the basic security scheme or model is affected. To enforce good password selection, you need to require passwords and to help users choose strong passwords. In addition, password aging is an important parameter to implement because it can make password cracking with brute force and dictionary attacks more difficult.

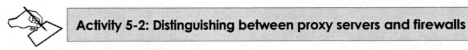 **Activity 5-2: Distinguishing between proxy servers and firewalls**

In this activity, you will determine whether the network requirements in the following scenarios are best met by a firewall, a proxy server, or both.

1. You are setting up a Web server as part of your network. Your network is configured with registered IP addresses, and users will be able to connect to remote Web sites directly. You need to limit traffic to HTTP traffic.

    _____

2. You are setting up Internet access for your network. Your ISP has given you two public IP addresses. One address will be used to configure a public Web server. All users must share the remaining address for Internet access.

    _____

3. You are setting up Internet access for your network. You do not want your local IP addresses to be visible on the network and you need to limit traffic to World Wide Web and FTP transfers only.

_____

Most direct Internet access solutions include both firewall and proxy server protection, often combined in a single multifunction device.

Optional Lab 5-1: Conducting a job search using Google Groups

In this optional lab, you will conduct a job search using Google Groups (*http://groups.google.com*).

1. Open **Mozilla Firefox**. Type *groups.google.com* in the Location box, then press **ENTER**. The Google Groups home page will appear (Figure OL5-1).

Figure OL5-1: Google Groups home page

NOTE:
In Step 2, if few or no links are found, type "Website" as one word or type a different city (or both).

2. Type *"Web site designer" AND <city>* (where <city> is your place of residence), then click the **Search Groups** button. This step retrieves all job listings containing the specified keywords.

3. Click several hyperlinks and view the job descriptions and requirements. Click the **Back** button in the toolbar to return to the search results page after viewing each hyperlink.

4. Enter keywords that describe a career in which you are interested, then click several resulting hyperlinks to obtain information about each position.

5. Close the browser.

6. Conduct job searches using several different search engines, such as *hotjobs.yahoo.com* and *careers.excite.com*. How do the various search engines differ in the way they operate and search results they provide?

 Optional Lab 5-2: Creating an HTML résumé

In this optional lab, you will create a Web-based résumé by saving it as an HTML file.

Note: The steps in this optional lab are written for the Microsoft Word 2003 word-processing application. If you are using another word-processing application or an earlier version of Microsoft Word, you can still perform this optional lab using steps similar to those shown. If you do not have access to a word-processing application, skip this optional lab.

Note: If you do not have access to a word-processing application but would still like to complete this optional lab, you can download OpenOffice, an open-source project that is free. Visit www.openoffice.org, then click the Download link to access the OpenOffice Downloads page.

NOTE:
The file size of the OpenOffice application is 63.5 MB (for Windows systems) and can take from 7 minutes (on a T1 connection) to 2.5 hours (on a 56-Kbps dial-up connection) to download.

1. Open Microsoft Word 2003.

2. Enter several lines of text to create the start of a résumé.

3. Use the tools in the Formatting toolbar to apply font, bold, italic, color and alignment attributes to selected text. Create and format tables and columns of information to add advanced formatting characteristics to your résumé.

4. Select **File | Save As Web Page** to display the Save As dialog box. Notice that the Web page file type is automatically selected in the Save As Type drop-down box.

5. Display the Save In drop-down list and click **Desktop** to specify to save the file on your Desktop.

6. Specify a name in the File Name text box, then click the **Save** button to save the document to your Desktop.

7. Open your browser, then use the appropriate commands to open the file you just created in your browser window. Notice that all the formatting attributes you applied in the original document render in the browser window.

8. Close the browser window, quit Microsoft Word 2003, then delete the file from your Desktop.

Lesson 5 Quiz

1. A network attack in which repeated attempts are made to guess user names and passwords using a file containing a long list of words is called:

   a. a back-door attack.
   b. a brute-force attack.
   c. a dictionary attack.
   d. a man-in-the-middle attack.

2. The action of using one key to encrypt and decrypt a message is called:

   a. hash encryption.
   b. PGP encryption.
   c. asymmetric-key encryption.
   d. symmetric-key encryption.

3. A network-level protocol that uses tunneling to encapsulate data packets into network packets is called:

   a. non-repudiation.
   b. Pretty Good Privacy (PGP).
   c. remote access server (RAS).
   d. Virtual Private Network (VPN).

4. A server whose primary goal is to enable the secure creation and management of digital certificates is called:

   a. a certificate authority (CA).
   b. Data Encryption Standard (DES).
   c. Public Key Infrastructure (PKI).
   d. Virtual Network Computing (VNC).

5. The practice of hiding internal IP addresses from the external network is called:

   a. information caching.
   b. Network Address Translation (NAT).
   c. packet-sniffing.
   d. spoofing.

6. A computer that holds various firewall components and services and is connected to a public network is called:

   a. a bastion host.
   b. an intranet.
   c. an extranet.
   d. a virtual LAN (VLAN).

7. You want to create a résumé that is compatible across all computer platforms and is completely invulnerable to viruses. In addition, you do not have your own Web page or access to a Web-space hosting service. You should save your résumé as:

   a. a text file.
   b. a Rich Text Format (RTF) file.
   c. a Portable Document Format (PDF) file.
   d. an HTML file.

Appendixes

Appendix A: Objectives and Locations*
Appendix B: Acronyms*
Appendix C: Works Consulted*

* Appendix found on Companion CD-ROM

CIW Foundations Glossary

absolute URL — A URL that gives the full path to a resource.

account lockout — A legitimate practice in which a user account is automatically disabled after a certain number of failed authentication attempts.

active partition — A logical partition that contains the files necessary to boot an operating system. This partition is read first at boot time. If no active partition exists, or if the operating system files are corrupted or missing, the computer will report error messages.

ActiveX — An open set of technologies for integrating components on the Internet and within Microsoft applications.

adapter — A device that provides connectivity between at least two systems.

Advanced Research Projects Agency (ARPA) — A U.S. Department of Defense agency that created the first global computer network.

Advanced Research Projects Agency Network (ARPANET) — A computer network, funded by ARPA, that served as the basis for early networking research and was the backbone during the development of the Internet.

antivirus software — Software that scans disks and programs for known viruses and eliminates them.

applets — Small programs written in Java, which are downloaded as needed and executed within a Web page or browser.

application programming interface (API) — A set of universal commands, calls and functions that allows developers to communicate with an application or operating system.

Application Service Provider (ASP) — A company that provides applications and services (over the Internet) to individual or enterprise subscribers that would otherwise need to provide those applications and services on their own servers.

application-level gateway — A firewall component that inspects all packets addressed to a user-level application; uses proxies to control and filter traffic on a connection-by-connection basis. Also provides authentication.

assignment — The appointment of a specific resource to a specific task.

assumption — A factor that is considered to be real or certain for planning purposes.

asymmetric-key encryption — An encryption method in which two keys (the private key and public key) are used to encrypt and decrypt a message.

attachment — A file that is sent with an e-mail message.

attenuation — The weakening of a transmission signal as it travels farther from its source.

AU — Audio file format used by UNIX servers, the majority of Web servers. Most Web browsers can read AU.

Audio Interchange File Format (AIFF) — High-quality audio format developed by Apple Computer.

Audio Video Interleave (AVI) — Standard Windows file format for video files.

authentication — The process of verifying the identity of a user who logs on to a system, or the integrity of transmitted data.

back end — A series of systems that fulfill requests made by a client. Back-end systems can include mainframes and servers containing information databases.

backbone — The highest level in the computer network hierarchy, to which smaller networks typically connect.

bandwidth — The amount of information, sometimes called traffic, that can be carried on a network at one time. The total capacity of a line. Also, the rate of data transfer over a network connection; measured in bits per second.

baseline — A recording of network activity, obtained through documentation and monitoring, that serves as an example for comparing future network activity.

bastion host — A computer that houses various firewall components and services and is connected to a public network, such as the Internet.

binary file — A file containing data or instructions written in zeros and ones (computer language).

blackhole list — A published list of IP addresses known to be sources of spam.

block-level element — A markup element that affects at least an entire paragraph.

blog — A collection of personal thoughts posted on a public Web site. Blogging is the act of adding entries to a blog.

Boolean operator — A symbol or word used in Internet searches to narrow search results by including or excluding certain words or phrases from the search criteria.

bottleneck — A point in network communication at which information is processed more slowly. Also, any element (a hard drive, I/O card or network interface card) that slows network connectivity rates.

browser e-mail — E-mail programs such as Outlook Express that come bundled with a Web browser and with which they may be integrated.

buffer — A cache of memory used by a computer to store frequently used data. Buffers allow faster access times.

bus — An electronic pathway that conducts signals to connect the functional components of a computer.

business logic — The coding (usually in SQL) necessary to create relationships in the data stored in a database.

business-to-business (B2B) — An e-commerce model in which a Web-based business sells products and/or services to other businesses.

business-to-consumer (B2C) — An e-commerce model in which a Web-based business sells products and/or services to consumers or end users.

byte — A measurement of memory needed to store one 8-bit character.

cable modem — A device that allows computers to communicate over a network by modulating and demodulating the cable signal into a stream of data.

callback — A process in which a remote access server returns a call to a remote client that has logged on in order to authenticate that client.

Carrier Sense Multiple Access/Collision Avoidance (CSMA/CA) — The LAN access method used by the IEEE 802.11 wireless specification and Apple LocalTalk.

Carrier Sense Multiple Access/Collision Detection (CSMA/CD) — The LAN access method used by Ethernet. Checks for network access availability with a signal.

Cascading Style Sheets (CSS) — A technology that allows greater style definition and formatting control of HTML elements. Formatting can be placed within the HTML or called remotely from an external style sheet.

channel — The cable or signal between two network nodes that enables data transmission.

character set — The group of symbols used to render text on a page.

circuit-level gateway — A firewall component that monitors and transmits information at the transport layer of the OSI model. It hides information about the network; a packet passing through this type of gateway appears to have originated from the firewall.

client — An individual computer connected to a network. Also, a system or application that requests a service from another computer (the server), and is used to access files or documents (such as a Web browser or user agent).

client-side script — Code embedded into an HTML page and downloaded by a user; resides on the client and helps process Web form input. Common client-side scripting languages include JavaScript and VBScript.

cluster — A group of sectors used as the basic unit of data storage.

clustering — The ability for multiple systems to act as a single host. Allows organizations to ensure high availability of data and to balance loads in busy networks.

coax — High-capacity two-wire (signal and ground) cable; inner wire is the primary conductor, and the metal sheath serves as the ground.

codec — A compression/decompression algorithm used by modern video and audio player plug-ins.

common field — A field contained in two or more database tables that forms a connection between the tables.

Common Gateway Interface (CGI) — A program that processes data submitted by the user. Allows a Web server to pass control to a software application, based on user request. The application receives and organizes data, then returns it in a consistent format.

Completely Automated Public Turing Test to Tell Computers and Humans Apart (CAPTCHA) — A test that uses a word-verification graphic designed to differentiate humans from automated senders during online transactions.

Concurrent Versions System (CVS) — A tool that allows programmers to control different versions of the pieces of a program as those pieces are developed.

constraint — A factor, such as budget or time, that limits a project manager's options.

cookie — A text file that contains information sent between a server and a client to help maintain state and track user activities. Cookies can reside in memory or on a hard drive.

customs — National departments responsible for controlling items entering and leaving the country.

daemon — A UNIX program that is usually initiated at startup and runs in the background until required.

data — Information being stored, usually in a database.

data source name (DSN) — A text string that is used to reference the data source by application programs.

database — A collection of data that can be sorted and searched using search algorithms.

database administrator — An individual responsible for the maintenance and security of an organization's database resources and data.

database management system (DBMS) — A program used to store, access and manipulate database information.

dead link — A hyperlink that, when clicked, sends a Web site visitor to a page or resource that does not exist on the server.

decryption — The process of converting encrypted data back to its original form.

deep URL — A URL that includes a path past the domain into the folder structure of a Web site.

demand priority — The LAN access method used by 100VG-AnyLAN networks. By prioritizing transmissions, hubs specify how and when nodes can access the network.

dictionary program — A program specifically written to break into a password-protected system. It has a relatively large list of common password names it repeatedly uses to gain access.

digital certificate — A password-protected, encrypted data file containing message encryption, user identification and message text. Used to authenticate a program or a sender's public key, or to initiate SSL sessions. Must be signed by a certificate authority (CA) to be valid.

digital signature — An electronic stamp added to a message that uniquely identifies its source and verifies its contents at the time of the signature.

Digital Subscriber Line (DSL) — A high-speed direct Internet connection that uses all-digital networks.

direct memory access (DMA) — A process that allows devices to bypass controllers and directly access memory.

disk cache — Storage space on a computer hard disk used to temporarily store downloaded data.

dithering — The ability for a computer to approximate a color by combining the RGB values.

document type declaration (<!DOCTYPE>) — A declaration of document or code type embedded within an HTML, XHTML, XML or SGML document; identifies the version and nature of code used. Denoted by the <!DOCTYPE> tag at the beginning of the document.

Document Type Definition (DTD) — A set of rules contained in a simple text file that defines the structure, syntax and vocabulary as it relates to tags and attributes for a corresponding document.

domain name — An IP address represented in words.

domain name server — A server that resolves domain names into IP addresses.

domain name space — The three-level domain name hierarchy (root-level, top-level and second-level domains) that forms the DNS.

Domain Name System (DNS) — A system that maps uniquely hierarchical names to specific Internet addresses.

dynamic — Always changing.

Dynamic HTML (DHTML) — A combination of HTML, script, styles and the Document Object Model (DOM) that provides Web page interactivity.

electronic commerce (e-commerce) — The integration of communications, data management and security capabilities to allow organizations and consumers to exchange information related to the sale of good and services.

Electronic Data Interchange (EDI) — The inter-organization exchange of documents in a standardized electronic form directly between participating computers.

e-mail client — An e-mail program that is independent of any specific Web browser, and that you can use to send e-mail messages.

emoticon — A combination of characters that you read sideways that helps convey emotion in an e-mail message.

emulator — A type of software that imitates a computer then allows non-native software to run in a foreign environment. Sometimes also a hardware device.

Encapsulated PostScript (EPS) — File format used for importing and exporting graphics.

encryption — A security technique to prevent access to information by converting it to a scrambled (unreadable) form of text.

event handler — A line of code that allows a language to respond to a specific event or user input.

event-driven — Reacting to particular user actions or the browser's completion of a specific task.

Extensible Hypertext Markup Language (XHTML) — The current standard authoring language used to develop Web pages and other electronically displayed documents. XHTML requires stricter code syntax than HTML.

Extensible Markup Language (XML) — A markup language that describes document content, instead of adding structure or formatting to document content. A simplified version of SGML.

Extensible Stylesheet Language (XSL) — A style language that provides formatting instructions for XML documents.

extranet — A network that connects enterprise intranets to the global Internet. Designed to provide access to selected external users.

field — A category of information in a database table.

File Transfer Protocol (FTP) — An Internet protocol used to transfer files between computers.

firewall — A security barrier that controls the flow of information between the Internet and private networks. A firewall prevents outsiders from accessing an enterprise's internal network, which accesses the Internet indirectly through a proxy server.

fixed-width font — A font in which every character, including the space character, has equal width. In proportional-width fonts, letters such as I and J have less width than M or B.

foreign key — A field in a related database table that refers to the primary key in the primary table.

frame — 1: A scrollable region of a Web page in which other pages can be displayed; a single element of a frameset. Each frame has its own URL.
2: Data passed between a system that contains addressing and link control information. Like all network protocols, IPX/SPX encapsulates its communications into frames.

frameset document — A Web page that defines a set of adjacent frames in which other Web pages are displayed.

front end — A client that acts as an interface to a collection of servers (for example, mainframes or PC-based servers). A Web browser is a typical front-end client.

fully qualified domain name (FQDN) — The complete domain name of an Internet computer, such as *www.CIW-certified.com*.

Gantt chart — A horizontal bar chart that graphically displays project tasks and durations.

gateway — A node on a network that serves as a portal to other networks.

Gnu Privacy Guard (GPG) — An open-source version of PGP, used for encrypting and decrypting e-mail messages, that does not use patented algorithms.

graphical user interface (GUI) — A program that provides visual navigation with menus and screen icons, and performs automated functions when users click command buttons.

hacker — An unauthorized user who penetrates a host or network to access and manipulate data.

hash — A number generated by an algorithm from a text string.

hash encryption — An encryption method in which hashes are used to verify the integrity of transmitted messages.

header — A block of information attached to a piece of data. The first part of a network packet. Can contain network addressing information or additional information that helps computers and applications process data.

help desk technician — An individual responsible for diagnosing and resolving users' technical hardware and software problems.

hexadecimal — A base-16 number system that allows large numbers to be displayed by fewer characters than if the number were displayed in the regular base-10 system. In hexadecimal, the number 10 is represented as the letter A, 15 is represented as F, and 16 is represented as 10.

home page — The first Web page that displays when you access a domain.

hop — One link between two network devices; the number of hops between two devices is considered a hop count.

host — A computer that other computers can use to gain information; in network architecture, a host is a client or workstation.

hosts file — A file that contains mappings of IP addresses to host names.

hub — A device used to connect systems so that they can communicate with one another; a repeater or a bridge.

hyperlinks — Embedded instructions within a text file that link it to another point in the file or to a separate file.

hypertext link — Highlighted or underlined text in a Web page that, when clicked, links the user to another location or Web page.

Hypertext Markup Language (HTML) — The traditional authoring language used to develop Web pages for many applications.

Hypertext Transfer Protocol (HTTP) — The protocol for transporting HTML documents across the Internet.

I/O address — A memory location that allows resources to be allocated to a system device.

illicit server — An application that installs hidden services on systems. Illicit servers consist of "client" code and "server" code that enable the attacker to monitor and control the operation of the computer infected with the server code.

image map — A set of coordinates on an image that creates a "hot spot," which acts as a hyperlink when clicked.

index — A catalog of the contents of a database. Each entry identifies a unique database record.

Information Technology (IT) — The management and processing of information using computers and computer networks.

infrared — A spectrum of light used for communication between various network-enabled devices.

inline images — Images rendered in a Web page.

instant messaging (IM) — A computer-based method of communication in which users can type and view messages sent to one or more recipients, and view the responses immediately.

Integrated Services Digital Network (ISDN) — A communication standard for sending voice, video or data over digital telephone lines.

interactive — The characteristic of some hardware and software, such as computers, games and multimedia systems, that allows them to respond differently based on a user's actions.

interface — A communication channel between two components.

Internet — A worldwide network of interconnected networks.

Internet Control Messaging Protocol (ICMP) — A subset of Internet Protocol that is most often used to determine whether a computer can communicate with the rest of the network.

Internet Message Access Protocol (IMAP) — A protocol that resides on an incoming mail server. Similar to POP, but is more powerful. Allows sharing of mailboxes and multiple mail server access. The current version is IMAP4.

Internet Protocol (IP) — The data transmission standard for the Internet. Every computer connected to the Internet has its own IP address, which enables a packet of data to be delivered to a specific computer.

Internet Service Provider (ISP) — An organization that maintains a gateway to the Internet and rents access to customers on a per-use or subscription basis.

interoperability — The ability of one computer system to communicate with another; often refers to different operating systems working together.

intranet — An internal network based on TCP/IP protocols, accessible only to users within a company.

interrupt request (IRQ) — A hardware line over which devices can send interrupt signals to the processor.

IP address — A unique numerical address assigned to a computer or device on a network.

IP Security (IPsec) — An authentication and encryption standard that provides security over the Internet. It functions at Layer 3 of the OSI/RM and can secure all packets transmitted over the network.

Java — An object-oriented programming language developed by Sun Microsystems that is fully cross-platform functional.

Java Virtual Machine (JVM) — The artificial computer that runs Java programs and allows the same code to run on different platforms.

JavaScript — An interpreted, object-based scripting language developed by Netscape Communications that adds interactivity to Web pages.

junction table — A database table containing foreign-key fields that refer to the primary-key fields from the primary tables in a many-to-many relationship.

Kerberos — A proprietary key management scheme between unknown principals who want to communicate securely. Uses symmetric algorithms and acts as a trusted third party that knows the identities of the organizations asking to communicate, but does not reveal them.

kernel — The essential part of an operating system; provides basic services; always resides in memory.

key — A variable value, such as a numeric code, that uses an algorithm to encrypt and decrypt data. Some applications encrypt and decrypt with the same key, whereas other applications use a pair of keys.

keyword — A word that appears on a Web page and is used by search engines to identify relevant URLs. Some words, such as "the" or "and," are too common to be used as keywords.

Layer 1 switch — A device that connects individual systems; a Layer 3 switch connects networks.

legacy model — A model that, because of its age, may not support modern technologies without manipulation or upgrades.

Lightweight Directory Access Protocol (LDAP) — A protocol that allows a network entity to access a directory service listing.

list server — A server that collects and distributes information from an authorized group of participants, called a listserve group.

listserve group — Users who subscribe to an e-mailing list through a list server.

LiveScript — The Netscape-developed scripting language that was the predecessor to JavaScript.

local area network (LAN) — A group of computers connected within a confined geographic area.

lossless compression — A type of data file compression in which all original data can be recovered when the file is decompressed.

lossy compression — A type of data file compression in which some file information is permanently eliminated.

Mail Delivery Agent (MDA) — An e-mail server program that receives sent messages and delivers them to their proper destination mailbox.

Mail User Agent (MUA) — A messaging component used as a stand-alone application by the user.

mailing list server — An e-mail server that regularly sends e-mail messages to a specified list of users.

malware — Abbreviation for malicious software. Malware is software designed to harm computer systems.

many-to-many relationship — In databases, a relationship in which one record in Table A can relate to many matching records in Table B, and vice versa.

markup language — A series of commands used to format, organize and describe information on a Web page.

media — Any material that allows data to flow through it or be stored on it; includes hard and floppy disks, wire, cable, and fiber optics.

Media Access Control (MAC) address — The hardware address of a device connected to a network.

Message Transfer Agent (MTA) — A messaging component that routes, delivers and receives e-mail.

meta search engine — A search engine that scans Web pages for <meta> tag information.

metalanguage — A language used for defining other languages.

MIME type — Identifies the contents of a file in the MIME encoding system using a type/subtype format; examples are image/jpg and text/plain.

modem — Abbreviation for modulator/demodulator. An analog device that enables computers to communicate over telephone lines by translating digital data into audio/analog signals (on the sending computer) and then back into digital form (on the receiving computer).

motherboard — The main circuit board in a computer, on which the microprocessor, physical memory and support circuitry are located.

Moving Picture Experts Group (MPEG) — High-quality video file compression format.

MPEG-1 Audio Layer-3 (MP3) — Popular compression standard for audio files; retains most of the sound quality of the source.

MPEG-2 — Current video compression standard.

Multipurpose Internet Mail Extensions (MIME) — A protocol that enables operating systems to map file name extensions to corresponding applications. Also used by applications to automatically process files downloaded from the Internet.

Multistation Access Unit (MAU) — The network device that is the central connection point for token-ring networks.

municipal area network (MAN) — A network used to communicate over a city or geographic area.

Musical Instrument Digital Interface (MIDI) — A standard computer interface for creating and playing electronic music. It allows computers to re-create music in digital format for playback.

narrowband — A specific set of frequencies established for wireless communication (usually for voice). Communicates at lower rates than broadband.

National Science Foundation (NSF) — An independent agency of the U.S. government that promotes the advancement of science and engineering.

needs analysis — Determining a customer's needs by acquiring information, processing and evaluating the information, then creating a plan of action to address the needs.

network — A group of two or more computers connected so they can communicate with one another.

Network Address Translation (NAT) — The practice of hiding internal IP addresses from the external network.

network engineer — An individual responsible for managing and maintaining a network infrastructure.

network interface card (NIC) — A circuit board within a computer's central processing unit that serves as the interface enabling the computer to connect to a network.

Network News Transfer Protocol (NNTP) — The Internet protocol used by news servers that enables the exchange of Usenet articles.

network operating system (NOS) — An operating system that manages network resources.

newsgroup — On Usenet, a subject or other topical interest group whose members exchange ideas and opinions. Participants post and receive messages via a news server.

node — Any entity on a network that can be managed, such as a system, repeater, router, gateway or firewall. A computer or other addressable device attached to a network; a host.

non-repudiation — The security principle of providing proof that a transaction occurred between identified parties. Repudiation occurs when one party in a transaction denies that the transaction took place.

object — An element on a Web page that contains data and procedures for how that item will react when activated. On a Web page, an object is typically a multimedia presentation.

object-based — Similar to object-oriented programming languages, but does not allow for inheritance from one class to another.

object-oriented — A style of programming that links data to the processes that manipulate it.

object-oriented programming (OOP) — Programming concept based on objects and data and how they relate to one another, instead of logic and actions; C++ and Java are OOP languages.

OCx — Optical carrier levels; defines the transmission speeds used in SONET/SDH.

one-to-many relationship — In databases, a relationship in which a record in Table A can have multiple matching records in Table B, but a record in Table B has only one matching record in Table A.

one-to-one relationship — In databases, a relationship in which each record in Table A can have only one matching record in Table B, and vice versa.

online service e-mail — An e-mail program that is part of an online service's software.

Open Buying on the Internet (OBI) — An open-technology standard used by organizations to exchange data in a common format; an alternative to EDI.

open source — Characterized by providing free source code to the development community at large to develop a better product; includes Apache Web server, Netscape Communicator and Linux.

Open Systems Interconnection (OSI) reference model — A layered network architecture model of communication developed by the International Organization for Standardization (ISO). Defines seven layers of network functions

order tracking — The ability to determine progress on delivery of a product. Businesses often provide order-tracking support to end users via Web browsers and e-mail clients.

P2P — A peer-to-peer network on the Internet.

packet — Data processed by protocols so it can be sent across a network.

packet sniffing — The use of protocol analyzer software to obtain sensitive information, such as user names and passwords.

password sniffing — A method of intercepting the transmission of a password during the authentication process. A sniffer is a program used to intercept passwords.

patch — Programming code that provides a temporary solution to a known problem, or bug.

patch panel — A group of sockets that manually switches data between inbound and outbound transmissions.

PC repair technician — An individual responsible for installing, modifying and repairing personal computer (PC) hardware components.

peer-to-peer network — A network in which each computer has both server and client capabilities.

peripheral port — A socket on a computer in which a peripheral device is connected.

permission bit — A file or directory attribute that determines access. Permission bits include read, write and execute permissions.

permissions — Instructions given by an operating system or server (or a combination thereof) that restrict or allow access to system resources, such as files, user databases and system processes.

Personal Digital Assistant (PDA) — A small, handheld computer used for personal information management.

personal information management (PIM) program — A tool used to schedule appointments and meetings, store contact information, and manage tasks.

planned maintenance — Any scheduled maintenance procedures, including preventive maintenance.

plenum — Space between building floors; usually contains air and heating ducts, as well as communication and electrical wires.

plug-in — A program installed in the browser to extend its basic functionality. Allows different file formats to be viewed as part of a standard HTML document.

Point-to-Point Protocol (PPP) — A protocol that allows a computer to connect to the Internet over a phone line.

Point-to-Point Protocol over Ethernet (PPPoE) — A protocol that implements PPP over Ethernet to connect an entire network to the Internet.

Point-to-Point Tunneling Protocol (PPTP) — A protocol that allows users and corporations to securely extend their networks over the Internet using remote access servers. Used to create VPNs.

pop-under window — A small browser window that appears behind the browser window you are viewing.

pop-up window — A small browser window that appears in front of the browser window you are viewing.

port — A logical opening in an operating system or protocol stack that allows the transfer of information. Not the same as a TCP or UDP port.

Portable Document Format (PDF) — A file format that can be transferred across platforms and retain its formatting; designated by the file name extension .pdf.

Post Office Protocol (POP) — A protocol that resides on an incoming mail server. The current version is POP3.

power spike — A short-duration high-voltage condition.

presentation responsibilities — The forms in which the data and business logic are presented on your screen. Presentation responsibilities include XHTML and HTML forms, and application-specific interfaces such as Web browsers.

Pretty Good Privacy (PGP) — A method of encrypting and decrypting e-mail messages. It can also be used to encrypt a digital signature.

primary key — A field containing a value that uniquely identifies each record in a database table.

print queue — A mechanism that stores print requests until they are passed to a printing device.

project — A sequence of tasks that must be accomplished within a certain time frame to achieve a desired result.

project management — The practice of applying skills and processes to activities in order to meet deadlines and achieve desired results.

project schedule — A document that lists the planned dates for performing tasks and meeting goals defined in a project plan.

proxy server — A server that mediates traffic between a protected network and the Internet. Translates IP addresses and filters traffic.

PS/2-style connector — The six-pin mini-DIN connectors introduced with the IBM PS/2.

query — A question posed by a user to a database to request database information. The database returns the query results based on the criteria supplied by the user in the query.

QuickTime Movie (MOV) — Standard file format for Apple QuickTime; uses the .mov, .moov or .qt file name extension.

QuickTime — A plug-in developed by Apple Computer for storing movie and audio files in digital format.

record — A collection of information in a database table consisting of one or more related fields about a specific entity, such as a person, product or event.

relational database — A database that contains multiple tables related through common fields.

relationship — A connection between two or more database tables that is based on a field that the tables have in common.

relative URL — A URL that gives an abbreviated path to a resource using the current page as a starting position.

replay attack — An attack in which packets are obtained from the network or a network host, then reused.

Request for Comments (RFC) — A published document that details information about standardized Internet protocols and those in various development stages.

reseller — A company that adds some value to an existing, then sells it to the public or to another company.

resource — A person, department or device needed to accomplish a task.

resource conflict — A situation in which two or more devices share a configuration setting.

restore point — A snapshot of a computer's settings at a particular point in time. Also known as a system checkpoint.

Return On Investment (ROI) — Profit earned as a result of a project relative to the value of resources required to complete it.

Rich Text Format (RTF) — Portable text file format created by Microsoft that allows image insertion and text formatting; an almost universal format.

root directory — Topmost hard disk directory (folder).

root-level server — A server at the highest level of the Domain Name System.

router — A device that routes packets between networks based on network-layer address; determines the best path across a network. Also used to connect separate LANs to form a WAN.

RSA — A popular, proprietary public key encryption algorithm.

rule — 1: In page design, a graphical line or lines; the word is related to "ruler," a tool of measurement that can be used to draw straight lines.
2: In a style sheet, a format instruction that consists of a specified selector and the properties and values applied to it.

sans-serif — A font style that does not use decorative strokes at the tips of characters. Includes the Arial font family.

scope — The goals and tasks of a project, and the work required to complete them.

scope creep — Gradual increases in project scope that can undermine the success of a project.

screen saver — A graphic or moving image that appears on your screen when your computer is idle.

search engine — A powerful software program that searches Internet databases for user-specified information.

Secure Copy (SCP) — A program used with Secure Shell (SSH) to transfer files between systems.

Secure Electronic Transactions (SET) — An Internet protocol that uses digital certificates to secure financial transactions.

Secure MIME (S/MIME) — Secure version of MIME that adds encryption to MIME data.

Secure Shell (SSH) — A protocol and command interface that provides secure access to a remote computer.

Secure Sockets Layer (SSL) — A protocol that provides authentication and encryption, used by most servers for secure exchanges over the Internet. Superseded by Transport Layer Security (TLS).

security analyst/consultant — An individual responsible for examining an organization's security requirements and determining the necessary infrastructure.

security manager — An individual responsible for managing the security measures used to protect electronic data.

segment — Part of a larger structure; common term used in networking.

selector — In a style sheet, any element to which designated styles are applied.

serif — A font style that uses characters with small decorative additions at the outermost points of the characters, called strokes. Includes the Times and Times New Roman fonts.

server — A computer in a network that manages the network resources and provides, or serves, information to clients.

server administrator — An individual responsible for managing and maintaining network servers.

server-side script — Code that resides on a server to help process Web form input. Server-side CGI scripts are commonly written in Perl.

Service Advertising Protocol (SAP) — A protocol designed to provide file and print services for Novell NetWare networks.

servlet — A small Java application that runs on a server.

shared domain — A hosting service that allows multiple entities to share portions of the same domain name.

shell — A command-based interface that allows a user to issue commands.

Simple Mail Transfer Protocol (SMTP) — The Internet standard protocol for transferring e-mail messages from one computer to another.

site map — A brief, hierarchical representation of a Web site that enables visitors to quickly identify areas of the site and navigate to them.

Small-Screen Rendering (SSR) — A browser technology developed for wireless devices that reformats Web pages to display on 176-pixel-wide cellular phone display screens.

smart card — A credit card that replaces the magnetic strip with an embedded chip for storing or processing data.

snail mail — Slang term for the standard postal service.

socket — The end point of a connection (either side), which usually includes the TCP or UDP port used and the IP address. Used for communication between a client and a server.

spam — Unsolicited and unwanted e-mail messages; the online equivalent of junk mail.

spam filter — An e-mail client program that identifies and filters out spam messages before they reach the e-mail Inbox.

spim — Spam that is delivered through instant messaging.

spread spectrum — Technologies that consist of various methods for radio transmission in which frequencies or signal patterns are continuously changed.

spyware — A software application secretly placed on a user's system to gather information and relay it to outside parties, usually for advertising purposes.

SSH File Transfer Protocol (S/FTP) — A file transfer protocol that allows the encryption of transmissions using the Secure Shell (SSH) protocol.

SSL/TLS-enabled FTP (FTPS) — FTP that runs on an SSL/TLS-secured connection.

stakeholder — A person or group with an interest in a project and the power to exert influence (either positive or negative) over the project and affect results.

standard — A definition or format that has been approved by a recognized standards organization.

Standard Generalized Markup Language (SGML) — A metalanguage used to create other languages, including HTML and XHTML.

Statement Of Work (SOW) — A contract to initiate a project; the contract contains project goals and specifies how those goals will be met.

streaming audio and video — Audio and video files that travel over a network in real time.

streaming media — A continuous flow of data, usually audio or video files, that assists with the uninterrupted delivery of those files into a browser.

Structured Query Language (SQL) — A language used to create and maintain professional, high-performance corporate databases.

switch — A device used to connect either individual systems or multiple networks.

symmetric-key encryption — An encryption method in which the same key is used to encrypt and decrypt a message.

Synchronous Optical Network (SONET) — High-speed fiber-optic system used as a network and Internet backbone. The European counterpart is the Synchronous Digital Hierarchy (SDH).

T1 — A digital carrier that transmits data at a speed of 1.544 Mbps.

table — A collection of data about a limited topic, organized into rows and columns in a database.

Tagged Image File Format (TIFF) — Commonly used graphic file format, developed by Aldus Corporation; uses the .tif or .tiff file name extension.

tags — Pieces of code, enclosed in angle brackets, that tell the HTML interpreter how to process or display text.

task — A unit of work that must be accomplished during the course of a project.

Telnet — The Internet standard protocol for remote terminal connection service.

text-level element — A markup element that affects single characters or words.

token passing — The LAN access method used by token ring networks. A data frame, or token, is passed from one node to the next around the network ring.

top-level domain — The group into which a domain is categorized, by common topic (company, educational institution) and/or geography (country, state).

trace — Thin conductive path on a circuit board, usually made of copper.

transceiver — A device that transmits and receives digital or analog signals.

Transmission Control Protocol/Internet Protocol (TCP/IP) — A suite of protocols that turns data into blocks of information called packets, which are then sent across the Internet. The standard protocol used by the Internet.

Transport Layer Security (TLS) — A secure protocol based on SSL 3.0 that provides encryption and authentication.

Trojan horse — A program disguised as a harmless application that actually produces harmful results.

troll — A Web user who publishes comments or submits feedback simply to annoy or anger.

trouble ticket — A record of a problem related to a service provided by an ISP or ASP. Used to record receipt of a complaint and track resolution of the problem.

tunneling protocol — A protocol that encapsulates data packets into another packet.

Unicode — A universal character set designed to support all written languages, as well as scholarly disciplines (e.g., mathematics).

Uniform Resource Identifier (URI) — A standardized method of referring to a resource.

Uniform Resource Locator (URL) — A text string that specifies an Internet address and the method by which the address can be accessed.

uninterruptible power supply (UPS) — A power supply that uses a battery to maintain power during a power outage.

update — A file or collection of tools that resolves system liabilities and improves software performance.

Usenet (User Network) — A collection of thousands of Internet computers, newsgroups and newsgroup members using Network News Transfer Protocol (NNTP) to exchange information.

user agent — Any application, such as a Web browser, cell phone, PDA or help engine, that renders HTML for display to users.

user name — A unique name or number that identifies you when logging on to a computer system or online service. In an e-mail address, the part before the @ symbol.

vector graphics — Resizable images that are saved as a sequence of vector statements, which describes a series of points to be connected.

viewer — A scaled-down version of an application; designed to view and print files.

virtual domain — A hosting service that allows a company to host its domain name on a third-party ISP server.

virtual local area network (VLAN) — Logical subgroup within a LAN created with software instead of hardware.

Virtual Network Computing (VNC) — A program that allows you to control a computer at a remote location.

Virtual Private Network (VPN) — A secure network between two sites using Internet technology as the transport; an extended LAN that enables a company to conduct secure, real-time communication.

Virtual Reality Modeling Language (VRML) — A three-dimensional graphic authoring language.

virus — A malicious program that replicates itself on computer systems, usually through executable software, and causes irreparable system damage.

Visual Basic — The Microsoft graphical user interface (GUI) programming language used for developing Windows applications. A modified version of the BASIC programming language.

Visual Basic Script (VBScript) — Scripting language from Microsoft, derived from Visual Basic; used to manipulate ActiveX scripts.

Voice over IP (VoIP) — A technology that transmits voice in digital form as packets of data using Internet Protocol.

Waveform (WAV) — Windows standard format for audio files.

Web application developer — An individual who develops primarily server-side Web applications.

Web architect — An individual who is responsible for creating the overview plan of a Web site's development.

Web-based e-mail — Free e-mail service from a provider such as Windows Live Hotmail or Yahoo! in which you request a user name. You can access your e-mail from any computer that has access to the Internet.

Web browser — A software application that enables users to access and view Web pages on the Internet.

Web page — An HTML document containing one or more elements (text, images, hyperlinks) that can be linked to or from other HTML pages.

Web site — A World Wide Web server and its content; includes multiple Web pages.

Web site analyst — An individual who analyzes Web site statistics to determine the site's effectiveness.

Web site designer — An individual responsible for the organization and appearance of a Web site.

Web site manager — An individual who manages a Web development team.

Webinar — An interactive Web-based seminar or training session.

What You See Is What You Get (WYSIWYG) — (pronounced whiz-ee-wig) A user-friendly editing format in which the file being edited is displayed as it will appear in the browser.

wide area network (WAN) — A group of computers connected over an expansive geographic area so their users can share files and services.

wideband — A large set of frequencies capable of carrying data at higher rates (for example, 1.544 Mbps). Usually carries digital signals. Includes DSL and cable Internet access.

wireless access point (WAP) — A device that enables wireless systems to communicate with each other, provided that they are on the same network.

Wireless Application Protocol (WAP) — A standard protocol that wireless devices use to access the Internet.

Wireless Markup Language (WML) — A markup language that presents the text portions of Web pages to wireless devices.

wizard — A tool that assists users of an application in creating documents and/or databases based on styles and templates.

World Wide Web (WWW) — A set of software programs that enables users to access resources on the Internet via hypertext documents.

worm — A self-replicating program or algorithm that consumes system resources.

X Window — A windowing system used with UNIX and all popular operating systems.

X.509 — The standard used by certificate authorities (CAs) for creating digital certificates.

xDSL — Collectively, the variations of Digital Subscriber Line (DSL), which include ADSL, RADSL and HDSL.

zone file — A file containing a set of instructions for resolving a specific domain name into its numerical IP address.

Index

Companion CD-ROM Contents

The *Network Technology Foundations* Self-Study Kit Companion CD-ROM contains the following files needed to complete the course labs:

💿 Network Technology Foundations_Self-Study Kit Companion_CD

📁 Answers	📁 Appendix	📁 Lab Files

📂 Answers

📄 ANSWERS_Activity.pdf	📄 ANSWERS_PreAssessment.pdf	📄 ANSWERS_Review.pdf
📄 ANSWERS_OptionalLab.pdf	📄 ANSWERS_Quiz.pdf	

📂 Appendix

📄 Appendix_A.pdf	📄 Appendix_B.pdf	📄 Appendix_C.pdf

📂 Lab Files

📁 Lesson01

📁 Lesson05

📂 Lab Files\Lesson01

📄 jre-1_5_0_06-windows-i586-p.exe

📄 phex_3.0.2.100.exe

📂 Lab Files\Lesson05

📄 fcinst.exe

Version 1.2